London Dry: The Real History Of Gin

Ted Bruning

White Mule Press, a division of
American Distilling Institute
PO Box 577
Hayward, CA 94541
distilling.com/books

ISBN 978-1-7322354-3-4

Dedicated to the memory of
Peter Lewis Bruning
1908–1985

Equal parts Booth's and Noilly Prat.
No ice.

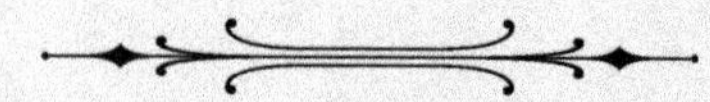

Contents

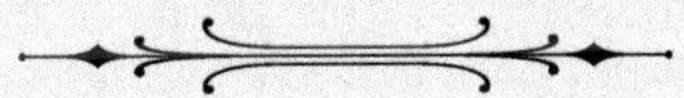

Foreword

by Charles Maxwell

Gin is an exciting, flavoursome and controversial spirit. Through the ages it has delighted its consumers, retailers and producers, while at the same time attracting a noisy and vociferous selection of bodies who have viewed it as a product of the devil himself.

The Worshipful Company of Distillers of the City of London obtained its Royal Charter over three hundred and eighty years ago, while my ancestor was apprenticed to a member of that company in 1681. But the origins of the spirit we call gin can be traced back over an even greater length of time than that. It is inevitable that over such a long period the facts of the history of this great drink have got somewhat blurred at the edges, and indeed for folklore and straight story-telling to have crept into the picture. To this must added the fact that any interpreter of its history can pick or choose which facts they wish to use, and in what light they wish to show them.

Ted Bruning in this excellent book has done a masterful job of burning off the fog and returning the stories to the fiction shelf. He concentrates, as the title of the work would suggest, on the great spirit gin, but he starts this history with the very origins of spirit distillation itself and traces it through to the present day. So we learn that the eight bolls of malt given to

Brother John Cor in Scotland in 1494 for the making of Aqua Vitae may have gone to create a spirit which, despite claims from north of the border, was unlikely to have anything to do with the making of whisky, but was more likely to have been infused with herbs and spices to make a much closer relative of gin.

The expression "Dutch courage", of course, came into use when English mercenaries went to the Low Countries, and while preparing for battle took a shot of the local spirit genever, which was soon abbreviated to "Gin" — right? Well, almost certainly wrong. If they were given any spirit at that time it was most probably brandy, as the availability of genever was seriously limited by a grain shortage in the sodden Netherlands.

Well, whatever else, the Gin Craze in London is a well-established fact. Ah, but here is where it is most important to know which elements in society wrote the history of that period. And while it is obvious that Hogarth's Gin Lane is a caricature, it well repays further research to find out how peoples' lives were lived at the time. But, dear reader, that is for you to discover, enjoy, and learn as you are led through The Real History of Gin in this excellently researched and written book. I at least can now sleep easier at night understanding that my family were not complete rogues!

— *Charles Maxwell is Master Distiller, proprietor of Thames Distillers, 11th generation of a great London distilling family, last managing director of Finsbury Distillery.*

Wkikmedia Commons

Introduction

As a beer-writer of more than 30 years' standing, I found my curiosity piqued when craft distilling in Britain seemed to be following a trajectory very similar to that of craft brewing. Both fell broadly into two waves: a first wave, with Martin Sykes of Selby Brewery the founding father of microbrewing and Julian Temperley of Somerset Royal Cider Brandy the founding father of microdistilling; then a second, with craft gin distillers obsessively exploring the possibilities of botanicals and craft brewers just as evangelical about hops. Both even had had their protofounders — Peter Maxwell Stewart of Traquair House in the former case and Bertram Bulmer of King Offa Cider Brandy in the latter.

On inspection, though, the similarities turn out to be more apparent than real. One great difference is that Britain's pioneering microbrewers were in almost all cases middle-aged mainstream brewers who had lost their jobs during the great waves of rationalization that saw more than half of the brewing plants in the country close down. All these gentry knew was brewing; all they had was their redundancy money; it was inevitable that some of them were going to put the two together if only to make a living. Today's craft distillers are different. Few of them have much of a background in the industry and few if any of them have been pushed into their new vocation by need.

Like chefs, they are driven by the quality and the possibilities of what they cook up.

Nor is there that all-pervading sense among craft distillers, as there always has been among microbrewers, that the mainstream industry has debased the product in the name of Mammon and that its misdeeds have to be corrected by someone of purer motives and higher ideals. If anything the reverse is true: The innovations that the big mainstream companies have been introducing to their own portfolios and marketing in recent years, especially in vodka and whiskey, have fed the consumers' appetite for both quality and novelty, and it's from the ranks of these energized consumers that many of the new-wave distillers have emerged. Perhaps as a result there seems to be none of the rancor and mutual disdain between mainstream distiller and newcomer that once — and to the detriment of the whole industry — plagued the relationship between old-established family brewers and parvenu micros.

To take the dissimilarities one step further, a great bone of contention between large and small brewers was the established brewers' monopolistic stranglehold over the pub trade through the tie and, in the "free" trade, tied loans. Microbrewers were desperate for local trade, which they were barred from; in response, they had to develop a nationwide distribution system of independent wholesalers to get access to what genuine free trade there was, which took years; and then, after the 1990 Beer Orders more or less dismantled the biggest tied estates, batter at the doors of the successor pub companies for admission — a process which, again, took years. Thanks partly to the internet, and partly to upmarket wine-merchants who are positively promiscuous in their desire to stock the best, the problem has more or less disappeared and craft distillers face far less formidable obstacles in getting at their consumers than the pioneering microbrewers of 30 years ago.

These reflections, together with the practical research involved in writing *The Craft Distillers' Handbook*, aroused the urge to know more. I had already researched the history of

Scotch for other projects, so I was familiar with the background up to the point where the stories of whiskey and gin began to diverge in the mid-16th century. After that point the story of whiskey was if not straightforward at least well rehearsed; the story of gin, however, was shrouded in myth and propaganda, especially when treating of the supposed gin craze in 18th-century London. It was especially annoying to find that the same baseless and one-sided calumnies were rehearsed over and over again as if they were gospel: not one of the many writers on the subject challenged the source material they so wantonly trotted out, so that not only were the same untruths repeated *ad nauseam*, they were often repeated in the same form of words!

I did, during the course of my reading, come across stray references to *The Mother Gin Controversy*, a paper by Professor Peter Clark of *The English Alehouse* fame published in the Transactions of the Royal Historical Society in 1988. Professor Clark is one of those historians who likes to roll up his sleeves, delve beneath the mulch of accepted history, and uncover the corms and rhizomes of contemporary records that always end up embarrassing the less rigorous. *Mother Gin*, as I found when I was very kindly sent a copy, dealt in depth with only one aspect of the gin craze — the 1736 Gin Act — but in a way that very strongly suggested that the entire thing was a propaganda job stunted up by a very narrowly based clique of post-Puritan churchmen who resented their exclusion from the first tier of power and influence. And so, on examination, it proves to be: There never was a gin craze, just very empty vessels with very squeaky wheels. Moral panics were ever thus!

Other myths, half-truths and inaccuracies, swarming like ivy, have obscured the true outlines of the history of gin. Gin palaces, cocktails, tonic water, bathtub gin, even Rick's Café Americain — none of them, it turns out, are quite what you've been told they are.

For reasons I shall explain in the text, I have decided to abandon my pursuit of gin's history at the point where its history ends and the current "ginaissance" begins, a point which

I have chosen to fix in the year of the revival of gin-making in London: 2009, when Sipsmith and Sacred were both founded. Anyone who hoped for an exposition of what has happened since then — of what is still happening now — will be disappointed; but no coherent narrative has as yet emerged, and none will for quite some time, I suspect.

Before plunging into gin's story, though, I would like to apologize to the Netherlands. I took a conscious decision at the point where the paths of British and Dutch gins diverged to follow only the former. There seems to be a Dutch entrepreneur behind every major development in distilling in the 16th, 17th, and 18th centuries — Dutch sailors may even be responsible for Menorcan gin! — and Dutch gin or genever is delicious and venerable; but its history is its own and demands separate treatment, preferably by a Dutch author. However, and to bring us London Dry enthusiasts down to earth, the world's biggest gin brand by many a country mile is the (self-proclaimed) genever-style Ginebra San Miguel from the Philippines, which sold 21 million 9-liter cases worldwide in 2016 compared to 15 million of Gordon's, Bombay Sapphire, Tanqueray and Beefeater combined.

I am used to reading headlines on both business and food and drink pages proclaiming that gin is taking over the world. It isn't. It's still a minority taste and always will be; and despite the headlines the category itself is led not by London Dry brands but by a genever. And here there really is a point of similarity with craft brewing: no, the whole world isn't drinking tea-infused sour North American IPA, however well publicized it may be. It's drinking Bud.

But then, who wants to read (or write) about Bud?

A Present From Persia: Boiled Wine and Salt

It's one of the great ironies of history that distilled spirits should have been brought to us by a religion and a culture that doesn't drink — such a great irony, in fact, that some of the most distinguished Western historians and researchers in the field of wines and spirits have denied it, for all the evidence.

Distilling, the science of separating mixed materials by manipulating their different condensation points, is one of the fundamental technologies on which human society rests — extracting metal from ore by smelting is, at bottom, a branch of distillation — but its origins are complicated by spontaneous discovery and are therefore much fought over. The science first entered Western literature in the 4th century BCE with a mention in the *Meteorology* of Aristotle, who contemplated the possibility of desalinating seawater by capturing and condensing the vapor arising from salt-pans.[1] At about the same time the metallurgists of India were developing an expertise and sophistication in separation techniques that the West would not match for quite some centuries, while the Chinese were distilling medicines and cosmetics from various botanicals using a four-stage condenser very unlike the western pot-still but not dissimilar to the kind of emergency desalinating condensers used at sea.[2] None of these societies existed in isolation, and once Alexander the Great had advanced as far as the Indus, Greece, China and southern India were in direct contact with each other; commercial and cultural intercourse between them was, if not quite commonplace, at least not unusual. How and indeed whether the knowledge of distillation was transmitted between these cultures is an ill-documented tangle on which a verdict has not been reached and probably never will be; but as the Romans and Byzantines were familiar with perfumes and cosmetics made by the distillation of aromatic oils from flowers and spices, there is every possibility that it occurred.[3]

It is often claimed, but unsupported by any documentary evidence, that wine was also subjected to distillation in classical antiquity. This claim appears to be based on the conspiracy principle: "they could have, so they might have, so let's assume they did;" but then we know of a great many feats the ancients had the power to achieve but never did. But by the late 8th century CE the scientists of the Islamic Enlightenment had started looking into the practical applications of the knowledge that every substance changed its state of matter at its own particular temperature, and one of the substances being investigated was indeed wine. We can now be absolutely certain that the earliest known writer on the subject, the Persian philosopher Jabir Ibn Hayyan (721–815) or Geber, called the Father of Chemistry, was experimenting with distilling wine, which as a devout Muslim he dismissed as being of little use for anything else. It's therefore all the more strange that two of the most distinguished Western authorities of modern times — the journalist of whiskey Alfred Barnard and the leading authority on the wine trade André Simon — should both have denied it, and that even more modern writers have continued to attribute it to medieval alchemists. Simon[4] writes:

> The process of distillation does not appear to have been applied to wine before the end of the 11th century, when a certain Marcus Graecus gave us

> the earliest known recipe for the distillation of Aqua Ardens or Ardent Water in a manuscript entitled *Liber ignium ad comburendos hostes* which is preserved at the Bibliothèque Nationale, Paris. A certain Doctor Albucasis, who lived at Cordoba, Spain, during the 12th century, has also left us a detailed description of the apparatus then in use for the distillation of rose water and of wine. In the 13th century, Raymond Lulli in his *Theatrum Chemicum* and Arnaud de Villeneuve, in his treatise *De Vinis*, show us that the distillation of wine had then been placed on a more scientific basis, and that the virtues of distilled wine were beginning to be appreciated. "Some people call it Eau de Vie," wrote de Villeneuve, "and this name is remarkably suitable, since it is really a water of immortality. Its virtues are beginning to be recognised: it prolongs life, clears away ill-humours, revives the heart and maintains youth."

Almost none of the above is entirely factual. *Liber Ignium* is a short late-13th century manuscript of uncertain provenance, comprising for the most part recipes for Greek fire or napalm; it records "aqua ardens" as an ingredient. Albucasis or Al Zahrawi (936–1013) was an Andalucian Muslim surgeon and author of a medical encyclopedia that remained a standard work for centuries and contained a description of distilling apparatus used to make both rosewater and alcohol; and the *Theatrum Chemicum* is a much later collection of English philosophical verses one of which does indeed mention Ramon Llull. Finally, *de Vinis* is a book of medicinal recipes recommending wine as a vector for medicinal herbs and mentioning *aqua vitae* without elaboration. And no mention of Geber!

Barnard[5] does at least refer to Jabir, but denies his achievement:

From what is known of the Egyptian, the Arabian, and even the Chinese races, it is probable that the secret of the power of the alembic was known to them in ages, the records of which have been lost in the long course of events. Smith[6] writing in 1729 attributes the invention of the art of distillation, by general consent of all learned men, to the Arabian physicians. M (Louis) Lenormand, a great authority, in his work entitled *L'art du Distillateur des eaux-de-vie et des esprits*, published in Paris in 1817, takes the same view. Speaking on the subject he says: '*Les Arabes s'occupèrent, de temps immémorial, à extraire, par la distillation, les parties aromatiques des fleurs et des plantes, dont leurs princes faissaient un très grand usage. L'on croit que ce sont eux qui, les premiers, ont soumis le vin à la distillation, et qu'ils en ont extrait la liqueur qu'ils appelaient aqua vitœ, et que nous avons nommée eau-de-vie. Les Arabes, dans les incursions qu'ils firent en Europe, portèrent successivement leurs procédés en Italie, en Espagne et en France.*' Morewood,[7] however, is of a different opinion. He gives credit to the Arabians as the "improvers" of the art, but looks to other nations for its origin; he is rather of the opinion that the art was long known in the east, by the Egyptians, the inhabitants of India, and the Chinese.

Leaving the discovery of the art shrouded in the mystery of bygone ages, we pass to that period when learned writers began to give it prominence in their works. Rhazes, Albucasis and Avicenna, three celebrated Arabian physicians and philosophers who lived about the 10th and 11th centuries, mention the distillation of roses, a process in their country much in esteem as affording a perfume

> greatly valued by their kings and nobles; but they do not allude to the distillation of wine. Geber, commonly called the Arab, who lived according to generally accepted account in the seventh century, in his celebrated work on chemistry gives an elaborate account of distillation, but only refers to it as a means of extracting the aroma of plants and flowers; he makes no reference to the distillation of wine.

Barnard and Simon might very well have been guilty of chauvinism: in the 19th century (until rudely disabused of the notion at Gallipoli) the West tended to write off the Ottomans and by extension other Islamic nations as decaying, degenerate and effete. It must have been hard to attribute to their forebears such titanic achievements in theoretical and applied science, in art, in architecture and in literature.[8] On the other hand, they might simply have lacked a reliable translation of the works of Geber and others, an omission which has only recently been put right — too late, alas for Reay Tannahill who in *Food in History* (Penguin, 1988) wrote: "It is generally accepted that the distillation of spirits was discovered in the 12th century by the alchemists;" and for Andrew Barr, who in *Drink: A Social History* (Pimlico, 1995) asserts that there was "no conclusive proof of any spirits having been distilled before the 12th century." *The History of Science & Technology in Islam*,[9] co-edited and largely authored by the Syrian chemist Ahmad Yousef al-Hassan, was completed in 2002 and made available online but was only published in print in 2017, five years after Professor al-Hassan's death, as Volume IV in the six-volume *Different Aspects of Islam*, part of UNESCO's General & Regional Histories project. Prof al-Hassan's new translations of original Arabic texts leave us in no doubt that Jabir and his successors were perfectly familiar with the distillation of wine and the properties and uses of the spirit it produced:

The distillation of wine and the properties of alcohol were known to Islamic chemists from the 8th century. The prohibition of wine in Islam did not mean that wine was not produced or consumed or that Arab alchemists did not subject it to their distillation processes… Some historians of chemistry and technology assumed that Arab chemists did not know of the distillation of wine because these historians were not aware of the existence of Arabic texts to this effect.

The first reference to the flammable vapours at the mouths of bottles containing boiling wine and salt[10] occurred in *Kitab ikhraj ma fi al-quwwa ila al-fi`l*[11] by Jabir ibn Hayyan. He says: "Fire which burns on the mouths of bottles due to boiled wine and salt, and similar things with characteristics which are thought to be of little use, these are of great significance in these sciences." This flammable property of alcohol from distilled wine was utilized extensively from Jabir's time and onwards and we find various descriptions of the alcohol-wine bottles in Arabic books of secrets and military treatises.

Among the early chemists who mentioned the distillation of wine is al-Kindi (d. 873) in *Kitab al-Taraffuq fi al-'itr.*[12] He says after describing a distillation process: "…and so wine is distilled in wetness and it comes out like rosewater in colour."

Al-Farabi (c. 878–c. 950) mentioned the addition of sulfur in the distillation of wine.

> Abu al-Qasim al-Zahrawi (d1013) (known in the west as Albucasis) mentioned also the distillation of wine when he was describing the distillation of vinegar from white grapes. He says: "...and similarly wine is distilled by anyone who so desires."
>
> Ibn Badis (d. 1061) described how silver filings were pulverized with distilled wine to provide a means of writing with silver, which indicates that alcohol was collected as a product and was utilized in various ways. He says: "take silver filings and grind them with distilled wine for three days; then dry them and grind them again with distilled wine until they become like mud, then rinse them with water."
>
> We find in the military treatises of the 14th century that old grape-wine became an important ingredient in the production of military fires. One manuscript contains five such recipes, with warnings that such distillates can ignite easily and they should be stored in containers buried in sand.[13]

This is far from being the end of medieval Islam's scientific contribution to our present-day drinking culture. Al Razi or Rhazes (854–925), for instance, was the first to identify, isolate, and refine ethanol to purity, and Arab alchemists and philosophers made increasing progress in their investigations of alcohol, its nature, and its uses even as the Islamic Golden Age of science and technology began to peter out in the mid-13th century. But through all these five centuries, the principal use of spirits of wine or *araq al-nabidh* (sweat of wine, from the droplets running down the outside of the still) remained as a solvent in the manufacture of inks, lacquers, medicines and cosmetics, and as the active component in Greek fire.

Not that people didn't drink it too, though. In the 150 years between the death of Muhammad in 632 and Jabir's prime, Islam had expanded from the Arabian Peninsula to absorb Egypt, coastal North Africa, and Iberia; Palestine, Syria, Iraq, and Lebanon; and Persia and the coast of the Indian Ocean as far as the Indus itself. This huge empire was peopled by millions of vanquished Christians, Jews and Zoroastrians who ran, among other things, vast commercial vineyards in Syria and southern Spain which under Islamic rule were mostly but not entirely given over to table grapes, the sweeter the better. The propertied classes of the conquered regions converted to Islam reasonably rapidly for obvious reasons, but the process was much slower among lesser folk who continued to enjoy a drink; their Muslim rulers, being teetotal but tolerant (and, like the British in India, heavily outnumbered), let them get on with it. Some of the Muslim élite themselves weren't above visiting infidel-run taverns from time to time; and from one of them in the 9th century comes what sounds like our first historical mention of spirits as a beverage when the notoriously dissolute poet and bon viveur Abu Nawas, a contemporary of Jabir's, was out on the town enjoying a drinking session with a friend. He tasted three kinds of wine in succession, each time asking the bartender (khmmar) for a stronger drink and ending up with a wine "the colour of rain-water, but as hot inside the ribs as a burning firebrand" — araq, perhaps; or as it was sometimes called, *ma'al-hayat*: the water of life.[14]

But it was as a solvent in the manufacture of paints and dyes and the extraction of active medicinal compounds from herbs rather than as a recreational beverage that the water of life or *aqua vitae* came to Christendom. On the cusp of the Christian and Muslim worlds, in Salerno just south of Naples, there was the world's oldest medical school, with documented roots in Republican Rome. By the 11th century the school had amassed a vast collection of texts in Latin, Greek, Hebrew and Arabic. Its tutors and lecturers included the leading physicians of the age, some of them from North Africa such as Constantine the

African (from Ifriqiya or Tunisia). Constantine, who converted to Christianity soon after arriving at Salerno in about 1065 (possibly under duress), devoted his life to translating Muslim, Greek and Jewish medical works into Latin; among the 37 books he is known to have translated were several of the works of Jabir ib Hayyan, which were much-copied and soon spread throughout Christendom.[15]

For Salerno's students came from all over Christendom, including Britain; and after their studies were completed they returned to their home monasteries carrying their newfound knowledge with them. To understand how rapidly and how far this sort of information could be disseminated one has to forget an atlas whose principal lines are international boundaries and instead picture one whose principal lines connect cathedrals and monasteries. Gradually the tides of war and politics severed the southern and eastern extremities — the churches in Persia, India, Ethiopia, Armenia — from the main bodies of the Mediterranean shores and northern Europe; but Christendom remained a cultural and political entity within which people and ideas moved with little friction or hindrance, crossing often and with ease the boundaries between and within the Muslim and Christian worlds, so that a discovery made in one far-flung corner could pervade the entirety within a generation. And part of the Salernitan curriculum from at least 1140, when a text[16] was published on the subject, was the use of spirits of wine or *aqua vitae* as a solvent in herbal tinctures.

Sadly for the claims to primacy of the Scots and Irish, knowledge of distilling is documented as having come to England first. Before his death in 1152 the widely travelled natural philosopher Adelard of Bath, whose journeys took him to Syria and the Crusader states, stopping off for extended stays in Muslim-controlled Sicily and at Salerno (he it was who introduced Arabic numerals to Britain), appended several encrypted recipes involving *aqua vitae* and including a number of Arabic terms to his copy of the 10th-century book of artisan formulae for paints, dyes and the like, the *Mappae Clavicula*.

Meanwhile many of Jabir's writings were translated into Latin by an English monk, Robert of Chester, in the 1140s.

But documentation in this period is always patchy, and there is a clue but no more than a clue in Giraldus Cambrensis's *Topography of Ireland* that Irish monks were versed in distilling at much the same time. In 1170 an Anglo-Norman knight, Hugh Tyrell, looted a "great cauldron" from a convent in Armagh. It took a cart pulled by two horses to get it back to his headquarters at Louth, where it set fire to his lodgings and burnt down half the town. Was it a still? Maybe; but the apothecary's alembic of the period was a bench-top affair and unlikely to require a cart to carry it, so if it was indeed a still it was likely to be producing something rather different from a solvent for potions and lotions. Tradition also has Henry II's soldiery, on campaign in Ireland at about the same time, discovering (and mispronouncing) *uisce beatha*; while a later and entirely apocryphal report supposedly from 1276 has Sir Robert Savage, lord of Bushmills, treating his men to "a mighty draught" of it immediately before battle. Author, broadcaster and distiller Peter Mulryan, however, gives the story a thorough debunking: "The tale was in fact lifted and misquoted from a book published in 1812; it should read that every soldier was given 'a good dose of good wine or ale.'"[17]

The first apparent documentation of *aqua vitae* as a beverage comes from the year 1405, when both the *Annals of Clonmacnoise* and the *Red Book of Ossory* report the death at Christmas of Richard MacRanall, chieftain of the now unlocatable Mountyreolas, of "a surfeit of *aqua vitae*," to which one redactor wittily appended: "it was not *aqua vitae* to him, but *aqua mortis*." Of course, he may have overdosed on a prescribed medicine rather than simply had far too much to drink; but the cardinal point is that this cannot be unequivocally stated, although it so often is, to be the first historical record of whiskey. The *Red Book* was Bishop Richard Ledred's day-book or book of ordinaries, maintained from his arrival at the See of Ossory in 1317 until the early 14th century and containing a mass of apparently miscellaneous data connected with charters, rentals, and other matters of day-to-day administrative importance including the following account of distillation, which is the earliest in Ireland and probably dates from the mid-14th century when the Black Death was raging.

> "*Aqua vitae* is either simple or compound. The simple is that which, without any mixture, is drawn from wine, and is called *aqua vini*; and this, being drawn simply, should in like manner be used simply, without any mixture with wine or water. Simple *aqua vitae* is to be made in the following manner: take choice one-year-old wine, and rather of a red than of a thick sort, strong and not sweet, and place it in a pot, closing the mouth well with a clepsydra[18] made of wood, and having a linen cloth rolled round it; out of which pot there is to issue a lyne arm (*cavalis*) leading to another vessel having a worm. This latter vessel is to be kept filled with cold water, frequently renewed when it grows warm and the water foams through the *cavalis*. The pot with the wine having been placed previously on the fire, distil it with a slow fire until you have from it one-half of the quantity of wine that you put in."

This is an accurate description of the distilling process in a rude and imperfect way. The manner in which the passage is worded would seem to imply that it describes what was easily understood and tolerably well known. But from it we remain uninformed whether the product which trickled from the still of the fourteenth century entered into use as a general beverage, or was intended only for medicinal purposes. The unhappy end of MacRanall, as just narrated, would appear to prove

> that, among persons of his rank at least, its use as an ordinary drink could not have been unknown.
>
> It is to be observed that the knowledge of the art of producing alcohol, so far as the *Red Book* throws light upon it, was confined in this case to ecclesiastics, and that the passage affords no information to what extent it was known to the body of the people, or practised among them. It is also obvious that this distillation was effected from foreign wine... Neither this, nor any other document of the period known to us, communicates information as to knowledge having been possessed of the extraction of alcohol from materials of native growth.[19]

Not only did monks produce their own spirits of wine, but a great deal was imported from the Muslim-controlled wine-growing districts of Andalucia, including the city of Jerez. So the spirit that killed MacRanall was undoubtedly brandy or at least its precursor. For evidence of whiskey, gin, or any other cereal-derived spirits we need to look elsewhere.

Materials of Native Growth: The Democratization of Distilling

The next stage in our investigation directs us away from the vineyard and into the cornfield and, concomitantly, removes us from reliable documentary sources. Surviving documentation is poor enough from the period when the producers and users of distilled wine were literate professionals such as monastic infirmarers prescribing tiny doses as medicine and alchemists speculating volubly on the nature of matter. Once it was discovered in northern and eastern Europe that cheap and plentiful native malt liquor could be distilled just as successfully as expensive imported wine, then the whole nature of spirits manufacture began to change, to become much more workaday and down-to-earth, the province of the artisan and burgess as much as the scientist and pharmacist; and reliable contemporary documentation dries up almost completely. From what survives the best we can say is that cereal-based spirits of broadly similar types began to appear in different parts of the beer-drinking world at about the same time: that is, in the 15th to mid-16th centuries. The charter myths pertaining to the origins of many of these native spirits, however, are diverse, often contradictory, and usually unattributed.

Of all of them the origins of vodka are the hardest to fathom, not least because Russia, Poland and Ukraine all vie for the honor of having invented it and whatever an authority from one country proclaims as indisputable fact, its opposite numbers from the others will denounce with equal force as obvious falsehood. And did we mention Belarus, Lithuania and Latvia?

Because this book is really about gin, this is not the place to try to unravel the worms in vodka's can; but at least two of its charter myths appear to be complete fabrication. One is that *zhiznennia voda*, water of life, is recorded in 1533 in the Novgorod Chronicle. Well, *zhiznennia voda* does indeed mean water of life, but the Novgorod Chronicle doesn't mention it and indeed couldn't have for the year 1533 because it ended in 1471 when Novgorod was defeated (and soon afterwards annexed) by the Grand Duchy of Moscow. Nor was Russia's first distillery recorded in the city of Khlynovsk in the Vyatka Chronicle for 1174, as you might have read. The date itself is not impossible, given rumors and legends from late 12th-century Ireland; but Khlynovsk was only a trading post founded at about that time in the valley of the river Vyatka by merchant adventurers from Novgorod. It gradually grew until it did indeed become a city, which was renamed Vyatka in 1780, Kirov in 1934 and Vyatka again in 1992. In the 18th and 19th centuries the city and district had several distilleries, including one at Urzhum founded in 1833 and still celebrated under its modern name, Royka, for its distinctive rye vodka. But nothing is recorded before then, in chronicles or elsewhere.

The most plausible charter myth for the emergence of vodka is the story of a Greek monk named Isidore who in 1430 taught the brothers of Chudov Abbey, which is actually inside the Kremlin complex, to distil a wash made of bread because they had insufficient wine.[20] It ticks most boxes: the date is about right, the monastic setting is right, and wine in medieval Russia was an expensive import. If there were only enough wine in reserve to provide for the Blessed Sacrament then the base for the infirmarer's distillate would have had to be sought elsewhere, and it's not terribly difficult to make an alcoholic wash from a mash containing up to 40% bread provided there is sufficient malted grain present to supply the enzymes required to convert the bread's unfermentable starch into sugar. Kvass can be brewed from rye bread, and the Toast project in Britain today finds a use for waste bread from bakeries, sandwich shops and supermarkets that would otherwise be thrown away by making beer with it (and very good beer it is too). The only thing lacking from the Isidore story, in fact, is a reliable contemporary source.

More level-headed modern authorities such as David and Deborah Christian place the origin of grain-based distillate in Russia in the late 16th century, which is rather later than developments in other northern and eastern European countries but which, given the sketchy foundations of earlier claims, is the date we probably ought to accept.[21] But one very important fact is that until the mid-19th century, when triple distillation and charcoal filtration became commonplace, vodkas, like all other grain-based spirits, were customarily flavored with herbs, spices, fruits and grasses whose origins are clearly medicinal. It's a tradition that survives today in variants such as bison-grass vodka or *zubrowka* in Poland.

One might expect the story of the origin of *kornbrand*, Germany's native cereal-based spirit, to be clear, precise and drilled into orderly rows. Not a bit of it. A political map of Germany in the late Middle Ages shows a galaxy of more than 300 intermingled kingdoms, principalities, duchies, statelets and free cities, some of them independent but many of them forming the scattered holdings of individual dynasties or powers. But Germany's fractal subdivisions did not imply that German universities, schools and monasteries were in any way disconnected from the Judaeo-Islamic-Christian intellectual complex: Albertus Magnus of Cologne (c1200–1280) was the most renowned philosopher and alchemist of the period and was also a dab hand with the alembic. Spirits of wine were virtually a commonplace throughout the German-speaking world much earlier than elsewhere, especially in the wine-growing regions of the south: municipal regulations and taxes on brandy are recorded in Nuremberg, Vienna, Frankfurt and elsewhere from the 14th century onwards. Apothecaries are recorded as distilling their own spirits of wine as early as the late 12th century to use in making medicines, and so are 15th-century innkeepers, presumably to use in making merry:

> From the publications at Augsburg in 1483 of a treatise by Michel Schreik, *Verzeichniss der Ausgebranden Wasser*, and at Bamberg in 1493, of a poem dealing with the merits and demerits of alcohol, it is evident that in Germany the use of spirits was, during the 15th century, no longer restricted to medicinal purposes. In 1496, the municipality of Nuremberg was already taking measures to check the abuse of spirits, a decree issued that year "forbidding the sale of distilled waters on Sundays and other holidays, in private houses, as well as by druggists and other merchants, in their shops, in the market, in the street, or elsewhere, so as to put a stop to their excessive consumption."[22]

We don't encounter an unequivocal record of grain-based distilling until 1545, however, when the town council of Nordhausen in Thuringia banned it. Medieval Nordhausen had distillers of wine among its populace: in 1507 they were significant enough to be worth taxing. But the city, which is very nearly in the geographical center of Germany, was also at the very northern extremity of Europe's wine-producing region — as indeed it still is: the Saale-Unstrut winegrowing district, Germany's most northerly, lies a few miles to the east on the same latitude. And 1550 or thereabouts was the climax of the Little Ice Age, which saw sporadic crop failures, rising prices, shortages of all sorts of commodities and even famines across Europe. With the cultivation range of vines ebbing southward the city's *Brennherren* had evidently switched from grape to grain to charge their stills with at some time between 1507 and 1545, which can only have reduced the retail price of their Weinbrand or, as we should now call it, Kornbrand or just Korn, and made it affordable as a recreational beverage for the common people. We mustn't forget that it takes 10 times as much malt to make a mug of Korn as it does to make the same mug of beer; even if the proof spirit is watered down by half, distilling still consumes five times as much grain as brewing. In a period of climatic unpredictability when grain-crops were already under pressure, cheaper Korn can only have meant more expensive bread and beer; hence the city council's ban. It was not the only reaction of its kind — an almost identical ban was introduced in Scotland in 1579, although it exempted noble households — but they seldom lasted long: expensive malt could always be padded out with rye and oats, and landowners also realized that here was an incremental demand that would allow them to increase output without risking a fall in prices. And vineyards forced out of business by climate change could always be turned over to marginal arable land well-suited to rye and oats, given that they tended to be sited on poor, thin soils on sloping ground. (Nordhausen's own vineyards all appear to have failed by the beginning of the 17th century.)

Of all the new generation of grain-based cereals, the *akvavit* of Scandinavia is of peculiar interest in that it may have arrived from both western and eastern Europe more or less simultaneously, but very late. For many early medieval Scandinavians, especially Norwegians and northern Swedes, short growing seasons and low summer temperatures made grain-harvests unpredictable and, rarely for Europe, honey was as accessible a source of fermentable sugar as malt — in fact the Baltic littoral is probably the last stronghold of mead-making (and distilling) in Europe. Ale, mead and a strong hybrid were the staple alcoholic beverages and if Vikings on the rampage seemed to be drinking more than usually prodigious amounts of ale it may well have been because they didn't get very much of it at home. So it's no surprise that there's no record at all of distilled spirits until 1400, when distilling seems to have arrived in Denmark.[23] In 1531 a Danish lord, Eske Bille, wrote to the Archbishop of Norway offering him a gift of water (meaning in this context spirit) that "helps for all illness that a man can have internally or externally." A medicine of high enough status to make a prestige gift of this sort can only have been wine-based, and the royal distillery founded by Christian III in 1555 was presumably working with wine. But at the very same time vodka was emerging as the favored beverage of the Slavic states to the south and east, and Scandinavia — Sweden in particular — was as open to cultural and commercial influences from Russia as from Germany. The retail license for *akvavit* recorded in Stockholm in 1498 might have related to either grain or wine-based spirits, since nothing is specified; but once the Lutheran reformer Gustav I (1523–1560) had dispossessed Sweden's monasteries the country's distilling trade soon passed into the hands of lay apothecaries who, we can safely assume, quickly switched from wine to cheaper and more readily available malt and rye to start distilling something that sounds very like vodka.

British monks and apothecaries had as long a tradition of making and writing about the distillation of wine as any of their continental counterparts. Adelard of Bath and Bishop Ledred of Ossory we have already met; the *Compendium Medicinae* of Gilbertus Anglicus (c. 1180–1250)[24] takes the use of *aqua vitae* or *aqua ardens* in medicine as a given; the British Library's Sloan Collection MS964 attributes the late reawakening of the sexual appetite of Queen Isabella (d. 1358), wife and betrayer of Edward II and mother of Edward III, to an elixir distilled from the lees of strong wine and infused with 20 herbs and spices including cloves, ginger, nutmeg, galangal, cubebs, grains of paradise, long pepper, black pepper, caraway, cumin, fennel, parsley, sage, mint, rue and oregano;[25] and Henry VI's Master of Stillatories or court apothecary Robert Broke (1432–1455) appears to have either overseen or at least benefited from the replacement of earthenware distilling equipment with glass.[26] Fragments of glass alembics from the 14th and 15th centuries regularly turn up in architectural digs at abbeys across Britain, and references to the purchase and use of distilling equipment by monastery infirmarers are equally commonplace. All these worthies worked with wine; and compared to the uncertainty and confusion that surrounds the great switch from grape to grain in most European countries, in Britain it can be narrowed down to a day, a month and a year: June 1, 1494, as recorded in the Scottish Exchequer Rolls. One of the most famous and yet most misinterpreted Latin sentences in the history of alcohol reads: *"Et per liberacionem factam Fratri Johanni Cor per preceptum compotorum rotulatoris, ut asserit, de mandato domini regis ad faciendum aquavite, infra hoc compotum viij bolle brasii"* or: "Delivery has been made to Brother John Cor, on the order of the Comptroller, as he reports, (and) by mandate of the lord king under that account of eight bolls of malt for making aqua vitae." Almost universally, this one sentence is hailed as marking the birth of whiskey. It does no such thing. It's closer, if anything, to the birth of gin.

What the apothecary is doing with the eight bolls of malt charged to his account is making pure alcohol (or as pure as he can get it, which was probably not very) as a base for medicinal tinctures and, possibly, the alchemical experiments of which James IV was so fond. A "boll" was a dry measure whose weight fluctuated according to when and where it was cited: according to a trade almanac of 1863 it amounted to 320 lbs of barley, so Friar John's allowance might have come to as much as 2,560 lbs or 1.15 tons — enough to make 3,852 liters of wash at 8% ABV or thereabouts or, after going through the still twice, 350-odd liters of not-very-pure alcohol. That's not actually a huge amount: even watered down by half it wouldn't have kept the court merry for very long. It would have been quite enough, however, to provide a good supply of drams (a dram being, when eventually standardized, an eighth of an apothecary's ounce) of crystal-clear(ish) spirit to be infused with a blend of wisely chosen healing herbs and spices. Absolutely nothing like whiskey, in fact, but quite a lot like gin, and very like the other grain-based spirits evolving north of the wine belt: vodka, as we have seen, commonly carried a charge of botanicals until the mid-19th century; *akvavit* was (and still is) flavored with herbal grists almost always based on caraway; and overproof *korn* or *ansatzkorn* was often the foundation of liqueurs such as *zirkenschnapps*, infused with pine-cones, which had been recognized as a pungent and powerful panacea since the *Materia Medica* of Dioscorides. In fact distillers in the northern half of German-speaking and German-influenced Europe became extraordinarily versatile in devising strong compounded spirits: perhaps because they had to compete with the Obstbrände of Austria, Bavaria, and Switzerland, the *eaux de vie de fruits* of Alsace, and the myriad *palinkas* of Hungary and the northern Balkans, they came up with a huge range of spirit-based infusions that included Kirsch, Kummel, Bärenfang, Danziger Goldwasser and Silberwasser and many, many others. (Alas, though, the biggest seller among them, Jägermeister, is a modern interloper having been formulated only in 1935.)

The flavorings, even the gold and silver, were all regarded or at least promoted as having therapeutic qualities long after production had passed from the hands of high-minded infirmarers to commercially minded apothecaries, long after the patrician and expensive wine base had been succeeded by the plebeian and affordable ale base, long after the expression "purely medicinal" had ceased to have any actual meaning. In fact our next record of Scotland's proto-whiskey (or, more properly, proto-gin) comes in the form a monopoly over its production granted by James IV to the Edinburgh Guild of Surgeon Barbers in 1505, and in 1577 Ralph Holinshead's Chronicle was still singing *aqua vitae*'s praises as a sovereign remedy which "being moderately taken it cutteth fleume, it lighteneth the mind, it quickeneth the spirits, it cureth the hydropsie, it pounceth the stone," and "kepyth... the stomach from wamblying."

But what can it have been like, this gin/whiskey precursor? Well, pretty much indistinguishable from the other malt distillates of the time — unaged and therefore clear; double-distilled, or it would not have been potable; and suffused with medicinal herbs and spices either in the second distillation or perhaps as a tincture. In 1695 James Lightbody, known as "Philomath," published a treatise on brewing and distilling entitled *Every Man His Own Gauger* in which he gives the recipe for "Irish *usquebaugh*" as follows:

> Take of good spirits, 12 gallons. Put therein of aniseeds, nutmegs, sugar, carroway-seeds, of each four ounces, distil the whole to proof spirit, put thereto liquorish, raisins of the sun 2 pound, and 4 lb. of sugar, let it drain through a flannel bag, and fine it down with the whites of eggs and wheat flour. This is the only way that natives of Ireland make this liquor, which is approved of to exceed all the other new ways of making it, being but imitations of the original.

George Smith's *Compleat Body of Distilling* (1725) gives various recipes; but he, along with many others, always refers to *usquebaugh* as a compound by rectification of proof spirits.[27] One recipe he gives requires five gallons of rum, six of "malt brandy," and gallons of water as required; then mace, cloves, nutmeg, cinnamon, coriander seed, ginger, cubebs, raisins, dates, licorice, saffron and sugar. The spices were to be rectified with the spirit in the still; the saffron should be bagged and hung "at the worm's end," the fruit and licorice were infused in hot water and strained into the spirit, and finally the sugar was dissolved in it. The price of the ingredients came to £2 17 shillings 1½ pence, and the resulting 10 gallons of "fine usquebaugh" would sell at £1 a gallon. It may not sound much like whiskey to us, and even as late as 1755 Dr. Johnson, in his dictionary, defined *usquebaugh* as being "drawn over aromaticks;"

again in 1825 Walter Hamilton, perhaps building on Johnson, defines *usquebaugh* in his *Concise Dictionary of Terms Used in the Arts & Sciences* as: "A strong compound distilled spirit *drawn* on *aromatics*, dried fruits, and spiceries, originally taken as a dram." It seems from these recipes and references that as late as the early 19th century, *usquebaugh* — but for the absence of juniper — was still closer to gin than to whiskey.

Usquebaugh would also have been far too strong to drink unless it was watered down by at least a half from its original 80-odd% alcohol by volume; and perhaps it was the watering down that persuaded people that it was much more than a medicine but a beverage in its own right. Not that its medicinal efficacy was ever forgotten or ignored: not only was *aqua vitae*, to Holinshead, "a sovereign liquor" against all kind of ailments (although only "if it be orderlie taken"), but it was also easy to make. The standard household brewing and washing copper, with the addition of a tight-fitting or well-luted lid and either a tapered condensing pipe or a coil of copper tubing (the more expensive option) immersed in cold water, was all the equipment required. And small-scale distilling was a great boon to farmers, for whom prolonging the shelf-life of their produce and if possible concentrating it to facilitate transportation was a permanent economic goal. Distilling meant that after good harvests they no longer had to sell their surplus barley at glut prices but could process and store it almost indefinitely against the inevitable lean years. And it was the storage that transformed a naïve, unsophisticated, herb-infused spirit close to gin into whiskey. Left in oak barrels (the standard method of storage in northern climes) until the time came to it take it to market, the limpid *aqua vitae* took on color and flavor from the tannin and vanillin in the oak, and continued to mellow as the aldehydes were metabolized and as a percentage of the alcohol ("the angels' share") gently evaporated through the porous wood. The longer it was kept, the smoother it became... and the higher the price it fetched.

That was the origin of whiskey, a farm-made spirit intended to even out the fluctuations in the value of different harvests and therefore likelier to be well-matured in oak than their urban cousins, which were born in a milieu where there was plenty of custom and a guaranteed quick turnover for a good fresh panacea — towns and cities being hotbeds of contagious diseases, with a constant demand for medicines that were if not especially efficacious at least pleasant to drink. By the end of the 16th century distilling had become a standard component of household economies wherever cheap wine, lees of wine, wine pomace, or a grain-based wash were available. In Scotland and Ireland the product, stored from good year to bad, was whiskey; in Russia vodka distilling was made a seigneurial monopoly as soon as the landowning classes discovered what a lucrative sideline their peasants had stumbled on; in the German-speaking territories of northern Europe, the Balkans, and throughout the romance countries artisan distilling of all sorts throve and diversified and slivovitz, barrack, hefebrand, anise and nocino became firm fixtures in the local culinary canons.

Perverse as it may seem, the two domains where artisan distilling of malt liquor never seems to have become widespread were the very two where gin was to take such firm hold: England and the Low Countries.

A Bush So Commonly Known: Juniper the Wonder Drug

The reason why grain spirits took so much longer to emerge in England and the Low Countries than elsewhere in northern and eastern Europe was simple: there was less demand for them. In Germany, Scandinavia, Russia, Poland, Scotland and Ireland distillers turned to grain-based wash because there were neither native vines nor money to import wine in the necessary quantity. In the two great North Sea mercantile powers there were no vines either, or too few; but there was plenty of money and hence plenty of imported wine.

At the start of the modern period English wine-shippers were establishing new sources of supply following the loss in 1453 of Gascony, which for three centuries had been part of the Angevin Empire and which had supplied England with all the wine it could drink. At the same time, the reconquest of Iberia from Muslim control was almost complete, and the vineyards that had for so long produced mainly sugar-rich table-grapes needed new markets. Affluent English wine-drinkers began to change their tastes, since the port, Canary, and Madeira, the sherry (or sack) so beloved of Falstaff and the Malmsey also immortalized by Shakespeare were sweeter and heavier than the table-wines of Bordeaux and the Loire. Even though these wines were not yet fortified, a development that was not widely adopted until the late 17th century, they created — and satisfied! — a demand for a stronger, higher-status drink than ale or beer and thus held back the rise to popularity of brandy.

Not that there was any lack of interest in medicinal distilling in England; and as monastic influence in medicine and science was waning (a process that was well under way before the final dissolution in the 1530s), the baton was increasingly being passed, as in Scotland, from infirmarers who jealously doled out their precious *aqua vitae* dram by dram to apothecaries whose interest lay in selling as much of it as they could. In this work the latter were guided by a translation of Hieronymus Brunschwig's *Liber de Arte Distillandi* (Strasbourg 1500) by one Lawrence Adams, printed and published in London in 1527 under the wonderfully wordy title *The Vertuose Boke of Distyllacyon of the Waters of all maner of Herbes for the help and profit of surgeons, physicians, pothecaries, and all manner of people.*

"Aqua Vitae," says the Vertuose Boke, "is commonly called the mistress of all medicines, for it easeth the diseases coming from cold. It giveth also young courage in a person, and causeth him to have a good memory and remembrance. It purifyeth the five wits of melancholy and of all uncleanliness, when it is drunk by reason and measure; that is to understand five or six drops in the morning, fasting, with a spoonful of wine, it comforteth the heart and causeth a body to be merry." Other similar works followed, all part of a great tide of manuals and handbooks offering instruction in all manner of trades that flooded out of London's nascent printing industry and quickly — impossibly quickly, it would have seemed to the previous generation — found their way to a newly literate class of artisan entrepreneurs desperate for knowledge.

These manuals included two entirely separate translations of the *Euonymus*[28] by the Swiss doctor, botanist, zoologist and general polymath Conrad Gessner, known in his lifetime as the Swiss Pliny and author of 72 books including the first ever on mountaineering. Peter Morwyng's *Treasures of Euonymus* went to three editions within a year of publication; the version by George Baker, *The New Jewell of Health*, followed shortly and was more successful still.[29] One of Gessner's recommendations was that spoilt wine or wine lees should be preferred over sound wine. As the *New Jewell* has it: "The burning water, or water of life, is sometimes distilled out of pleasant and good wine, as the white or the red, but oftener out of the wine lees of a certain eager-savour or corrupt Wine. Further, when out of pure wine a water of life is distilled, I hear that out of a great quantity of good wine, a little yield or quantity of burning water is to be distilled, but out of the lees of wine, a much (greater) yield and quantity (are) gathered."

Morwyng's take on the same passage includes the insight that the sale of lees to distillers was a highly profitable sideline for wine-merchants: "Burning-water, or aqua vitae," he writes, "is drawn oute of wyne, but, wyth us, out of the wyne lies only, specially of them that sel it, and by this onely almost get their livying. And peradventure it is never a whit the worse that it is drawne oute of lees; for Lullus teacheth that it may be wel destilled of corrupt wine, yea, if it be distilled often it shal be made the more effectuall (that is to say), hotter and drier, etc."

By 1577, when in England Holinshead was still eulogizing about *aqua vitae*'s miraculous therapeutic and medicinal properties, across the North Sea things were changing. As a semi-autonomous province of Burgundy the late medieval States General — modern Holland and Belgium and the Flemish-speaking county of modern France north of Calais — had traditionally had access to the wines of Burgundy, to the produce of surviving vineyards in Flanders, and to imports from both Spain and France. In the late 15th century a long series of wars broke out which led to the Spanish taking control; in 1585, the seven northernmost provinces — effectively, modern Holland — broke away, with the loss to the Dutch of their supplies of Spanish wine. This had far-reaching consequences, for the people of the Low Countries' thickly clustered and prosperous cities had been developing a taste for brandy. Indeed they coined the term *brandewijn*, by which we refer to distilled wine to this very day, and several cities soon had thriving distilling industries. And it seems clear that not all of the output of these businesses was intended to be used medicinally: the late 15th-century BL Sloane MS 345 contains two brandy recipes, *Gebrandewijn te maken* (to make brandy wine) and *Eenander manyr om brandewijn te maken* (another way to make brandy wine), which are included with the kitchen recipes. This, and also the fact that the old term *aqua vitae* was replaced by the new word, is good evidence that by the end of the 15th century the drug had become a drink. The tax levied on brandy by city authorities in 1497 reinforces the suspicion.[30]

Faced with the loss of a large part of their wine supply (the Flemish vineyards having succumbed to climate change in the first half of the 16th century), the burghers of the breakaway provinces fell back on two expedients. One was to lend money to enable the winemakers of the Charente, whose product was too thin and acidic to be of potable quality but was ideal for distillation, to set themselves up as distillers. The rationale was that since brandy was no more than concentrated wine it would be much cheaper to transport if it were distilled at source and rehydrated at home. They never seem to have got round to the rehydration part; but they did found the Cognac industry, some of whose output had already started finding its way to the London market in the mid-16th century.[31]

The second expedient was to pad out the precious wine in their wash with malt liquor. They did not immediately follow the lead of their Scandinavian and German neighbors and produce all-grain spirits like *akvavit* and *korn* partly because they were prosperous enough not to have to and partly because grain, too, was in short supply. Not only had independence shorn the seven United Provinces of the richer agricultural land in the south, but much of their remaining land, having yet to be drained, was not much more than swamp and while well-suited to stockrearing was all but useless for arable. Nevertheless, says Eric van Schoonenberghe:

> In the 16th century the consumption of brandy rose rapidly. Many cities introduced taxes on brandy, which was increasingly being distilled from beer and mead... However, the upper class continued to drink brandy from wine while the commoner resorted to drinking the cheaper brandy. Already in 1552 a physician from Antwerp, Philippus Hermani, protested against the growing consumption of brandy distilled from beer in *Een Costelijck Distileerboek*[32] and in 1588 the pastor Casper Jansz Coolhaes did so in *Van seeckere seer costelijcke wateren.* According to these authors brandy from grains has less flavour, wine distillate is the only healthy one, one can only speak of brandy if it is distilled from wine, and grains can only be used for the purpose of making bread. Notwithstanding these warnings the production and consumption of brandy made from beer and mead rose enormously in the second half of the 16th century. The distillers no longer processed other brewers' beer, but made their own and distilled it two or three times to obtain corn brandy or malt spirit.

Two developments made it possible to use so much grain for distillation: one was the reimposition of feudal practices on peasant farmers in Eastern Europe, which created a new source of cheap corn, and the other was the gathering pace of land reclamation in the United Provinces themselves, reaching a climax in the early 17th century. The evolution of cereal-derived spirit into a drink we would recognize as gin came about as a marriage between the new sufficiency of grain and the very high regard in which Dutch herbalists had long held that near-ubiquitous bushy conifer, the juniper.

The juniper was believed by many in the region to be the wonder drug of its time. Its little black berry (really a miniature cone), its oil, even the smoke and ashes of its wood had therapeutic properties such that, according to the 17th-century English herbalist Nicholas Culpeper, the whole plant was "scarce to be paralleled for its virtues." He wrote:

> For to give a description of a bush so commonly known is needless. They grow plentifully in divers woods in Kent, Warney Common near Brentwood in Essex, upon Finchley Common without Highgate; hard by the New-found Wells near Dulwich, upon a Common between Mitcham and Croydon, near Amersham in Buckinghamshire, and many other places.
>
> The berries are a most admirable counter-poison, and as great a resister of the pestilence as any growing: they are excellent against the biting of venomous beasts, they provoke urine exceedingly, and therefore are very available to dysuries and stranguaries. It is so powerful a remedy against the dropsy, that the very lye made of the ashes of the herb being drank, cures the disease. It provokes the terms, helps the fits of the mother, strengthens the stomach exceedingly, and expels the wind. Indeed there is scarce a better remedy for wind in any part of the body, or the cholic, than the chymical oil drawn from the berries; such country people as know not how to draw the chymical oil may content themselves by eating ten or a dozen of the ripe berries every morning fasting. They are admirably good for a cough, shortness of breath, and consumption, pains in the belly, ruptures, cramps, and convulsions. They give safe and speedy delivery to women with child, they strengthen the brain exceedingly, help the memory, and fortify the sight by strengthening

> the optic nerves; are excellently good in all sorts of agues; help the gout and sciatica, and strengthen the limbs of the body. The ashes of the wood are a speedy remedy to such as have the scurvy, to rub their gums with. The berries stay all fluxes, help the hæmorrhoids or piles, and kill worms in children. A lye made of the ashes of the wood, and the body bathed with it, cures the itch, scabs and leprosy. The berries break the stone, procure appetite when it is lost, and are excellently good for all palsies, and falling-sickness.[33]

But appreciation of the digestif and healing properties of juniper went back long before Culpeper's time, and as van Schoonberghen asserts, it was the Dutch who appreciated them most. The German-speaking world produced 28 medical tracts singling out the juniper for special praise during the medieval period, with the earliest dating from the 13th century when the French-Flemish Jacob van Vitri devoted an entire chapter to it in his *Historia Orientalis* (1244). At much the same time the Augustinian canon Thomas van Bellingen from Brussels, a pupil of Albertus Magnus, produced *Liberde natura rerum,* a compendious bestiary and herbal compiled from the works of Ancient Greek philosophers such as Aristotle, Hippocrates, and Galen, the Islamic scientist Avicenna, and the 12th-century herbal *Circa Instans,* which also gave special attention to the power of the juniper's berry and oil. But the oldest documentary reference to the use of juniper in beverages comes in *Der Naturen Bloeme*, a rhyming nature encyclopaedia by Jacob van Maerlant (1235–1300) written between 1266 and 1269 in Damme, an outport of Bruges. Wine in which juniper berries have been seethed — "*seiden jenewere in wijn*" — is recommended as a digestif and therefore as the immediate predecessor of gin; but gin proper is only described and strongly advocated in a much later tract, *Sequuntur propietates et virtutes granorum juniperi et olei granorum*, written in 1496 partly in Latin and partly in Middle Dutch (Wellcome Historical Medical Library MS618). Some recipes in the manuscript come from the practice of Jan Spierinck, the personal physician of the Duke of Brabant and three times dean of the University of Louvain. One such, supposedly written by a Dr. Hubertus, recommends leaving the berries to macerate overnight in *aqua vitae* rather than boiling them in wine — a method of compounding practiced to this day. In the recipe *Gebrande wijn te maken* we encounter rectification proper: brandy's medicinal properties, we are told, can be greatly enhanced by adding a cloth bag filled with carefully selected herbs including powdered *gorsebeyn* or juniper bays and redistilling the brandy. Substitute grain spirit and add some of the other recommended herbs — bay-leaf, cloves, and nutmeg among them — and you have straightforward gin.

This timeline clearly rules out the traditional attribution of the invention of gin to a professor from Leyden, Franciscus de le Boe or Sylvius (1614–1672). Sylvius, founder of iatrochemistry,[34] was as accomplished in the practice of distillation in the preparation of drugs as any chemist of the time, and made free use of juniper derivatives. However in 1606, eight years before Sylvius was born, the Dutch States General had issued an ordinance levying taxes on all distilled wine and anise, genever and fennel waters (water here meaning, as so often, distilled spirit) when sold as beverage rather than physic. In the States' ordinance on brandy of October 1583 there is no mention of a tax on the sales of herbal waters; at that time, therefore, the Government still classed these drinks as medicinal. "The fact that a tax on these medicinal drinks was introduced in 1606 indicates that they were no longer seen as a medicine, but rather as a largely consumed stimulant," says van Schoonberghen.[35]

This takes us back to the separation in 1585 of the United Provinces in the northern Low Countries from the Spanish Netherlands in the south. The consequent loss of trade with Spain reduced the north's supply of wine, as we have seen, and hence made it too dear and too scarce to distil. As people fell back on grain-based "brandy" it was reclassified as a beverage;

but as far as the better-off were concerned it was no substitute for the real thing. Independent compounders and rectifiers therefore set up in business in most cities to produce a drink that would satisfy the refined taste of the more affluent burghers. "The upper class appreciated malt spirit's organoleptic characteristics less than brandy distilled from wine," says Van Schoonberghen. "This urged the producers to aromatize the malt spirit, especially with juniper. This was also the origin of specialization, *viz.* malt distillers producing the raw spirit while compound distillers aromatized it."

Juniper not only satisfied demand for a more sophisticated drink, it had practical advantages as well. Like the hop, which was beginning its rise to popularity in English brewing at about the same time, the juniper turned out to be both prolific and, compared to other herbal crops, easy to manage. It was hardy and drought-resistant, thrived in both acid and alkaline soils, and needed little or no input. The berries were straightforward to harvest since the bush's natural height rarely exceeded a meter or two. The branches and cones being very densely packed were easily accessible to the picker; and since the berries were slow to mature there were normally ripe and unripe fruits on the bough simultaneously, making for a long rolling harvest rather than a single annual labor-intensive burst.

More than that, though, juniper is delicious. Crush a few of its dark, sticky little cones and you release a wonderfully clean, pungent aroma that has been used as a substitute for black pepper for centuries, especially in rich game dishes that need a lift and in sweet pastries that would otherwise be syrupy and cloying. The oil has been a staple in cosmetics since as far back as the time of the Pharoahs, and a handful of twigs or branches thrown on the fire (or barbeque!), especially when twinned with rosemary, drives away the most pernicious of odors and refreshes the air with an antiseptic piney fragrance. And this is not just hyperbole: the cone is packed with terpenes, the oily hydrocarbons that give fruit and flowers their scents and flavors, dominated by up to 50% pinenes both alpha, which is water-soluble, and beta, which is only soluble in ethanol — hence gin's peculiar pungency. Its other flavor components are also at the sharper end of the terpene spectrum: borneol, a component of camphor; myrcene, the dominant terpene in cannabis and also present in bay, cardamom, parsley, hops, lemongrass and verbena; sabinene, present in black pepper, tea-tree and nutmeg; and limonene, self-explanatory and the most versatile of all terpenes, used as a solvent in paint-stripper and also in 3-D printing. The only exception is farnesene at around 5% of oil content, whose warm floral aroma also found in lavender and bergamot adds depth and fullness to the juniper's piquancy.

Juniper was only one of a number of herbs — or as we now say, *botanicals* — with which the earliest versions of gin were commonly either infused or rectified. Others included the roots of angelica, an umbellifer all too easily confused with hemlock but with similar therapeutic properties to juniper itself (nowadays mainly crystallized and used as a cake decoration); liquorice, thought good for respiratory ailments; and orris or iris, aged, dried and ground to create a dark floral background. These fairly humble ingredients were available locally, but the more exotic spices now commonplace in botanical grists were more problematical. Medieval gastronomers delighted in sharp, pungent spices to enliven their diet of boiled and baked meat, root vegetables, cabbage, leeks and onions, pulse-based pottage, cheese, bread and the occasional apple or well-boiled pear. But in the mid-15th century the Mongols cut the overland spice road of central Asia and the Ottomans captured Constantinople, until then the principal *entrepôt* for the Oriental trade. The sea-routes to the spice isles were in the hands of the Portuguese, who made hay while the sun shone and throughout the 16th century mercilessly exploited their monopoly. Even the prosperous burghers of the Low Countries found their spices getting more and more expensive until they were out of the reach of all but the wealthiest; so in 1595 the Dutch decided to challenge the Portuguese by sending their own merchant fleets to the East Indies to establish trading posts and therefore a regular source of supply of spices and other exotic commodities. Before long it was possible to add cloves, cinnamon and cardamom to the register of favorite botanicals, along with the acid zest of new sweeter strains of orange and lemon (notably portingales from Portugal, supplanting bitter Seville oranges from Spain), and the picture was more or less complete. But not quite: the story of the juniper's part in the evolution of gin had a coda.

While the distillers of the United Provinces were turning to their newly plentiful sources of grain to replace their dwindling supplies of imported wine, the distillers of the Spanish Netherlands were being forced to use imported wine rather than their own grain. The ban imposed in 1601 by the Governor General, Archduke Albert of Austria, on the distillation of grain and, interestingly, cider was an act of blatant protectionism and remained in force until Spanish rule finally came to an end in 1714. Only Hasselt, which was not strictly part of the Spanish Netherlands but belonged to the Principality of Liège, was not forced to abide by Albert and Isabella's edict and continued to distil "wachtelwater," its own kind of gin. But in the Spanish Netherlands proper, the obligation to use expensive Spanish imports had had the effect of holding the distilling industry back. Only with the succession of the Austrian branch of the Habsburg family were farmers in the southern Low Countries not only allowed but positively encouraged to start distilling grain again in order to re-energize the depressed agricultural sector. However they rarely flavored their spirit with juniper even though they still called it gin; and to this day some distillers in East and West Flanders produce gin without juniper.[36]

Dutch Courage: Friends, Foes, and Fighting Spirit

By the opening of the 17th century, the United Provinces had discovered its national drink, a grainy, malty spirit either compounded or rectified predominantly with juniper berries, with the addition of herbs and roots from its own gardens and spices from its newly founded Oriental trading-posts. Two centuries before the invention of the column still made it possible to produce near-neutral spirit, early gin was probably very similar to the *moutwijn* — a wash of malt and other grains pot-distilled to around 50% ABV — which is the basic building-block of today's *oude* and *yonge* genevers and *korenwijn*. The residual malt gives today's version a roundness and mouthfeel as close to whiskey as to gin; and with gin's characteristic aromatics to lift and enliven it, it soon became more popular than the fennel and aniseed-flavored spirits that were its early competitors.

Across the North Sea the English, as close commercially, politically and culturally to the Dutch as they were geographically, were soon familiar with genever (which they still called *brandy*). It's not actually true, though, however often repeated, that the first Englishmen to taste it were either the soldiers in the Earl of Leicester's campaign of 1585–1586 or the mercenaries who fought for the Dutch against the Spanish in the 1590s:

genever, as we know, was not regarded as a beverage but as a medicine until the tax reforms of 1606, and given Holland's scarcity of grain was probably not made in copious enough volumes to satisfy the English soldiery anyway. It's probably true that they did indeed discover hard liquor in the late 16th-century Low Countries, but the hard liquor they discovered was most likely to have been French brandy from the stills financed by Dutch merchants in the Charente. Nevertheless, and even though the expression "Dutch courage" wasn't to appear in print until 1814, the English soldiers who fought both alongside and against the Dutch in the century between Leicester's expedition and the War of the Spanish Succession were well aware that Dutch generals were wont to follow Ramon Lull's advocacy of "the marvellous use and commodity of burning waters in war, a little before the joining of battle, to stir and encourage the soldiers' minds."

English military leaders at the time don't seem to have been terribly impressed, as witness *Instructions to a Painter*, Sir Edmund Waller's verse celebration of the Duke of York's naval victory over the Dutch in the Battle of the Four Days fought off Lowestoft in 1665:

> The Dutch their wine and all their brandy lose
> Drained of that from which their courage grows…
> Bacchus now, which led the Belgians on
> So fierce at first, to favour us began.
> Brandy and wine, their wonted friends, at length,
> Render them useless, and betray their strength.

The generals soon changed their minds when they re-encountered gin as allies of the Dutch during the Nine Years' War and the War of the Spanish Succession, as Defoe recounted in a pamphlet published in the wake of an increase in malt tax and to defend the malt distillers against moral reformers[37]:

... the Dutch Sutlers carry'd into the Camps in Flanders, during the late long Wars against France, a certain new distill'd Water call'd Geneva, being a good wholesom Malt Spirit, if rightly prepar'd, wrought up with Juniper-Berries; a Thing not only wholesom, but really physical [i.e. medicinal], and for many Years allow'd to be so by the most celebrated Physicians. It was strange to observe, how this Liquor prevail'd in the Army; how the Soldiers were surprized at the Goodness of it; the Spirit, the Vigor it put into them: They declar'd publickly to one another, there never was any such Liquor heard of in the World; it put a perfectly new Spirit, and new Life into them; and invigorated them at such a rate, that it made them quite a new kind of People.

At first, like the Champaign and Burgundy, it was drank among the Gentlemen only; a Drink for Generals, and for Officers: Nay, they tell us in Holland, that even the great D[uke] of M[arlborough] gave it a Character as a Thing that inspir'd Nature with a new Flame; and put a sort of Vigor into the Mind, which Nature itself was a Stranger to before; and that he recommended the (moderate) Use of it, to the greatest Men, when they were going at any time to engage the Enemy. It is a great Mistake to argue from hence, that the Dutch always made their Soldiers mad with Drink, before they led them out to fight; for what I am saying of them now, is of the Generals and Officers, before the Soldiers came to have any fellow-feeling of this Article. At first, no doubt the Dutch made a fine Spirit of it, and as perfect as it was possible to be expected: But as the Dutch are hardly to be charged with any Deficiency in

> needful Craft, and that they saw plainly what was good for the High, was also good for the Low; and that the poor Soldiers Money was as good to them as the great Generals, if they could but make it out in Quantity; they soon came into the old Trading Maxim, viz. that Cheapness causes Consumption, and found out a Way to make a Sort of the same Spirit, and drawn perhaps from the same Ingredients; that being made meaner in Quality, should be proportioned to the Purse, as well as to the Palate of the common Soldiers. And thus the Soldiers in the Confederate Camp, came to the honour of Drinking upon a Level with their Officers, or at least, flattering themselves that they did so, which indeed was almost the same Thing; and if there was any apparent Difference, it was such that neither Officers or Soldiers were nice enough in their Palates to judge of…
>
> Our soldiers tasting this Liquor, brought the Desire, as well as the Fame of it, over with them at the ensuing Peace; and our Distillers preparing it as well here, as the Dutch abroad, they supply'd the People with it, wrought from our own Corn the Product of our own Land, very much to our Advantage, as has been said already: the Encrease of the Demand, afterwards encreasing the Consumption of our own Malt, to a very great degree.

These martial examples notwithstanding, the English seem to have come to the idea of spirits as a beverage very late. Tudor and early Stuart apothecaries regarded *aqua vitae* highly as a physic, as did their patients: Shakespeare mentions *aqua vitae* six times, four of them as a medical restorative (*Romeo & Juliet* III, 2 and IV, 5; *Twelfth Night* II, 5; *Winter's Tale* IV, 4), once as part of a gentleman's travelling kit (*Comedy of Errors* I, 1), and only once as (apparently) a drink in the *Merry Wives of Windsor* when Ford says: "I will rather trust a Fleming with my butter, Parson Hugh the Welshman with my cheese, an Irishman with my aqua-vita bottle…" (II, 2). Gervase Markham in *The English Housewife* (1615) gives 16 recipes for various medicines and cosmetics, including a dye, all based on distillates of wine, wine lees, or ale and using an almost comical miscellany of herbs, roots and spices. The following is typical:

> To make the imperial water. Take a gallon of Gascon wine, ginger, galingale, nutmegs, grains, cloves, aniseeds, fennel seeds, caraway seeds, of each one dram, then take sage, mints, red roses, time, pellitory, rosemary, wild thyme, camomile, and lavender of each a handful, then break the spices small, and the herbs also, and put all together into the wine, and let it stand so twelve hours, stirring it divers times, then distil it with a limbeck, and keep the first water, for it is best: of a gallon of wine you must not take above a quart of water; this water comforts the vital spirits, and helps inward diseases that come of cold, as the palsy, the contraction of sinews, also it kills worms, and comforts the stomach; it cures the cold dropsy, helps the stone, the stinking breath, & makes one seem young.

Markham's contemporary Hugh Plat includes in *Delights for Ladies* (1609) a similar section entitled Secrets of Distillation and comprising 25 spirit-based recipes, all for medicines and cosmetics, and as late as 1663 Samuel Pepys describes his one and only encounter with gin as a cure for constipation, reporting: "I had a couple of stools forced after it, and did break a fart or two." Markham's list does, however, include a single recipe that he specifically designates a beverage rather than a medicine: his "very principal aqua composita" includes balm, rosemary flowers, dried red rose leaves, penny-royal, elecampane root ("the whitest that can be got"), liquorice, cinnamon, mace, galingale, coriander seeds, caraway seeds, nutmeg, aniseed and borage; all finely chopped, steeped in ale for a day and night, and distilled. This, says Markham, "was made for a learned physician's own drinking;" and if its battery of 14 botanicals seems a little inflated, well, there are artisan gins being concocted today that are just as elaborate.

At the same time small-scale artisan distilling of beverages was just beginning to emerge, not so much after the Irish and Scottish model of farmers adding shelf-life and value to glut harvests, but along lines more suited to a nation of shopkeepers: as extensions to existing retail businesses. Peter Clark in *The English Alehouse* records a pub called the Aqua Vitae House in Barking in 1572, three such operations licensed in Salisbury in 1584, and a customer asking to be allowed to have a little lie-down after trying the *aqua vita*e made by Goody Streat at her alehouse in East Grinstead.[38] However Clark uncovered few mentions or traces of spirit-retailing at such an early date in the alehouse inventories he studied: more common, perhaps, were the "strong-water shops" of which Daniel Defoe, in the above-mentioned pamphlet, records:

> These were a sort of petty Distillers, who made up those compound Waters from such mixt and confus'd Trash, as they could get to work from, such as damag'd and eager, or sour Wines; Wines that had taken Salt Water in at Sea; Lees and Bottoms; also damag'd Sugars, and Melasses, Grounds of Syder, and innumerable other such like. For till then there was very little Distilling known in England, but for physical Uses. The Spirits they drew were foul, and gross; but they mixt them up with such Additions as they could get, to make them palatable, and so gave them in general, the Name of Cordial Waters. And thus the strong-

> Water-Shops usually made a vast Show of Glasses, labell'd and written on, like the Gallypot Latin of the Apothecarys, with innumerable hard Names to set them off. Here, as at a Fountain, the good Wives furnish'd their little Fire-side Cupboards, with a needful Bottle for a cherishing Cup: And hence, as from wholesale Dealers, all the little Chandlers Shops, not in London and its adjacent Parts only, but over great Part of England, were furnish'd for Sale; and to the personal Knowledge of the Writer hereof, and of Thousands still living, not the Chandlers Shops only, but just as is now complain'd of, the Barbers Shops (Barber Chirurgeons they were then called) were furnished with the same, and sold it by Retail, to the poor People who came under their Operations.[39]

The trade was apparently substantial enough in the 1590s for two businessmen, Robert Drake and Michael Stanhope, to buy a royal monopoly granting them the right to license all distilleries in and around London making "aquacomposita, aquavitie, beere venigar, or allegar onlie and for no other intent or purpose by anie person or persons whatsoever to be sould or put to sale" for a term of 21 years. In April 1600, we find their deputy Gerson Willford licensing William Catcher of the Red Lion, East Smithfield, to brew ale or beer for the purpose of distillation (but not to distil wine or wine lees) and sell it in London, Westminster, and Southwark at a license fee of 6 pence a barrel. The patent was evidently not as profitable as Drake and Stanhope had expected, since it lapsed in 1601, perhaps because the English already brewed such strong beer, "calling the same doble-doble," that the authorities constantly tried to ban it,[40] and to distill it would surely have been both gilding the lily and tempting fate. Nevertheless, distilled spirit was becoming enough of a commonplace to strike a familiar chord in satirical drama: in 1622[41] we find it being uttered for sale in a tavern in John Fletcher and Philip Massinger's *The Beggar's Bush*, III, 1. (Interestingly, the play is set in a heavily fictionalized Bruges and the spirit is being cried for sale as "brand wine").

By the 1620s London had around 200 compound distilleries,[42] selling much of their output as ship's stores which (until the capture of Jamaica in 1655) crews might fall back on when and if the beer or cider they habitually carried ran out or became spoiled and, according to critics complaining in 1640, much of the rest via "'shops and drinking-houses' retailing liquor 'so fierce and heady' that a pint 'will make half a score of men and women drunk.[43]'" Sailors who had acquired a taste for spirits at sea wanted hard liquor ashore as well, a demand that soon spread to landlubbers; and it was (ostensibly, at least) in response to the indiscriminate and unregulated spread of distilling for beverage that the Distiller's Company of London was formed. The moving spirits behind the new livery company — 69th in order of precedence — were two fairly minor courtiers: Sir William Brouncker, who had virtually beggared himself buying a Viscountcy, and the queen's physician, Thomas Cademan, a recusant Roman Catholic. The two were already in business together as distillers in St. James's, and to overcome opposition from the Apothecaries' Company, which petitioned that allowing them a charter would infringe its monopoly, they sought the advocacy of the king's own physician Sir Theodore de Mayern. A Swiss-born Huguenot refugee with degrees from both Heidelberg and Montpellier, he had attended Henry IV of France until the king's assassination in 1610 and had then joined the court of James I. First and foremost a chemist, he had assisted at the secession of the apothecaries from the grocers to form their own livery company in 1617. Once again his lobbying was successful, and the Distillers' Company of London (never to be confused with the 20th-century Distillers Company Ltd.) received its charter from Charles I in August 1638 with Cademan as Master. The Company was, on the face of it, intended to regulate and prevent abuses and protect the public, declaring in its charter:

> That no Afterworts or Wash (made by Brewers, etc.) called Blew John, nor musty unsavoury or unwholesome tilts, or dregs of beer or ale; nor unwholesome or adulterated wines, or Lees of Wines, nor unwholesome sugar-waters; musty unsavoury or unwholesome returned beer or ale; nor rotten corrupt or unsavoury fruits, druggs, spices, herbs, seeds; nor any other ill-conditioned materials of what kind soever, shall henceforth be distilled, extracted or drawn into small spirits, or low wines, or be any other ways used, directly or indirectly, by any of the Members of this Company, or their successors at any time hereafter forever.

Many of these practices were and remain industry commonplaces — how could there be marc without lees of wine? — and some had even been recommended by Gessner and his English translators. As for "unwholesome wines," the thin, acidic whites that the Dutch had selected as the feedstock for their French brandy were pretty well undrinkable in their virgin state. Given what else we know — that Brouncker was all but broke, that de Mayerne was notoriously acquisitive, and that patents and monopolies were more about profiting from fines and licenses than protecting the consumer — it seems more than likely that the founders of the Company were in it for gain. Perhaps the malpractices they list were no more substantial than "body odor" or "night starvation" of our own times — maladies entirely fabricated so that their inventors might profit from the cure (or in this case, the fine). But if so, it was a plan that never materialized. The Company's monopoly on granting licenses and levying fines only extended to a 21-mile radius of London, and when in November 1642 Civil

War broke out its courtier-founders were suddenly out of favor and in no position to lobby for further advancement.

London, still at this time the principal seat of English distilling, was securely in the hands of Parliament from the moment the war started until the Restoration nearly 18 years later; and you might expect that a government of Puritans would zealously and rigorously purge it of frivolities such as distilled spirits, just as it purged it of maypoles and Christmas. But it didn't, and for two main reasons. One was that spirit beverages still existed side by side with spirits-based medicines and were in many cases produced by the very same enterprises, so that you couldn't harm one without harming the other. Another was that while the Puritan ethos may have dominated politically, Puritans themselves were a minority and their culture was not universally shared, even within the loose and fractious grouping of interests that constituted the government. The Lutheran strand in English Protestantism, as opposed to the Calvinist strand in the Kirk, valued hard work, enterprise, ingenuity and initiative to the point where worldly success could be taken as a mark of divine favor — the sacrament of wealth that underpins the contorted Lutheranism of the United States to this day. If a brewer or an apothecary were to increase his wealth and social standing by diversifying into distilling then provided he could contrive to appear godly he would find no enemies among the ruling coalition. What held distilling back was the state of the wartime economy: one of Parliament's first acts after hostilities began was to impose a near-universal purchase tax, the excise (from the Dutch *accijs*), which was so onerous that it provoked a serious riot in 1647 when the butchers of Smithfield resisted the officers sent to collect it. But excise was an exigency of war, quickly taken up by both the Royalist and Scottish Parliaments and intended as a temporary measure, not a punitive one; for while the Puritans and their fellow-travellers sought to suppress any public junketings they considered ungodly, they could hardly suppress alcohol itself when beer was food for the worker, wine the reward for the diligent and strong waters the medicine for both.

Excise proved far too profitable to be temporary, however; and although reduced from eight pence a gallon to two pence (four pence on imports) soon after the cessation of hostilities the duty on spirits was to be part of the lasting legacy of the revolution. Another such bequest was rum, which had James II not been so stubborn a Catholic might have evolved into our national spirit.

In 1655, as part of a foreign policy aimed at undermining support for the exiled Charles II, Cromwell sent Vice-Admiral William Penn (father of the founder of Pennsylvania) to capture Santo Domingo (today's Dominican Republic) from the Spanish and establish a colony for disgruntled ex-Royalists (Barbados, occupied in 1627 and originally colonized mainly from the West Country, had more recently used to settle Scottish prisoners of war). Penn was beaten off, however, and instead invaded the less strongly held neighboring island of Jamaica. In Barbados the British settlers had established plantations of tobacco; sugar-cane was first planted in the late 1630s by Protestant Dutch refugees from Brazil and rapidly became the island's dominant crop[44]; and from its waste product, molasses, the thrifty and inventive Dutch distilled a spirit which they called *rumbullion*. The etymology of the word is contested, but its likeliest origin is a combination of the English adjective *rum*, meaning odd or strange (as in "a rum do and no mistake") well-recorded in Elizabethan texts and only recently obsolete, and *bouillon*, French for a hot drink but also signifying "boiled." Jamaica also had sugar plantations, and sugar planting with rum production as a profitable sideline became one of the foundation stones of the slave trade, the economic expansion of Britain's American colonies (before being superseded by tobacco and cotton), and indeed the whole British Empire.

The rum produced in ever-growing quantities by the colonists soon caught on in the west-facing British ports that handled much of the West Indian and American trade: its popularity in Bristol and Plymouth at first, followed by Liverpool and Glasgow, lasted well into our own times. But rum was only one of a whole crop of new-fangled spirits that competed for public favor in the aftermath of the Restoration, of which Daniel Defoe observed (with a nod to Waller, perhaps):

> Our Drunkenness as a National Vice, takes its Epoch at the Restoration, or within a very few Years after... Joy, Mirth, good Cheer, and good Liquor, were the Solace of the common People. They rejoiced that after a long Usurpation, the King should enjoy his own again; that after a long Series of Blood and Confusion, and a Civil War in the Bowels of their Country, the People should enjoy a publick Peace and Tranquillity; that Trade should flourish, and Plenty succeed Misery and Want. These were the several Reasons of their Joy; and very merry, and very mad, and very drunken, the People were, and grew more and more so every Day. As to the Materials, Beer and Ale were considerable Articles; they went a great way in the Work at first, but were far from being sufficient. Strong Waters, which had not been long in Use, came in play; the Occasion was this: In the Dutch Wars, it had been observed, That the Captains of the Hollanders Men of War, when they were to engage with our Ships, usually set a Hogshead of Brandy abroach, afore the Mast; and bid the Men drink lustick, then they might fight lustick.[45]

French brandy, often called *Nantes* after the port from which much of it was shipped, was of course the natural drink of Charles II's Francophile court and its imitators; the Spanish and Portuguese exported brandy too; and rum, as we have seen, was slowly capturing the heart of the West Country and especially its Atlantic ports. Also finding favor in the rural west, however, was the distillate of the region's age-old rival to ale and beer: cider.

During the Commonwealth and after the Restoration, a number of influential tracts were published urging landed gentry ruined by requisition and sequestration to help rebuild the incomes of their neglected and war-damaged estates by planting cider-apple trees in hedges, on headlands, and on any other unproductive or underexploited ground they might own. Two of the most influential of them, *Pomona* (1664), compiled and edited by the diarist John Evelyn, and *Vinetum Brittanicum* (1676) by John Worlidge, assumed that most orchardmen were distilling at least some of their produce; and given the ubiquity of household stills among the bourgeoisie assumed by Markham and Plat it is unreasonable to assume that many cidermakers denied themselves the profit of a sale or the pleasure of a tipple. The probate inventory of the Spread Eagle in Midhurst, East Sussex, taken in 1673, includes a small pewter still — and Sussex being cider country, it is not merely possible but probable that the late innkeeper, Henry Courtney, had been making cider brandy for his guests.[46]

Distillation, although never a hugely significant contributor to the economy of the western counties, was nevertheless earnestly promoted by some: *Aphorisms upon The New Way of Improving Cyder, or Making Cyder-Royal* (1684) by Richard Haines (a Sussex ciderist better known for his Gospel commentaries), advocated the manufacture of a liqueur composed of a hogshead of cider blended with the distillate of a second hogshead — exactly the same as modern *pommeau* — as a native product that could compete successfully with imported spirits. An instinctive protectionist, Haines shared the view that a growing trade gap, especially in new luxury products such as coffee, chocolate and brandy, was the source of the economic slump of the 1670s. The total annual value of these he put at £2 or £3 million. On the other hand, he said, English manufactures had decreased. His remedies were both to stimulate and protect the manufacture of English goods and to ban imports that he saw as superfluous such as "that outlandish, robbing, and (by reason of its abuse) Man-killing Liquor, called BRANDY."[47] Cyder-Royal never caught on, but in the Britannian Magazine (1691) a writer named William Worth argued that "brandy made from beer, cider, perry or fruit wines is little inferiour to that of France," and there is a passing reference in William Ellis's *The Compleat Planter and Cyderist* (1756) to "many hogsheads of perry carried by wagons to Worcester to the distillers to draw a spirit from it, which is sold for 10 shillings per hogshead." (A tax of four shillings a hogshead was imposed in 1759, but it was the measures adopted in 1823 against moonshining in Scotland that finally killed off artisan and domestic distilling in England).

But however hard rum and cider brandy might be promoted in the cities and shires of the west, and whiskey in the far north, the market that mattered was London. In the second half of the 17th century London was at the tail end of a long growth spurt which saw its population increase tenfold between 1520 and 1690, while the national population only doubled. Between 1650 and 1700, according to the Cambridge Group for the History of Population's best estimate, London's population grew from 400,000 to 575,000[48] despite the plague of 1665 as rural migrants streamed into the city from a countryside impoverished by war and recession and now made hostile by the final wave of enclosures. And although they encountered squalor, overcrowding, jerry-built shacks, crime, contaminated water, sewage in the streets, disease, infant mortality and all the miseries that haunt any city that has outgrown itself so rapidly, they also encountered work, wages and a dazzling choice of goods — including drinks — to spend it on. For many incomers, the range of drinks shipped into the capital meant finding alehouses and taverns that stocked the drinks of their hometowns. Alongside clear, pale beers from Burton (just rising to prominence as a major brewing center thanks to the switch from firewood, which was in very short supply, to clean, steady-burning and above all plentiful coke to fuel its many maltings), they could enjoy imports of the strong Kentish beer beloved of Pepys, the even stronger Norfolk Nog and nostalgic tankards for migrants still homesick for Derby, Dorchester, Lichfield, Nottingham, Doncaster, Devon and elsewhere. Cider was sold in an increasing number of alehouses, and alongside the wines traditionally sold in taverns there was now a growing choice of spirits. Pepys in his diaries recorded the names of 20 alcoholic beverages he found in various establishments including six varieties of beer (two of them customarily sold hot); both metheglin and mead; cider; sherry and a variant, Bristol Milk; other wines including Muscadet, hypocras and "Ho Bryan" (actually Haut-Brion, the first wine to brand itself by its point of origin) in the Royal Oak in Lombard Street; and French brandy and other unspecified spirits which probably included brandy from Spain and the Canaries. Defoe, born in 1660 and writing many years later, listed without further elaboration "Aqua Vitae, Aqua Mirabilis, Aqua Solis, Aqua Dulcis, Anniseed Water, Cinamon Water, Clove Water, Plague Water and Cholick Water, which in short was Geneva"[49] as popular spirits in the London of his youth.

The aniseed water he singled out for special mention may actually have been either a wormwood infusion such as arak, very similar to modern pastis, ouzo, and raki, imported from the eastern Mediterranean, or more probably a domestic copy based on the easily made "malt brandy" favored by the urban proletariat. It paid less tax than beer, and the huge increase in the amount of cheap coal being shipped into London from Newcastle ate into one of the brewer and distiller's biggest costs: fuel to heat mash tun, kettle and still. The arrival of cheap, strong glass also made it possible to distribute bottled beers and spirits through retail channels other than the traditional on-trade: Defoe doesn't recall "anniseed-water" as being on sale in taverns, the coffee-houses then coming into vogue,[50] or alehouses, but in shops (including specialist "strong-water shops") and bumboats, and the streets:

> Aqua Vitae and Anniseed Water, were the Captains or Leaders; and the strong Inclinations of the People ran all into those two: And in a little while the latter prevail'd over the former too; and as Anniseed Water was the only Liquor for some Years, the Quantity that was drunk of it, was prodigious great: In a word, it was the Geneva of those Times, it was not only sold in the Chandlers Shops, and in the Barbers Shops, as above; and perhaps in Bulks and Stalls too; but it had this particular Article attending it, (which we are not yet arrived to with the Geneva) viz. That it was cried about Streets, of which, the Memory of the famous Anniseed Robin, will be a never-dying Testimony; who was so well known in Leaden-Hall, and the Stocks-Market for his Liquor, and his broad-brim'd Hat, that it became proverbial, when we saw a Man's Hat hanging about his Ears, to say, he looks like Anniseed Robin. This Part, viz. of going about the Streets, and into the Fields, to Shows, and Musters of the Trained Bands, to cry a Dram of the Bottle, has not been so long omitted, but that we can all remember it: And the Bumboats, who continue to this Day, crying a Dram of the Bottle, in the River, among the Ships, are a Remainder of that Custom, and which was never left off at-all.[51]

As distilling and spirit retailing grew in volume, an important economic imbalance between imported spirits and domestic produce began to emerge. "In 1684, the whole of English-made spirits on which excise was paid amounted to 527,000 gallons, whilst there were 202 tuns, 36 pieces, and 19 casks, equal to about 29,000 gallons of foreign spirits imported into London during the month of February 1683," says André Simon. "In 1694, the produce of all the stills in England amounted to

754,300 gallons of spirits. In the same year, in spite of the prohibition of French spirits, there were imported from Holland, Spain, Portugal and the Canaries, in the port of London alone, about a million and a quarter gallons." (Simon's figures are of duty-paid goods only, net of the smuggling observed by the chief excise officer Charles Davenant in southern England 1678–1689). This was in the in the face of urgent pleas for a protectionist policy from English producers and their advocates. The arguments of the ciderist Richard Haines had been prefigured in 1673 by a petition to Parliament got up by the brewers, identical in sentiment and near-identical in language:

> The Grand Concern of England explained in several proposals to the consideration of Parliament that brandy, coffee, mum, tea and chocolate may be prohibited, for they greatly hinder to consumption of barley, malt, and wheat, the product of our land.
>
> Before brandy, which is now sold in every little alehouse, came into England in such quantities as it now doth, we drank good strong beer and ale, and all laborious people (which are far the greatest part of the kingdom), their bodies requiring, after hard labour, some strong drink to refresh them did therefore every morning and evening used to drink a pot of ale or a flagon of strong beer, which greatly promoted the consumption of our own grain, and did them no great prejudice; it hindered not their work, neither did it take away their senses nor cost them much money, whereas the prohibition of brandy would be otherwise advantageous to the kingdom and prevent the destruction of His Majesty's subjects, many of whom have been killed by drinking thereof, it not agreeing with their constitution.[52]

The sheer length of the subtitle with which Haines prefaced his Aphorisms is the most eloquent summary both of the argument for domestic production and the urgency with which it was propounded: "For the Good of those Kingdoms and Nations That are Beholden to Others, and Pay Dear for Wine, Shewing That Simple Cyder, frequently Sold for Thirty Shillings per Hogshead (vis Three half-pence a Quart) may be made as Strong, Wholesome, and Pleasing as French wine usually sold for Twelve-pence a Quart; Without Adding anything to it, but what is of the Juice of Apples; and for One Penny or Three-half-pence a Quart more Charge, may be made as good as Canary commonly sold for two Shillings. As also, how one Acre of Land worth now Twenty Shillings, may be made worth Eight or Ten Pound per Annum." To drive home the message, it is dedicated to "All Kings Princes and States, who have no wines of their own Production," including the "Kings of the two Northern Crowns" and the States General of the United Provinces.

But the protectionists of the 1670s were spitting into the wind: the Francophile late Stuart kings and their ministers were free trade Tories, not protectionist Whigs, and their Parliaments were of the same stuff. Only a reluctant and ineffectual intervention on the Protestant side of the interminable Franco-Dutch war prodded Charles II into banning French imports including wine and brandy in 1678: the ban didn't have much impact thanks to smuggling and high-level corruption, though, and was lifted as soon as the even more Francophile and openly Roman Catholic James II succeeded his brother in 1685.

Then came 1688…

FROM "GOOD AND WHOLESOME BRANDY"

Christmas 1688 came three days early for the Church of England: On 22nd December that year (and at his second attempt), the unbending Roman Catholic James IImanaged to escape to France, to be succeeded by his equally unbending Protestant elder daughter Mary and her Dutch husband William, who would reign with her as King William III.

William, ruler of the United Provinces since 1672, had invaded England with a considerable armed force a month earlier, having been invited by an English ruling class dismayed at James's refusal to summon Parliament, dismiss his Catholic ministers and confidantes, and disinherit his infant son. Instead of counterattacking the invaders promptly with the army he still controlled, James delayed and forfeited its support too; a few days after the defection of its leaders (including the young John Churchill), England had a new regime. And since Holland was almost permanently at war with France, the new government's very first action was to reinstate the blanket ban on trade that James had lifted; while the second was to pass the not unrelated "Act for encouraging the distillation of brandy and spirits from corn and for laying several Duties on low wines or spirits of the first extraction."[53]

The preamble to the Act declared its protectionist purpose unambiguously: "whereas good and wholesome brandy, aqua vitae, and spirits may be drawn and made from malted corn; for the encouragement therefore of the making of Brandy, strong waters, and spirits from malted corn, and for the greater consumption of corn and the advantage of tillage in this kingdom." The Act itself was quite a short one: only 12 clauses, mostly concerned with administrative detail but with three key provisions aimed at boosting the distilling industry. Duty on low wines, set at 4 pence a gallon by Charles II in 1661, was reduced to 1d a gallon on British corn spirit and 3 pence on spirits of cider and perry, and increased to 8 pence for low wines drawn from "foreign materials" and a shilling for the distillate of brewer's wash or "tilts" (cask lees of ale so called because they were collected in the bilges of the barrels, which had to be tilted to let the liquid flow out of the bung-hole), perhaps a nod to the London Company of Distillers' notion of quality control. At the same time though, the Company's monopoly on production of low wines was abolished and a separate clause was inserted allowing anyone to set up as a distiller without either the tradesman's customary seven-year apprenticeship or even a justices' license. Finally, a bounty of 3 pence a gallon was to be paid on exports.

The act was probably the biggest opportunity in history for a nascent domestic industry to invest in expansion, but it was all too sudden for the English distillers. In 1684, according to Andre Simon, duty was paid on 527,000 gallons of English-made spirits and 377,000 gallons of imports. The English-made spirit, apart from cider brandy, seems to have been mostly made from tilts, for even in the era (i.e., before 1825) of the 16-ounce pint and hence the 128-ounce gallon the big barrels in common use by brewers and wine shippers — 54-gallon hogsheads, 72-gallon puncheons, 108-gallon butts and 216-gallon tuns — held easily enough tilts to be worth distilling. But the common people who favored these waters and cordials only marginally outdrank the aristocracy and bourgeoisie with their imported French and Spanish brandy — if at all, given that Simon's figure only represents the legally imported spirit on which duty was actually paid while the additional quantity that was smuggled is unknowable.

While in England the distilling industry in the later 17th century seems to have been a small-scale operation run almost as a sideline by brewers, cidermakers and wine-merchants, or by the scavengers who collected their barrel-lees, in the United Provinces it had matured and prospered, and by the 1690s the river port of Schiedam was witnessing the birth of true mass-production. A few miles inland of the Hook of Holland, the old fishing town was by then a major transhipment node for goods arriving both from Germany and Belgium for onward export and from the North Sea and the Dutch East and West Indies for inward distribution. By the end of the 17th century it had become more than just a busy seaport and was also a manufacturing center with more than 30 gin distilleries, some of which are still operating today including Nolet (founded 1691) and de Kuyper (1695). (In Amsterdam the venerable house of Bols had been founded even earlier, in 1575: Bass claims to possess the world's oldest trademark, but Bols is surely the oldest brand-name). The development of distilling in Schiedam and other such centers had been boosted by a diaspora of Protestant southerners, many of them skilled and experienced distillers, following the partition of 1585. Just as the German diaspora of the mid-19th century included skilled brewers who founded brewing industries as far afield as Milwaukee and Mexico, members of this diaspora were responsible for establishing distilleries in the Antilles, Barbados and Brazil; and when the English in 1664 seized control of New Amsterdam they found that the Dutch settlers there had already been producing gin on Staten Island for 20 years! A community of 7,000 of them also settled in London where some entered the distilling trade; most of the Protestant refugees, though, migrated north to the United Provinces where they contributed their energy and expertise to the processes of expanding the output and refining the technology of the distilling industry; so as barley production in East Anglia, Lincolnshire, and East Yorkshire increased alongside enclosures and improved techniques and outstripped the capacity of the English distillers to process it, there was only one market developed enough to sell it to: Holland.

How much British malt was sold to Holland in the years immediately following the Glorious Revolution it's hard to know: nearly 40 years later Defoe estimated the amount of barley used by English distillers as 200,000 quarters or (very roughly) 35,000 tons a year, with at least another 100,000 quarters being malted and sold to the Dutch. This barley, he claimed, was poor stuff grown on marginal land which, had it not been recently improved, would never have been cultivated.[54] We do have a rather better estimate, thanks to tax records, of the coal exported to Holland from Tyneside and central Scotland to mash and distil it, though: 40,000 tons in 1700 rising to 140,000 tons by the mid-century, alongside 25,000 and 75,000 tons respectively from Belgium.[55] The English distilling industry, with such enormous potential markets and potential capacity behind it, caught up soon enough; but in the meantime Dutch merchants routinely perpetrated a fraud on the English Exchequer so egregious that it can only have been connived at, or at least conveniently ignored, by excise officers.

The fraud as described by Defoe operated as follows: the Dutch merchant would place an order for (say) 20 quarters of barley, pay the two shillings malt tax per quarter, and send his raw seed complete with "tails" — the thin, half-ripened heads that would normally be discarded — to the maltings. There the sodden grain would puff up somewhat, and even the shoots would bulk it out a little, which was all quite normal; but it would be measured unscreened, with the tails bulking it up to 40 or even 60 quarters. Once the malt was loaded for export the merchant could reclaim or "draw back" the duty — not just the 40s he had paid on his original order of grain, but 80 shillings or even 120 shillings on the exaggerated volume of malt he had loaded. As if that weren't enough, his export bounty of

30 shillings for 20 quarters was also fraudulently inflated to £3 or even £5. This illegal profit of £2–4 drawback and £1, 10 shillings to £3 bounty must surely have been shared with the excise officer and the maltster; even so, it cut the Dutch distillers' costs to the point where they were able to undercut their native competitors when they reimported the finished product and, said Defoe:

> The Dutch were doubtless look'd upon as great Benefactors to our Commerce, and who by taking off yearly so great a Quantity of our Corn, were so great an Advantage to our Landed Interest, our Navigation, and our Poor; and while the Product, let it be what it will, was consum'd abroad, and their Geneva and other Spirits reach'd no farther than their Camps and Fleets (and withal while they did not cheat us in the Draw-backs too, if ever that time was) they were really so. But here you will see that it is possible, in the general turn of things, and the Changes which matters of Trade, in common with the rest of human Affairs, are subject to, what is a publick Good today, may be a publick Grievance tomorrow; and what a Law is made to encourage at one time, may require a Law to prohibit and prevent at another: And this is the true Case of the Dutch Distilling Trade, as it shocks with, and at this time interferes with our own.

By the time Defoe's pamphlet was published the influence of the Dutch had already begun to wane as England's production capacity inexorably rose; but by then they had already done the job of turning juniper-infused jenever from the medicine Pepys took for constipation into the people's favorite. At the time of the Glorious Revolution the two branches of what was to become the gin industry had already separated:

larger enterprises (although not, at this early stage, very large enterprises) commonly known as "malt distillers" produced the base spirit, paying excise duty on the low wines or "spirits of first extraction" from the wash still.[56] This they ran through the spirit still to concentrate and purify for sale to retailers, many of them very small, who either compounded (infused) or rectified (redistilled) it with their chosen botanicals — aniseed, as we have seen, being the most popular — watered it down to a potable strength, and (allegedly; although this is a subject we shall return to) padded it out with all sorts of noxious extenders.

The provisions of William & Mary's Act cutting the duty on low wines from four pence to a single penny a proof gallon was accompanied by successive increases in duty from two pence a quart in 1688 to three pence in the 1720s to pay for the seemingly perpetual war against France. Nobody in the government seems to have been able to predict the effect these contradictory measures would have: they appear to have been taken somewhat by surprise when spirits suddenly became enormously popular while, in London, average annual beer sales fell from 1.152 million barrels in the years 1715–1724 to 986,000 in the following decade.[57] The native malt distillers with their limited capacity simply couldn't keep up with demand when sales soared from 850,000 gallons (500,000 gallons domestic, 350,000 imported) in 1685 to more than 2,000,000 gallons in 1690 (1,250,000 imported). It was reported that the Dutch distillers were so hard put to it that to keep up with demand they shipped their jenever as new make, without the customary two or three months' maturation in oak, which might explain some of the bad press it got. It was also reported that English malt distillers were resorting to installing new stills in back rooms, filling extra storage tanks by means of "private pipes and stop-cocks," and even distilling on the Sabbath, the implication being that they were as interested in evading duty as in satisfying the demand of compounders and rectifiers.[58]

The English industry's attempt to keep up was aided by a punitive tariff of four shillings two pence a gallon on imported spirits and an even more punitive six shillings eight pence on French brandy and, as Defoe observed, by changing tastes:

> It is evident, that as well by the Dearness of French Brandy, and the Corruption and Fraud of the Dutch Importation, as by the improv'd and still advancing Goodness of the English Malt Spirit, which I shall make appear is coming fairly up to be equal to the best French Brandy; the great and opinionated Gust of the People to French and Foreign Brandy, is already much abated, and the Consumption of our own Product gains Ground on them every Day, to the great Advantage of the whole Nation.[59]

The "improv'd and still advancing Goodness of the English Malt Spirit" was due in large part to the publication of books of recipes and instruction such as George Smith's *Compleat Body of Distilling* (1725), which went through edition after edition for the rest of the 18th century and into the 19th and allowed the hundreds of small compounders and rectifiers that sprang up, especially in London, to supply a huge range of flavored spirits (and medicines, since it was intended for apothecaries as well) of good and consistent quality. But the cunning of those rascally Dutch, it appeared, was inexhaustible. Defoe fumed:

> Nor have the Dutch done with us yet; but let us examine it thorowly, and we shall see a greater Fraud yet. The Dutch, I know not by what Error on our Side, are allow'd to import here foreign Brandy, the Duty upon Importation being 4s 2d per Gallon, or thereabouts; whereas the French Brandy pays 6s 8d per Gallon. This our People take up with, and call it French Brandy; and having sufficient Proof that it comes from abroad, are satisfied with it as such. The Dutch tell us, it

> is not French, tho we have good Reason to believe that all the real Brandy that is in it is French, by which we are cheated that way. But that is not the Case; 'tis apparent, the Dutch mix their own Malt Spirits with this Brandy, and send it to us, while our People, deluded with the Notion that it must be right Brandy, because it comes by a foreign Permit, eagerly buy it for right Brandy, and give a Price accordingly.

But given time, the advances being made in industrial technology began to tell. In the early years of the 18th century new equipment was just beginning to become available, practical versions of scientific instruments were slowly evolving, and the trend towards bigger and more profitable malt distilleries capable of consistently achieving a high-quality base spirit was clearly observable. In particular, improvements in the smelting, refining, and processing of sheet copper made possible not only the very large haystack boilers — upright cylinders with flat bottoms and domed tops — that provided the steam for Savery and early Newcomen engines but also much larger pot stills and brewery coppers than had previously been available: the "great copper" described by Michael Cambrunne, a Hertfordshire brewer and author of *The London & Country Brewer* (1759), held 20 barrels or 720 gallons (remembering always that a pint before 1825 measured only 16 fluid ounces), and weighed 5,760 lb. In this respect, gin distilling and porter brewing had the same requirement, and it would be fascinating to know how much crossover there was between the two. Porter was made by mashing the malt grist three times, blending the worts,[60] then boiling them with hops in a giant copper kettle before fermentation and maturation in huge upright coopered tuns. Distillers achieved a similar or even better extraction by fermenting the worts without troubling to run the liquid off the grain beforehand[61] and distilling the resulting wash in a copper still (copper was favored for many reasons, one of them being that it converts foul-tasting sulphides into flocculent sulphates, which precipitate easily), often over an indirect heat source such as a sand-bed or a *bain marie* for a more even distribution of heat without the hot-spots that would caramelize the wash, and for finer temperature control. In all cases a very large and pressure-resistant copper vessel was crucial to the process; and the success of Newcomen's engine — the first started work in 1712 at Dudley and 133 were in operation around the country by the time of his death in 1729 — as we have seen, prepared the nation's coppersmiths to meet increasing demand from the brewing and distilling industries. London brewers in 1699 brewed an annual average of 5,000 gallons each whereas by the middle of the 18th century the biggest porter brewers were producing 200,000–300,000 barrels, which will give some idea of the size of the various vessels and vats they required.[62]

Distillers, being parvenus not yet hidebound by tradition who didn't find innovation threatening, were also more forward-looking than brewers when it came to adopting hydrometers and thermometers. The hydrometer, a calibrated glass float that measures the density of liquids, was known to the ancients and to Galileo but was only rediscovered as a practical implement for assessing the purity of coinage by Robert Boyle in 1675.[63] It was used by distillers long before being introduced into the brewing industry because establishing proof-strength was regarded as vital.[64] In 1730 an instrument-maker known only to history as Mr. T. Clarke designed a more durable copper version, because in the busy working environment of the distillery a delicate glass instrument "could not well be carried in the pocket." His version was calibrated to proof, specifically "for the use of those that deal in brandies and spirits" and was so accurate that after many distillers had used it to dispute duty assessments the authorities adopted it too.[65]

Thomas Cooke, one of London's leading malt distillers and master of the Distillers' Company in 1742, was an early adopter not only of the hydrometer but also of the thermometer. A practical mercury-filled model had been invented by

Gabriel Fahrenheit in 1714, to be followed by the Fahrenheit scale in 1727, but few British brewers had one before the end of the century and some still weren't using it until the middle of the next. Conveniently, the ideal mash temperature of around 150° F is also the highest temperature at which most people can just bear to put their hand in (hence the expression "rule of thumb"); it's also the temperature at which water that has been boiled and then left to cool stops producing vapor. It can be fairly reliably achieved by boiling 220 measures of water and then adding 100 measures of cold.[66] Most brewers were happy with these rather loose traditional methods; Cooke, however, wasn't, and dictated that: "the thermometer only can determine what should be done, and I think there can be no perfect work without the use of it."[67]

With gin so much cheaper than beer, and with the mainly London-based malt distillers so quick to embrace new and more efficient methods, Britain's spirits production ballooned from its 1694 level to peak at 8 million proof gallons in 1744. The sheer size of the industry is best understood by estimating the amount of wash the distillers brewed. It took 8–10 gallons of wash to make a gallon of spirit; so in 1743 the mainly London-based distillers brewed at least 64 million gallons of it, the equivalent of 1.7 million beer barrels — very much more, in fact, than the output of the city's beer brewers. The triumph of England's native distilling industry over foreign competition is perhaps best summarized by the Victoria County History's entry for Colchester, port city for the barley-growing region of Hertfordshire and Essex:

> In the early 18th century malt was exported from Colchester to Rotterdam to supply the Dutch distilleries; later in the period local maltsters and brewers established their own distilleries in Colchester and acquired many local inns. A malting established at the Hythe by 1706 was bought in 1727 by Richard Freshfield, who had a brewery in

> St. Giles's parish by 1735 and acquired a number of inns. Samuel Todd had established a distillery near Headgate by 1749, when he bought Second Mill, Lexden Road, with its malting house. The mill and malting business survived Todd's bankruptcy and were said in 1785 to be extensive, but the malting and kiln had fallen into disuse by 1787. In 1807 the Colchester brewery of Robert & Samuel Tabor acquired nine public houses within the borough. Samuel Bawtree and George Savill bought Hull (or Distillery) mill in 1811 and built a distillery on the site and a rectifying house in Culver Street. Thomas Andrews's brewery, recorded from 1774, passed *c.* 1815 to his kinsmen, the Cobbold family, who had maltings at the Hythe. Cinder ovens recorded at the Hythe in 1773 and 1786 probably provided coke for malting kilns until a gasworks was established in 1817.

Two other provincial distilleries from the period which are still familiar today are G&J of Warrington, founded in 1761 as Dakin's and bought by St. Helen's brewery Greenall Whitley in 1870, and Plymouth Gin, founded in 1793 as Fox & Williamson in the former Dominican Abbey which is still its home to this very day.

With the firm establishment of distilling as a new industry came a new word. *The Fable of the Bees* was a political pamphlet published in 1729 by Bernard Mandeville, an Anglo-Dutch political economist and satirist, to whom we owe the following idiomatic neologism: "the infamous liquor, the name of which, derived from Juniper berries in Dutch, is now, by frequent use and the Laconick spirit of the Nation shrunk into a Monosyllable: Intoxicating Gin, that charms the unactive, the desperate, and the crazy."

...To "Vesuvian bowls"

Long before gin had got its name — even before juniper came into its ascendancy, in fact — some observers had already been noticing a general increase in spirit-drinking across the country. Charles Davenant, a commissioner of excise under James II who went on to become a noted "political arithmetician," recorded "considerable brandy retailers" in East Sussex; and in Wiltshire: "abundance of brandy brought into every corner of this county." Much of the spirit was either smuggled or distilled illegally, he noted: "More brandy is drunk in this town [Canterbury] than is entered [i.e., tax-paid] in all the county."[68] Later, in 1703, he commented that spirit-drinking was "a growing vice among the common people and may in time prevail as much as opium with the Turks." Defoe, as we have seen, recalled the same phenomenon but with the detail that much of the retailing was carried on not in alehouses but in the shops of the compounders themselves and through the other shopkeepers and tradespeople they supplied. This specialization was certainly the norm in London, and dram-shops of one sort or another remained gin's principal retail channel until well into the 19th century in both London and the larger provincial towns and cities. In the countryside, though, ordinary alehouses seem to have started stocking spirits as a matter of course from about 1700.[69]

It was significant that Davenant expressed misgivings about the excessive consumption of spirits in particular: the late 17th and early 18th centuries contributed their fair share to the age-old canon of tirades against drink in general, including such gems as *Murder Within Doors: or, A War Against Ourselves. Proving There Are More Killed By the Vintners Than Are Saved By the Physicians* (1708) and the rather more sober *Dissuasive From The Sin Of Drunkenness* (1711) by Josiah Woodward, a significant player in the growing moral reform movement. As spirit-drinking gradually caught on the propagandists and pamphleteers started turning their attention to the newcomer with its shocking strength; and they didn't mince their words. One of the earliest such pieces, *A Satyr Against Brandy*, was also one of the most vituperative and set the literary tone for much of what was to come. The first 10 lines give a flavor of the 50 that follow:

> … damn'd *Stygian* Juyce, that dost bewitch,
> From the Court Bawd, down to the Country Bitch;
> Thou Liquid Flame, by whom each fiery Face
> Lives without Meat, and blushes without Grace,
> Sink to thy Native Hell to mend the Fire,
> Or if it please thee to ascend yet higher,
> To the dull Climate go, from whence you came,
> Where Wit and Courage do require your Flame;
> Where they Carouse it in *Vesuvian* Bowls,
> To crust the Quagmire of their spungy Souls.[70]

The Satyr was published in the brief pause between the two long and costly wars against the French, the Nine Years' War (1688–1697) and the War of the Spanish Succession (1701–1714), fought by William III and Queen Anne, when public morals notwithstanding no patriotic Englishman could question the economic contribution of this new industry. As Defoe said in 1713 in his thrice-weekly *Review*:

> First, the corn consumed... is our own produce, pays rent for our lands, employs our people, our shipping, etc., and secondly the importation of foreign spirits is prevented. Nothing is more certain than that the ordinary produce of corn in England is much greater than the numbers of our people or cattle can consume, and... when markets are low abroad and no demand for corn is made... the distilling trade is one remedy... for it helps to carry off the great quantity of corn in such a time of plenty... and (is) therefore to be especially to be preserved and tenderly used.

It was an argument Defoe elaborated at greater length in his later Treatise; but war in those days was never quite as total as it is today (how often and how deeply, for instance, does the life-and-death struggle with Napoleon a century later impinge on the society and consciousness of Jane Austen?), and the extent to which the distilling industry and its ancillary trades were flourishing, however vital the revenue generated, was becoming the cause of much unease. The moral conflict aroused by taxing vice was itself nothing new: a century earlier James I had laid a tax on tobacco of 6 shillings 10 pence per pound, which had not proved prohibitive as the king hoped but had only addicted his treasury to the very narcotic it had aimed to price out of the market. It was now a dilemma that many found less and less acceptable, wars or no wars, as summed up by the impish Mandeville:

> Thus the Merchant, that sends Corn or Cloth into Foreign Parts to purchase Wines and Brandies, encourages the Growth or Manufactury of his own Country; he is a Benefactor to Navigation,

increases the Customs, and is many ways beneficial to the Publick; yet it is not to be denied but that his greatest Dependence is *Lavishness* and *Drunkenness:* For if none were to drink Wine but such only as stand in need of it, nor any Body more than his Health requir'd, that Multitude of Wine-Merchants, Vintners, Coopers, *&c.* that make such a considerable Shew in this flourishing City, would be in a miserable Condition. The same may be said not only of Card and Dice-makers, that are the immediate Ministers to a Legion of Vices; but of Mercers, Upholsterers, Tailors, and many others, that would be starv'd in half a Year's time, if *Pride* and *Luxury* were at once to be banished the Nation...

Thieves and Pick-pockets steal for a Livelihood, and either what they can get Honestly is not sufficient to keep them, or else they have an Aversion to constant Working: they want to gratify their Senses, have Victuals, Strong Drink, Lewd Women, and to be Idle when they please. The Victualler, who entertains them and takes their Money, knowing which way they come at it, is very near as great a Villain as his Guests. But if he fleeces them well, minds his Business and is a prudent Man, he may get Money and be punctual with them he deals with: The Trusty Out-Clerk, whose chief aim is his Master's Profit, sends him in what Beer he wants, and takes care not to lose his Custom; while the Man's Money is good, he thinks it no Business of his to examine whom he gets it by. In the mean time the Wealthy Brewer, who leaves all the Management to his Servants, knows nothing of the matter, but keeps his Coach, treats his Friends, and enjoys his Pleasure with Ease and a

> good Conscience, he gets an Estate, builds Houses, and educates his Children in Plenty, without ever thinking on the Labour which Wretches perform, the Shifts Fools make, and the Tricks Knaves play to come at the Commodity, by the vast Sale of which he amasses his great Riches.[71]

Once the wars were won the need for revenue became less pressing, and the stage was set for a long series of political jousts between a newly energized puritanical wing of the church and the politicians who both represented and benefited from the landowning gentry and the tenant farmers who paid their rent from the proceeds of sales of grain. The two sides are somewhat blurred, and the relationships between them were such that they can scarcely even be described as sides.

The political establishment was in those days fluid, falling into two camps rather than parties. The Whigs were, by and large, representative of the big landowners who had supported the Glorious Revolution and therefore enjoyed an almost uninterrupted run in power of half a century. Their opponents, the Tories, represented the leftovers of the court party of Charles II and those who still supported James II and therefore bore the fatal taint of Jacobitism. But these two tribes were nebulous: they crossed the floor, they split into factions, they acted on personal grudges. Some of the Whig leader and proto-Prime Minister Robert Walpole's deadliest enemies were Whigs, but they generally caved in under pressure — and even more readily on a promise of office or a bribe.

The church side, on the other hand, was slowly becoming more organized but was, socially and politically speaking, somewhat marginal. Puritanism as a power bloc within the Church of England had disappeared in a puff of smoke in 1660; but the moral austerity of the Puritans was still very much a force and from the 1690s manifested itself in the formation of local Societies for Reformation of Manners, which used private prosecutions to uphold statutes against lewdness, neglect of the

Sabbath, and drunkenness that had fallen into desuetude, and the largely educational Society for the Propagation of Christian Knowledge which is still with us today.

The 30 years' on–off contest between the two sides started in 1721. The general background was a sharp rise in crime apparently consequent upon the end of the War of the Spanish Succession in 1713 and the discharge into society of thousands upon thousands of soldiers and sailors, many of them into a life of destitution, drink, and armed robbery.[72] The impression of London as a modern Sodom, sliding inexorably towards destruction in a welter of licence and vice, was dramatically reinforced in 1720 by the collapse of the South Sea Company and its devastating impact on investors at all levels of society ("walking ghosts," Defoe called them), while a new pandemic of bubonic plague swept across Europe, although fortunately it never crossed the Channel. But when in April 1721 the Privy Council ordered Westminster Quarter Sessions to appoint a committee to investigate rumors of "scandalous clubs" of young people who "in the most impious and blasphemous manner insult the most sacred principles of our holy religion, affront Almighty God Himself, and corrupt the minds and morals of one another," it was inviting a body dominated by evangelicals to give vent to years of frustration. The ranks of these scandalous clubs, such as the Bold Bucks who denied the existence of God and ate Holy Ghost Pie on Sundays,[73] were filled with the well-born and well-connected who were far beyond the reach of mere magistrates; but when the committee reported in October it took the opportunity to cite a long list of its pet moral and social peeves, from which all the modern Babylon's ills flowed. Drunkenness, gambling, prostitution and theatre (staging more variety, much of it risqué, than straight drama), those old targets, were the stew's main ingredients; but its special piquancy was supplied by that comparatively novel spice: gin. "Nor is there any part of this town wherein the number of... brandy and geneva shops do not daily increase, though they were so numerous already that in some of the largest parishes every tenth house at least sells one sort or another of those liquors by retail," claimed the committee. Further, this increase was: "the principall cause of the increase of our poor and of all the vice and debauchery among the inferior sort of people, as well as of the felonies and other disorders committed in and about this town." And it castigated: "the great destruction made by brandy and geneva-shops whose owners retail their liquors to the poorer sort of people and do suffer them to sit tippling in their shops, by which practice they are not only rendered incapable of labor, but by their bodies being kept in a continual heat are thereby more liable to receive infection." The main report was accompanied by annexes protesting at the gin-shops' exemption from the burden of billeting soldiers imposed on licensed alehouses, and at the "sanitary nuisances" they created.

The committee recommended a crackdown on unlicensed retailers; but of course spirit retailers had been exempted from licensing by William III in 1690, so nothing could be done. Everything therefore went quiet until 1724, when in a blistering annual address to the Society for the Reformation of Manners the Bishop of Lichfield relaunched the attack on spirit retailing. The following February the magistracy also renewed its offensive with a census of all spirit retailers in Middlesex. In October the chairman of the Middlesex Quarter Sessions, Sir Daniel Dolins, added his voice to the growing clamor for new legislation; and the fact that the census, when published in January 1726, revealed that the 6,187 spirit retailers the constables found in Middlesex — London excepting the City and Southwark — was much the same as when last counted in 1711,[74] did nothing to dampen things down. Satire came back to the fray too: The Tavern Scuffle, published in the same year, took the form of a rowdy discourse between Swell-gut the brewer and Scorch-gut the distiller, with Swell-gut naturally emerging the winner. And science weighed in as well, with a report from the College of Physicians labeling gin-drinkers as "diseas'd, not fit for business, poor... a burthen to themselves and neighbours, and too often the cause of weak, feeble, and distemper'd children." All this was rebutted by Defoe's *A Brief Case of the Distillers* (for which the Company of Distillers paid him £88 4 shillings 10 pence) forcibly restating the economic case for the native distilling industry, and everything went quiet again for another two years.[75]

It was Defoe himself who gave the moral reformers a third chance at legislation when he published his real opinion of gin, as well as on other pressing issues such as education, in a pseudonymous pamphlet entitled *Augusta Triumphans*:

> So far are our common people infatuated with Geneva, that half the work is not done now as formerly. It debilitates and enervates them, and they are not near so strong and healthy as formerly... If this abuse of Geneva be not stopped, we may go whoop for husbandmen, labourers, &c. Trade must consequently stand still, and the credit of the nation sink; nor is the abatement of the excise, though very considerable, any ways comparable to the corruption of manners, the destruction of health, and all the train of evils we are threatened with from pernicious Geneva... Our common people... get so drunk on a Sunday they cannot work for a day or two following. Nay, since the use of Geneva has become so common, many get so often drunk they cannot work at all, but run from one irregularity to another, till at last they become arrant rogues. And this is the foundation of all our present complaints.

A far cry indeed from "a good wholesom Malt Spirit, if rightly prepar'd... a Thing not only wholesom, but really physical, and for many Years allow'd to be so by the most celebrated Physicians"!

Upon this, both Westminster and Tower Hamlets Quarter Sessions ordered the Grand Juries under their supervision to go after spirit-sellers, even if they were exempt from licensing control, on the grounds that "those houses and shops, where People frequently get drunk with Geneva, or other spirituous liquors, are Indictable as disorderly houses whether they have or have not Licences." The new king, George II, issued a proclamation in October 1728 expressing concern over street crime and supporting the closure of "night houses, geneva shops and other tippling houses." Pressure for a new law was now irresistible, and Walpole reluctantly had a bill introduced that attacked the apparent villains — London's 1,500 compound distillers and its 6,187-plus spirit sellers — by requiring them to pay £20 a year for a license (effectively outlawing street sales), with a duty of five shillings a gallon on compounded or otherwise flavored spirits "commonly called gin." The malt distillers, of course, being the clients at one remove, as it were, of the great landed gentry, escaped scot-free.

In backing magisterial efforts to restrict gin consumption by controlling the retail trade, the government was taking the correct course. The moral reformers were right: in its enthusiasm to fund the war and cripple French commerce, the government of William III had gone too far. With all restrictions abolished, there were simply too many retailers. Curbing their numbers and proscribing the nature of their activities would undoubtedly have brought the problem of excessive consumption — if indeed the problem was real rather than merely perceived — under the control of the authorities. But still the 1729 Act was ineffective. The license proved impossible to enforce in the unpoliced metropolis, and the compounders dodged the duty simply by not compounding the malt spirit they bought in bulk from the distillers. Instead they watered it down to potable strength, "dulcified" it, and sold it unflavored as "parliament brandy" (and a dozen other nicknames), which the public embraced as enthusiastically as it had done gin. And perhaps, despite the condemnation of detractors, it wasn't all that bad: it can only have been like rather full-flavored vodka, or perhaps new-make whiskey; and if the compounders weren't allowed to add flavorings, there was nothing to stop the retailers or the customers themselves adding a shot of fruit cordial. Be that as it may, gin was now in the political arena: both reformers and distillers felt that if one piece of legislation failed it could always be amended. The 1729 Act was repealed under pressure from both sides and was replaced in 1733 — it would have been a year earlier, but it ran out of Parliamentary time — by an Act that described itself as encouraging British distilling. It dropped the 5 shillings duty but retained the requirement for compound distillers, grocers, chandlers and other retailers to take out licenses, and encouraged the use of informers to help control unlicensed street vending.

It didn't work either, and it's hard to see how it ever could have given its conflicting aims of encouraging the distillers while curbing the retailers. In truth, though, an 18th-century government lacked the ability to achieve either aim. A junta of Whigs could hardly lay any blame for anything at the door of its political sponsors, the landed gentry with their barley-growing tenants,[76] and their biggest customers, the malt distillers. Nor had it the resources to effectively tackle the hydra of small part-time retailers that had been allowed to grow unchecked for 30 years.

The 1733 Act didn't simply fall, however: it was pushed. The assassin was a young single mother who, by her own mother's account, was "never in her right mind, but always roving." Judith Dufour[77] worked in a silk mill and lived with her mother, but her two-year-old daughter Mary was in the care of the Bethnal Green workhouse. One cold Sunday morning in January 1734 Judith went to the workhouse to collect Mary for the day, exclaiming as she met her at the new stockings, petticoat and overcoat the parish had dressed the little girl in. Judith was next seen that evening, turning up the worse for wear for her night shift at the mill. Halfway through the shift she sent out for a dram, and then another, and then, drunk, confessed to her workmates that she'd sold Mary's new clothes for gin and left the little mite half-naked in a shed in a nearby market garden.

Horrified, the other women made her guide them to the place. When they got there Mary was dead; but in daylight it was seen that the little girl hadn't died of exposure but had been strangled. Judith was hanged, of course; but record numbers attended her trial and the public response was not the usual stone-throwing rage of the Georgian mob, but an overwhelmed silence at the pathos of it all. It also meant a new lease of life for the moral reform campaign and, in due course, a return to stone-throwing form for the Georgian mob.

Judith's tragedy created a poignant backcloth that gave popularity and power to two subsequent works of anti-gin propaganda. Dr. Stephen Hales's medical treatise, *A Friendly Admonition to the Drinkers of Brandy & Other Distilled Spirituous Liquors* which (although of necessity it contained its fair share of biblical fulminations since Dr. Hales was a churchman too) treated spirits as chemical rather than spiritual toxins and drinkers as treatable addicts rather than doomed sinners. Having said that, it did perpetuate the fallacy that spirits produced more dramatic physical effects than those caused by the same quantity of alcohol in less concentrated forms, a notion born of a merely hazy understanding of what alcohol actually was. Above all, though, it was positive: a counterpoise to the hellfire-and-damnation hyperbole of most pamphlets. Shortly afterwards came *Distilled Spirituous Liquors the Bane of The Nation, Being Some Considerations Humbly Offer'd to the Legislature* by Thomas Wilson, son of the mad Bishop of Sodor & Man and a social climber desperate for a benefice, which he eventually got thanks to the patronage of the most eminent anti-gin campaigners.

With sympathizers including the Queen herself, veteran judge and independent Whig MP Sir John Jekyll, and the Speaker of the Commons Arthur Onslow lined up behind them, the magistrates issued scathing blasts against gin at that September's Quarter Sessions, accompanied by a new census of spirit retailers revealing that the number had now grown to 7,022 (although not providing the all-important context of population growth). As Parliament began its 1736 session a propaganda war broke out, with both distillers and moderate journalists lambasting Wilson in pamphlets and newspapers, Wilson's supporters lambasting them back, and their supporters lambasting Wilson's supporters, all with unequalled vehemence and vituperation. Wilson's detractors were finally trumped by a series of highly sensational reports of gin-related tragedies, the most sensational of them being the case of a childminder, Mary Estwick, who in her drunken state dropped the baby she was looking after on to the fire. With the wind of public opinion set fair, Jekyll introduced a bill that proposed such huge impositions on the small men, the compounders and retailers, that gin would be effectively outlawed. Retailers would all need a £50 annual license and would have to pay an astonishing £1 a gallon in duty. Unlicensed retailing would attract a £100 fine; street selling, £10. Effectively the 1736 Gin Act made humble gin accessible only to the rich, which was as close as such a class-ridden society could come to outright Prohibition.

The bill became law in April and was due to come into force at Michaelmas. Throughout a tense summer an anxious government expected trouble. In July a Jacobite parcel bomb exploded in Westminster Hall, scattering pamphlets denouncing unpopular measures including the Gin Act. Later there were riots in the East End, mainly anti-Irish but including a measure of anti-Gin Act agitation. There was hostile press; there were satirical revues, pamphlets and ballads; there were mock funerals for Mother Gin. There was even a rather ham-fisted attempt at staging a Jacobite uprising, promising free gin to all who would take part. But with the capital studded with soldiers no wider unrest developed. On Michaelmas Eve there were wakes all over London, and in some other cities too, to drink off the last of the old duty-paid stock; some of the mourners drank so deep that the wakes turned out to be their own. But in the succeeding days there was unease but no unrest, with spirit retailers treating the 1736 Act just as they had its predecessors:

i.e., they ignored it. Precisely two of the £50 licenses were ever taken out.

It was one of the most counterproductive laws ever made. It echoed the 1733 Act in its reliance on informers, who were to receive half of the fines they generated. The honest apothecaries who thought they were exempt were low-hanging fruit and became its first victims, much to the anger of their friends, relations and patients. Street sellers were equally easy meat: those who couldn't pay the fine were sent to the Houses of Correction, which quickly overflowed into "spunging houses," pubs that rented out their attics and cellars as jail cells. Magistrates had to hold extra sessions to deal with all the street hawkers and market traders — many if not most of them women — who were paraded in front of them. But gin selling went on, either out in the suburbs where there were fewer informers, or in "puss-mew" houses, the 18th-century precursor of Prohibition speakeasies, where you (supposedly) spoke the password, put your tuppence through a slot in a door or window, and got your measure of gin in return.[78] And meanwhile public unrest — a more potent political force then than now — was growing. The Queen's carriage was mobbed by protestors, public anger was clearly rising, and the Commissioners of Excise were forced to admit that all the prosecutions, all the fines, and all the jail sentences had made no difference either to gin production or sales. In fact production of raw spirit continued to grow, because the malt distillers themselves were, as we have seen, economically speaking the scions of the landowning gentry who ran the Government.

Further, the Act had no real teeth until April 1737 when the Government slipped into another act entirely, the Sweets Act that reduced the duty on fruit wines, a clause providing for informers to get their bounty from public funds when their victims couldn't pay their fines, which was often. In that very same month an informer was mobbed, pelted with stones, and had to be rescued by excise officers in a carriage and from then on attacking, dragging, beating and "pumping" (18th-century waterboarding) informers became a popular sport among the mob, and convicted retailers were even rescued on their way to prison. Law officers were attacked, too, from constables to excise officers to the magistrates themselves.

That didn't stop the informers, though: after all, £5 was a fortune in 1737. They formed gangs who openly entrapped their victims, then blackmailed them, then turned them in anyway. Rewards were offered for the capture of anyone who attacked one of them: immediately afterwards came the first murder of an informer. There were three more over the winter, mostly following the same pattern of attacks by mobs in public. The New Year saw rioting becoming more frequent, along with mob rescues of people accused of vending and more attacks on informers. The response from the authorities was to crack down harder: they felt they couldn't afford to lose their authority altogether, and a royal proclamation urging the stricter enforcement of the Riot Act was followed by a new Act in 1738 making attacks on informers a felony and empowering private citizens to arrest gin-sellers. The first fruit was a perverse verdict when despite absolutely clear-cut evidence of guilt, a jury acquitted a man accused of leading a mob to attack a magistrate's house. After that, things went from bad to worse. Another informer was murdered, then another; and the mob made a parade of his cortege, mocked his funeral, then burned him in effigy.

The magistrates ran out of steam and the fund that paid the informers ran out of money. However hard the authorities struggled, the hydra could not be killed. Popular and press opinion had swung against the informers, and the exposure of corrupt excise officers running extortion gangs made the whole attempt at prohibition less popular still. Within a few weeks of the passage of the 1738 Act, the authorities had stopped even pretending to enforce it. There was one last great joke: a gang of informers were known to be in a house dividing the day's haul, when someone revealed their presence to a passing press gang. A quick swoop bagged the entire gang, who were soon leading a healthier life on the ocean wave; for by then Britain was at war again and gin fell out of the headlines.

To help fund the War of the Austrian Succession (1742–1748) two further acts were passed, in 1743 and 1747, both hoping to increase revenue by reducing the license fee to a manageable amount while controlling consumption by increasing the duty. The 1743 act came at the very peak of gin production: excise duty was paid on some eight million gallons that year, most of it distilled in London. The malt distillers saw the derisory duty on low wines, which had not been raised since 1690, double to two pence per proof gallon, while spirit duty paid by the compounders was put at six pence a gallon and the retail license fee was slashed to £1. The new act was an admission of the failure of the last — a candid one, too, for as the Secretary of State Lord Bathurst said in the Parliamentary debate: "We find by experience we cannot absolutely prevent the retailing of such liquors, because if we prevent their being retailed in an open, fair way they will be retailed in a clandestine smuggling manner."[79] He later conceded:

> Everyone knows that the 1736 Act did not diminish the consumption, nor prevent the excessive use of spirituous liquors. They were not, it is true, retailed publicly and avowedly, but they were clandestinely retailed in every coffee-house and alehouse, and in many shops and private houses, so that the use and even the abuse of spirituous liquors continued as frequent, though not so apparent, as before the Act was made; and the consumption rather increased than diminished, as appears from the amount of the duty for these last two years.[80]

That was fine by the reformers, who believed that vice belonged in holes and corners; but the moderate pragmatists feared that laws that were so openly flouted by so many undermined, possibly fatally, the whole notion of law itself. Besides, the government needed the increased revenue to fund a huge war loan of £1.8 million. The bill passed, with the sole concession that compounders and rectifiers themselves should not be allowed retail licenses.

To placate the undimmed fury of the prohibitionists, the government instructed magistrates not to issue spirit licenses to all and sundry but only to applicants already in the victualling trades, a stipulation that wiped out the takeaway trade carried on by grocers, chandlers, market stall holders, street hawkers and the shebeens that supposedly operated in back rooms, garrets and basements. Within a few months 1,000 licenses had been issued in London, 20,000 nationwide.[81] Production went into a steep decline, though, especially when duties were raised again in 1746, but excise revenue grew from nothing to £90,000. In return for the increased duty compound distillers were given back the right to apply for licenses, for which they paid £5, in the act of 1747. By 1749 the number of licenses issued in London had risen to 5,300, of which 600 had been awarded to compounders.

These developments, especially the fall in production, might reasonably be seen as the final answer to the "problem." The prohibitionists weren't done yet, though. In 1748 the War of the Austrian Succession came to an end and the Jacobites had been put firmly back in their box following the failure of the 1745. The outbreak of peace reopened the window for the moral reformers, now led by Thomas Secker, Bishop of Oxford, and still a very numerous cadre, to relaunch their lobby for prohibition. On board were two new recruits: Henry Fielding, satirist, novelist, failed lawyer, reformed roué, and near bankrupt, whose friends procured for him a magistracy in 1748 and the chair of Westminster Quarter Sessions in 1749; and a friend of Fielding's, the artist William Hogarth.

Fielding had long been under the influence of reformers such as Thomas Wilson, Thomas Lane, Dr. Hales, and the Bishop of Worcester and joined them in believing that the outright prohibition of gin was still the panacea for all London's ills, despite the total failure of efforts to date. In January 1751, just as that year's session of Parliament was opening and with all of 18 month's experience as a magistrate, he published his celebrated *Inquiry into the Causes of the Late Increase of Robbers* to immense acclaim, for all that the book was not much more than a reheated hodge-podge of all the propaganda that had gone before, freshly seasoned with a sprinkling of his (not very extensive) experience of life on the Bench. Gin was treated as the sole fountain of all vice and debauchery much as it had been and in much the same terms as ever, with a great blast at "luxury" (i.e., the natural outcome of paying workers a penny more than they needed for bare sustenance) thrown in. Its publication was followed almost immediately by the issue of Hogarth's two prints, *Gin Lane* and *Beer Street*, for sale at 1 shilling each or in a deluxe version at 1 shilling 6 pence,[82] which for all the freshness of their imagery and the brilliance of their execution had nothing new to say.

These were only two boulders in a landslide of prohibitionist propaganda, some of it, like Fielding's, rehashes of old material; others tackling previously ignored aspects of alcohol abuse, for instance Eliza Haywood's 1750 publication *A Present for Women Addicted to Drinking, adapted to all the different stations in life, from a Lady of Quality to a Common Servant*; and the economist (and vicar) Josiah Tucker's pamphlet, *An Impartial Enquiry into the Benefits and Damages from the Use of Spirituous Liquors*, which calculated that gin cost the economy just short of £4 million a year. There was also a great deal of press support for a new Gin Act and petitions from magistrates in London and, for the first time, other cities as well. A committee of enquiry into felonies and their causes drew testimony from doctors who put it all down to gin, public officials who put it all down to gin, tradesman who put it all down to gin. Parliament was in reforming mood and the prohibitionists had every reason to be confident. But the Government's care for its revenues proved more powerful than all the propaganda, however brilliantly it was presented. In the end, spirit duty and the license fee went up a little and the stipulation that licenses should only be allowed to alehouses, inns, taverns, coffee shops and other victuallers was restated.

And that was that. A pragmatic Parliament, by steering a course between extremes, had established the public consensus necessary for the law to function merely by restating and slightly strengthening the wise regime introduced in 1743. Magistrates and excise officers started straight away to enforce the provisions of the act, and found no obstruction to their doing so. After a pampered childhood and a consequently difficult adolescence, gin had grown up.

The Craze That Never Was

The preceding narrative leaves us with one question. How much of it, if any, was true? The pamphlets, books, satires, committee reports, acts of parliament — they all happened. But did they describe a world of fact in which London's working class was being eaten away by addiction, or one of fancy concocted from preconception, prejudice, misinterpretation and plain ignorance? Surely, given the sheer volume of evidence the latter is impossible? Or is it? Just reflect for a few moments on a single word: witchcraft. The resources devoted to detecting witches and the savagery that went into eradicating them — over centuries, not mere decades, and across a continent, not just in one city — were colossal; belief was universal. Yet there never was such a thing as a witch, nor such a canon as witchcraft. All of us can think of other instances in our own times when public scares and moral panics have been whipped up without a shred of evidence: the McCarthy hearings, for instance; and a far more recent manifestation in the British Labour Party.

A problem for those who want to look more closely at the whole episode is that apart from a few counterblasts, the only voice we have is that of the reformers themselves. The malt distillers kept a lofty silence, depending for protection on their ability to subvert and corrupt the government; the compounders were ill-served by their lobbyists; we only meet the retailers as defendants; and as for the drinkers — well, they were labeled as "the poor" or "the common sort," and the poor and the common sort rarely seem to have anything to say. So the story of those years that has come down to us is the story as told by the reformers. It is one of the rare occasions when the losers wrote the history, and their version of events was faithfully relayed by the seminal historian of Georgian London, Dorothy George, whose *London Life in the 18th Century*, published in 1925, largely followed the eminent Fabians Sidney & Beatrice Webb's *History of Liquor Licensing in England 1700–1830*, published in 1903. To be fair to the Webbs, they had not set out to write a social history: the book was a by-product of their much larger work on the history of local government and only set out to explain how the liquor licensing regime evolved as it did during an age of considerable political controversy. It was written when and indeed because liquor licensing had once again become a major political issue in their own time. According to the preface:

> A mere shred of history cut out of its context, beginning at 1700 and ending abruptly at 1830, cannot provide satisfactory reading... With this explanation of some of its imperfections, we offer the following sketch of what did happen between 1700 and 1830 as possibly contributing towards an understanding of the present problem.

Nevertheless their total and uncritical acceptance of the reformers' case along with the use of some wild and unsubstantiated coinages of their own, such as "a perfect pandemonium of drunkenness in which the greater part of the population of the metropolis seems to have participated," was enough to convince George; and her influence was such that most of those who came after have followed her as unquestioningly as the Webbs had accepted the contemporary literature. So powerful a narrative is it that the Gin Craze is now as much woven into London's mythic fabric as Oliver Twist and 221B Baker Street.

Just to make her position clear, George heads the very first chapter of London Life with the opening stanzas of the two short poems written by the dramatist (and clergyman) James Townley as captions for Hogarth's Gin Lane and Beer Street (1751):

> Gin, cursed fiend, with fury fraught,
> Makes human race a prey,
> It enters by a deadly draught
> And steals our life away.
> Beer, happy Produce of our Isle,
> Can sinewy strength impart,
> And wearied with Fatigue and Toil,
> Can chear each manly Heart.

While acknowledging the weakness of contemporary record-keeping, George accepts without question the contemporary opinion that deaths exceeded births in mid-18th-century London as a consequence of gin-drinking; that the decades 1720–1750 saw gin-drinking reaching critical levels damaging to the public good; and that the culprit, at a time of rising wages and falling prices, was luxury: that is, that most working people had some spare income left over after buying the necessities of life, which of course they spent on alcohol, or, put another way, that the poor were so dissolute because they weren't quite poor enough. This assertion she supports by referring to, among others, Corbyn Morris, a senior customs inspector and statistician who had become a researcher and essayist/pamphleteer to Henry Pelham, brother of the Duke of Newcastle. In his *Observations on the past Growth and present State of the City of London* (1751) Morris asserts:

> The diminution of births set out from the time that the consumption of all these liquors by the

> common people became enormous. As this consumption hath been continually increasing since that time, the amount of births hath been continually diminishing. Inquire from the several hospitals in the City, whether any increase of patients, and of what sort, are daily brought under their care? They will all declare, increasing multitudes of dropsical and consumptive people arising from the effects of spirituous liquors.

From the same year, George cites a representation to Parliament entitled *Considerations upon the Effects of Spirituous Liquors* which claimed that since 1740 child deaths and the reduced birth-rate had between them amounted to more than 9,000 a year and while "other trivial reasons for this great mortality, which in some degree have always subsisted, may possibly require some abatement; but still the real grand destroyer is materially evident." Swinging unambiguously behind this analysis, she writes: "The only explanation seems to be that usually given by contemporaries — the orgy of spirit-drinking which was at its worst between 1720 and 1751, due to the very cheap and very intoxicating liquors which were retailed indiscriminately in the most brutalising and demoralising conditions."

To take George's three main points in order, the "demographic deficit" was a cause of increasing consumption, not a consequence of it; that even in the peak year of consumption, 1743, not enough gin was sold to do any significant harm to the population at large; and that a surfeit of luxury — that is, disposable income — was not the root of increasing consumption so much as a lack of alternative consumer goods to spend it on. George's account of the period went more or less unchallenged until 1988, however, when *The Mother Gin Controversy in the Early Eighteenth Century*, a paper by Professor Peter Clark, was published in *Transactions of the Royal Historical Society*. Bypassing the contemporary propagandists on whom George had placed so much weight, he looked at excise records, probate inventories, Bills of Mortality and other primary sources and found that things were not quite as the contestants had described them. Was spirit drinking really the affliction of the poor? Was spirit retailing really such a sordid and miserable affair? Was alcohol abuse really so widespread and so extreme that it caused a crime wave, reduced the birth rate, and enfeebled the workforce?

As far as the most dramatic claim about gin-drinking is concerned — that it was the cause of a rising death-rate and a declining birth-rate — Clark concedes that the Bills of Mortality for the early decades of the century suggest a rise in mortality and a "more sluggish" movement in baptisms. But although London's "demographic deficits" were almost certainly expanding from the start of the century, as confirmed by parish register evidence for St. James, Clerkenwell — an important gin-selling area where the demographic deficit doubled in the years 1710–1740 — it is doubtful that gin-drinking was a factor. "The high levels of infant mortality at this time were mainly associated with endemic levels of smallpox and typhus," Clark points out. "Adult mortality rates remained relatively stable."[83] In other words, overcrowding, lack of sanitation, and poor hygiene killed the children, while gin didn't kill a noticeable number of those who survived to adulthood. As for actual alcohol-related deaths, the Bills of Mortality record an increase in deaths ascribed to excessive drinking from 17 in 1725 to 69 in 1735, "but this may only reflect greater official consciousness, and after 1736 recorded numbers fell back despite mounting levels of consumption."

Another plank in the reformers' platform which Clark's paper questions is that retailing and drinking gin were aspects of the squalor, misery, license, and general depravity (and in George's words, brutality and demoralization) that characterized "the poor." Clark found, however (as your intuition might have already told you), that the gin trade was by and large perfectly respectable; that retailing as a legitimate means of making a living was an alternative to rather than an aspect of squalor, misery, license, depravity, brutality and demoralization; and that its customers, of necessity, were sufficiently well-off to indulge themselves a little. Indeed, one of the few voices we hear from the huddled masses is that of a witness at the magistrates' committee of 1725, described as "a market-woman."[84] She testified:

> We market-women are up early and late and work hard for what we have. We stand all weathers and go through thick and thin… and if I spend three-farthings now and then in such simple stuff as poor souls are glad to drink, it's nothing but what's my own. I get it honestly, and… if it were not for something to clear the spirits between whiles and keep out the wet and cold; alackaday! It would never do!

The words of a perfectly respectable working-class woman, not the specimen of squalor and depravity that gin's detractors would have us believe! As for the seediness of gin's retailers, the mainstream pub trade during the reign of George II, as Clark demonstrates,[85] had come up in the world: licensed publicans were often businesspeople of substance and high social standing, running large and highly evolved multi-purpose houses offering food, games, and club rooms (pub-based social clubs were enormously popular at the time) as well as wide range of drinks. Establishing a gin-shop, either specialized or within a chandler's (or, in modern terms, a convenience store) or grocer's shop, offered less well-capitalized but again, perfectly respectable working-class entrepreneurs an affordable route into business and self-improvement. Clark says:

> These small general stores multiplied in town and countryside during the eighteenth century responding to rising demand and reflecting the growing sophistication of inland trade. Some, no

> doubt, as commentators said, were little establishments kept by poor folk, but surviving inventories for East London chandlers from the later 17th century indicate that there could also be more substantial traders. Thomas Fluck, for instance, of St. James, Clerkenwell, had a well-stocked shop selling brandy and other spirits, Cheshire and Warwickshire cheeses, butter, bacon, mops, soap, candles and thread, and had an estate worth nearly £44 at his death, partly in outstanding debts. Writers commented how orderly many of these shops were kept.

If the chandlers, grocers and apothecaries who sold gin alongside their more traditional stock in trade were generally respectable, argues Clark; so, as far as we can tell, were the gin-shops and dram-sellers that retailed little else.

> There is not much evidence to substantiate claims that specialist gin retailing was dominated by the impoverished and disorderly. Occupational backgrounds were often not very different from those of established victuallers… The relative respectability of many dram-shop keepers in the 1730s is confirmed when we correlate them with lists of ratepayers and the poor. Thus in Bethnal Green… they paid a rate [i.e., local tax] significantly higher than for the area as a whole. Admittedly, poor people may have been exempt from the rate, but only two or three of the ginsellers in 1735 had previously received a parish pension.

Jessica Warner in *Craze*[86] cites several examples of gin-shops consisting of "nothing more than an unremarkable room or two behind a storefront or residence" as well as chandler's shops where the customers, mainly women, habitually enjoyed a dram while carrying out their errands. But she finds no more excess or disorder than you would expect to encounter in any alehouse in any working-class district; certainly nothing like Fielding's "nurseries of all manner of vice and wickedness" where "practitioners in roguery assemble" to instruct "young idle fellows... in all the arts and tricks of their own profession, which is of robbing on the highway, picking pockets, forging hands, breaking open houses, clipping and coining, and all other crimes." Doubtless many gin-shops were indeed hubs for organized crime, but no more so than many low taverns and pubs.

To get at the motives underlying the allegations against Madam Geneva and her acolytes it's necessary to understand who her accusers were; and as with the actual witch-hunts of the 16th and 17th centuries they were mostly churchmen: inheritors of the Puritan mantle, seeking to impose a moral and social discipline which they themselves were both to define and enforce. They were motivated by one creed in particular, and one that is both ridiculous and abhorrent to any modern economic or social thinker: that to give the working classes anything to work towards was not to reinforce but to undermine their work ethic, and that they were best kept at their grindstones by being unable — just — to afford the necessities of life, let alone its pleasures. "A frequent taste of any kind of any kind of diversion is apt to grow upon the palate and to give too strong a relish for them," warned one anonymous pamphleteer, "and when the inclination is turned strongly towards them, the shop or work-room is like the confinement of the prison, and labor like a weight that goes uphill."[87] Gin was not the campaigners' sole or even first priority: lewdness, neglect of the Sabbath, public license especially gambling and the theatre (venue then for all sorts of morally dubious spectacles), and violent crime were as baneful to them as drunkenness: of the leading London justices, Sir Daniel Dolins also crusaded against homosexuality while Sir John Gonson chaired a standing committee of magistrates known as The Convention to coordinate efforts against the growing menace of organized crime as personified by its godfather, the self-styled Thief-taker General Jonathan Wild, hanged in 1725. To the aid of these churchmen and magistrates rallied doctors, many of them also in holy orders; political satirists; and straightforward opponents of the Whig ministries of Sir Robert Walpole (1720–1742) and Sir Henry Pelham (1743–1756). None of these crusaders set out to lie; but they were completely unprepared to collect and interpret statistics and had none of the historic data they needed to give what figures they did collect any context and meaning. The personnel they had at their disposal, even for so simple a task as counting gin retailers, were woefully few and unreliable at that, for many of the parish constables who did the counting were spirit retailers themselves. Nor, it seems, were these unqualified census-takers primed to discover the volumes that individual retailers actually sold, or whether gin was their principal commodity or part of a much broader trade. Finally, the reformers analyzed what the constables brought them through the prism of dogma, which distorted their view and doubtless led to much exaggeration. And for them, as for almost all political campaigners, the end came to justify the means; and their end, in modern parlance, was to take back the streets of London. In short, as with all witch-hunters, their goal was power.

For anyone of a traditional cast of mind London has always been a rather terrifying place, ever-changing, uncontrollable, and free. This was even more so in the 18th century when, following a period of stagnation after the Restoration, its population suddenly started growing again. From 500,000 in 1675, it grew to 575,000 in 1700, 675,000 in 1750 and 900,000 in 1800.[88] The increase was largely driven by the renewal of the enclosure of farmland, which drove workers off the land and beggared many of the tradespeople who had depended on their custom. Most of these refugees ended up in the regimented brick-terraced laagers of the mill towns where there was at least enough work to feed their families, although at the price of their freedom. The younger exiles, including a disproportionate number of single young women, headed Whittington-like to London, a city of opportunity with the promise of unlimited work in semi-skilled and unskilled trades such as domestic service, building, and general laboring; often with better wages and conditions than they had endured in the countryside, and the possibility of advancement too. Add the astonishingly high rate of infant mortality and the short average lifespan and it becomes clear that as London's population grew, it skewed dramatically towards people of working (and drinking) age; hence it was the demographic deficit — population growth based on adult immigration rather than child-rearing — that drove the increase in gin-drinking. And since house-building had not kept up with the influx, the new young working-class Londoners lived much of their lives in public — in alehouses, in theatres, at sports and games, in gin-shops — where shocked and disapproving vicars could hardly help but watch them shamelessly carousing, drinking, dancing and flirting[89] and persuade themselves that civilization itself was gravely endangered thereby. Overcrowding was also one reason why so little was spent on consumer durables: it would be pointless to buy nice clothes if you had nowhere to keep them and they were sure to be stolen anyway. What disposable income the working class of 18th century London actually had could only feasibly be spent on transient pleasures: bare-knuckle boxing, racing, bloodsports, theatre, gambling… and gin.

The presence of so many single women among the gin-drinkers was particularly shocking. Single women in urban alehouses in earlier times had generally been (or been seen as) prostitutes. Now, though, the city's alehouses welcomed working women, free, independent and bent on well-earned recreation after their labors. Often they preferred sweetish, possibly fruit-flavored, shorts (for fruit cordials were still on the market and figure in all the distillers' recipe-books of the period, even if gin, in London at least, had by and large eclipsed them) to the quarts of strong, heavy beer preferred by many of the menfolk: not only were sweet shorts easier to drink, they were cheaper, too.[90] And so many women were involved in retailing gin as barmaids, shopworkers, market women and street hawkers[91] that drinking it as well as selling it hardly seemed worthy of comment, as it might have done back home in the countryside. Indeed the femininity of gin was, in the eyes of its enemies, one of its most appalling aspects: not only did it (or so they thought) undermine women's ability to produce and rear the laborers and soldiers of the future, it gave them an economic power that was rightfully a man's, and it also implied a sexual freedom (surely more imagined than real) that made of London a modern Babylon.

But the fact that prudes and fogeys often witnessed young working men and women downing gin, and that they reveled in horror-stories like that of Judith Dufour, is not in itself evidence of excessive consumption. The same is true today. You might be shocked by the sight of young drinkers vomiting outside kebab shops and fighting over minicabs on a Friday and Saturday night in even a modest provincial town center, but the wider truth is that alcohol consumption is declining among almost all demographics except the affluent middle-aged who do their drinking in private and who do plenty of it; and young people are more likely than ever to be dry during the week even if they do push the boat out at weekends. So back in 18th-century London, were these raucous youngsters really engaging in George's "orgy of spirit-drinking," or were appearances deceptive?

First, what were they drinking? The base spirit sold by the malt distillers to the compounders must have contained enough malted barley to convert all the insoluble starches in the various unmalted grains into sugar, or the wash wouldn't have fermented. The malting barleys of East Anglia and the northern Home Counties had been selected for their suitability for brewing over many generations and carried enough of the vital diastatic enzymes to enable quite a small proportion to convert much larger quantities of unmalted (and therefore untaxed) grains. As well as unmalted barley these would have been principally rye and oats since wheat was expensive and maize hadn't yet arrived. In brewing, rye imparts a refreshing sharpness while oats give smoothness and body; that they were used mainly to pad out the expensive malted barley did not imply, therefore, any ill-effect on the quality of the spirit. If anything they should have improved it.

It's often said, in various forms of words, that 18th-century gin was "sold at the strength it came off the still — much stronger than today's watered-down version,"[92] but there's every reason to conclude the very opposite. If the new-make spirit was anything like the "malt wine" on which Dutch distillers based their jenever it will only have been distilled to 50–60% alcohol, leaving plenty of congeners to create whiskey-like grainy and toasty flavors. By various accounts it was delivered from the malt distillers at "one in five under proof," proof being 57.15% ABV; the spirit therefore arrived at the compounder/rectifier at about 46% ABV, today's export strength. Commercial recipes then recommend sweetening it with syrup to reduce its volume by a further 10% to an ABV just above today's standard bottle strength (although it was in the compounder/rectifier's interest to stretch it as far as possible). At this point the compounder simply steeped the botanicals in the spirit, while the rectifier added them to the still along with plenty of water and then redistilled the spirit to extract their aromatics. Both methods are legitimate and have their apologists. The final product was usually served in "quarterns," or measures of a quarter of an old-style 16 oz. pint. Surviving recipes suggest that the compounder/rectifier diluted the final product to below today's standard 37.5% ABV, while the usual habit of adding a splash of water or a shot of fruit cordial brought the strength down further still, maybe to as little as 30%. At that concentration a quartern would have contained no more than four modern units[93] of alcohol; and quarterns were often shared. A common practice was to serve a "quartern three-out" — i.e., one quartern among three customers or, in modern terms, a rather generous single standard pub measure each. Hardly a lethal dose!

But of course, how many quarterns people actually drank is as significant as how much alcohol each quartern delivered. In the mid-18th century the population of England was about 6.5 million; the population of London (where 80% of the nation's gin was made) was 675,000, and the amount of British-made spirits of all varieties (but mainly gin) on which duty was paid peaked in 1743 at 8 million proof gallons[94]: very roughly, then, a proof gallon per head per year. Translating this into consumption, though, is a complicated business. For a start, there was competition: in the West Country, especially in the port cities, imported rum was also popular; while the middle and upper classes appear to have preferred French and Spanish brandy and drank very little gin. Even if only half the population (10% of which was concentrated in London) ever drank gin at all, that would give an average national consumption of two proof gallons per head per year. That doesn't give a true picture of consumption, though, as averages seldom do: London was gin's principal market, and per capita consumption in the capital was much greater than in the provinces, even if consumption outside London was gradually catching up. Clark says:

> One can find clusters of specialist gin-sellers in the larger towns and ports. But the impression is that most retailing outside the capital was done by established victuallers. In a mock debate in the Craftsman in August 1736, Mr. Hearty admitted that gin drinking "has got too much footing amongst us in the country," but he adds, "not to such a degree as some people seem to imagine." In 1736 no provincial center joined in the parliamentary clamour against Mother Gin.

This does not, sadly, give us a clear impression of what proportion of 1743's 8,000,000 proof gallons was sold outside London; but let us assume that the provincial gin distillers such as those we encountered in Colchester were able to fulfill the demand of the provinces, and that the London distillers sold their entire output of maybe 5.5 million proof gallons to the less affluent half of the capital's 675,000 inhabitants. That's still only 16 old-style 128 fl. oz. proof gallons, or 3,000-odd units per head per annum, 57 per week, or eight per day — the alcoholic equivalent of a daily quart pot of porter or four pints of today's best bitter.[95] If we further accept the allegation that gin was on sale all day through numerous channels and the implication that almost everybody drank everywhere all the time rather than on the modern pattern, then nobody would even have been over the legal drink-drive limit, let alone incapacitated by drink. Even accepting that eight units a day is rather more than the Department of Health recommends today, and that everybody drank beer as well, drinking on this scale is still not enough to produce a noticeable effect on mortality in a city where sanitation was unknown and where contagious and environmental diseases roved unchecked. And that is at the very height of the gin boom: in no other year was this figure achieved. Of course, there will have been many people who regularly drank well over this average, but then there will have been a corresponding number who drank below it; so one is very sorely tempted to ask: what craze? As Jessica Warner notes: "Concerns over drunkenness bore very little correspondence to actual consumption." Or to conclude, in Clark's customarily measured tone: "In general then, the spirits trade was more limited in its scale and conventional in its organization than alarmist propagandists asserted. They also misrepresented its effects. Gin became the progenitrix of most of the social and economic problems afflicting the country."

In their desperation to maintain control over the chaos always threatened by the city's licentious working class, the mainly middle-class moral reformers — and there was scarcely a peer (other than the Lords Spiritual) nor a senior MP among them — resorted freely to millenarian hyperbole and hypocritical scaremongering. The double standards were unapologetic and even occasionally explicit: Henry Fielding's admonition to "let the great therefore answer for the employment of their time to themselves, or to their spiritual governors"[96] is quite nakedly so, as is his justification:

> Society will receive some temporal advantage from their luxury. The more toys which children of all ages consume, the brisker will be the circulation of Money, and the greater the increase of trade. The business of the politician is only to prevent the contagion from spreading to the useful part of mankind; and this is the business of persons of fashion and fortune too, in order that the labour and industry of the rest may administer to their pleasures, and furnish them with the means of Luxury. To the upper part of mankind time is an enemy, and… their chief labour is to kill it; whereas, with the others, time and money are almost synonymous; and as they have very little of each to spare, it becomes the legislature, as much as possible to suppress all temptations whereby they may be induced too profusely to squander either the one or the other.

This outright denial of the rights and status of the working class might diminish Fielding somewhat in the eyes of admirers of his novels, but by the time he wrote these astonishing (to us) words he was sick and prematurely aged (he died three years later aged only 47), and the rather brutal thread that runs throughout *An Enquiry* might charitably be attributed to his infirmities. His attitude, though, was widely shared and extended not only to the working class but by natural extension to their drink of choice. Because they were an inferior sort with inferior rights, gin must therefore be a horrid, fiery, and noxious poison that was not only harmful but tasted dreadful too. *Satyr Against Brandy* set the tone, dubbing it:

Essence of Ember, scum of melting flint,
With all the Native sparkles floating in't;
Sure the *Hack-Chymist* with his Cloven foot,
All *AEtna*'s simples in one Lymbeck put.

Thomas Wilson, that harsh man, was not slow to calumniate the object in whose destruction lay his chance of preferment, claiming absurdly that it was distilled not so much from malt as from "rotten fruit, urine, lime, human ordure, and any other filthiness from whence a fermentation may be raised, and by throwing in cochylus indice and other hot poisonous drugs."[97] Defoe, once he was no longer being paid, joined in the campaign of defamation: to the Defoe of 1726 (the Defoe in the pay of the Company of Distillers) a spirit "drawn from the corn… carefully extracted from the gross and humid Parts, and faithfully prepared without any Adulterations or corrupt Mixtures, must be as wholesom to the Body… as any Spirit extracted from other Principles of any kind whatsoever" and therefore "equal to the best French Brandy"; to the Defoe of 1728, it had become simply "that nauseous liquor called geneva." Dr. Johnson in his dictionary of 1755 dismissed it as "a distilled spirituous water, made with no better an ingredient than oil of turpentine, put into the still, with a little common salt, and the coarsest spirit they have, which is drawn off much below proof strength." This is a libel born of ignorance and snobbishness; there is no evidence to suggest it, and much to suggest that the gin produced by London's 1,500 compounders and rectifiers, all in competition with each other, was a sophisticated product which at least matched beer in quality; while the very existence of so many competing compounders must logically have been the precursor of a heliotropic progress towards high quality. For they could scarcely have competed with each other on price, since gin was so cheap anyway; they can therefore only have competed by making better and better products.

It is therefore very surprising to find modern writers echoing, without a shred of independent evidence to support them, these highly partisan and utterly unfounded sentiments. Jessica Warner states, "Aside from its name, this beverage bore little resemblance to what now passes for gin. It was made from the worst possible ingredients, and because of this it was flavored with fruits and other additives in order to mask its harsh and musty taste." (She is not alone in this assertion; indeed the repetition of virtually the same form of words — the word "mask" in particular appears over and over again — by so many writers suggests a single and unquestioned source.) However, in the days before nitrogen testing, moisture testing and other modern laboratory techniques, distillers found they were able to use poorer-quality malting barley than brewers because what they were after was the sugar and nothing but the sugar, whereas brewers wanted the malt's own flavors to carry through to the end product. The quality of the grain did not therefore impact the quality of the gin — in fact, the less of the grain's character that made it to the still, the better.[98] And the idea that it was flavored with "fruits and other additives" to "mask its harsh and musky taste" is wrong on two counts. First, new make — spirit fresh from the still — is not really potable whether it is intended for the finest single malt whiskey or own-label discount hooch. Some of today's craft distillers do bottle small amounts of new make for connoisseurs, although more for amusement than pleasure. But even at proof any spirit burns and irritates and needs to be brought down to standard bottle strength or less before it can really be enjoyed. Secondly, the admixture of "fruits and other additives" is the whole object of the exercise. They were not originally added to mask the "awful taste" of the spirit, as is often (and against all the evidence) asserted, but to surrender their active volatiles to it. The spirit itself was no more than a neutral solvent for the "aniseed, juniper berries, elderberries, cherries, raspberries, and other fruits" that Warner so excoriates, as well as botanicals more obviously medicinal in origin.

In a similar vein, Patrick Dillon conjures a bootleg industry of rogue compounders in the slums of St. Giles's during the prohibition years of the late 1930s and early 1940s giving up "the old way of flavoring by slow distillation" as too expensive and too time-consuming and instead adding neat flavorings to the raw spirits and giving them "a quick stir."

> One guide for publicans published a recipe. To 120 gallons of raw spirit, twenty under proof [i.e. 46% ABV], it added a splash of turpentine (for taste), half an ounce of sulphuric acid (for kick), the same of bitter almonds (for bite), a gallon each of lime and rosewater (for the bouquet), plus eight ounces of alum boiled up in water and a pint of wine spirits… In St. Giles's, they didn't bother with the rosewater. It was a moot point, anyway, whether any of the drinkers much cared what their gin tasted like.[99]

Even assuming that the "bootleggers" of St. Giles's actually existed when, after all, they were only continuing the trade of which they had been legal and respectable practitioners only the day before, and accepting the slur that working-class Londoners were in some way too brutish or ignorant to detect poor quality and go elsewhere for better, this is a complete misrepresentation both of the process he describes and the ingredients he lists. Compounding, or steeping, or infusing, or macerating was and still is a perfectly respectable method of flavoring spirits. Most modern distillers, certainly in Britain, prefer rectifying; but a blind tasting to establish the superiority of one method over the other would probably not yield any very conclusive result. In terms of quality, compounding facilitates the use of extracts, oils, tinctures, tisanes, gums, powders and processed formats in general which might affect the flavor to an extent, but only to a very well-informed palate. One is reminded of the Campaign for Real Ale's utter rejection of the use of hop oils and extracts instead of whole hops: it was never cited as a problem — nor even noticed — by less particular beer-drinkers.

As for the ingredients, each of the substances listed has a perfectly legitimate purpose. Let's start with turpentine, or reduced pine resin, still used today in the making of retsina. Pine resin, as we have already noted, is stuffed full of terpenes including alpha and beta pinenes, camphene, carene, linalool and geraniol, all known to brewers as the fresh, clean, outdoors-y aromatics found in some hop varieties. It's one of many tree resins including palm, birch, maple and sapodilla sap that have several common culinary uses, and medicinally it has been used by doctors from Hippocrates and Dioscorides to the manufacturers of Vick's as an antibacterial to treat cystitis, neuralgia, rheumatism, sciatica, nephritis, genito-urinary and pulmonary infections, bronchitis and blocked noses. To an 18th-century gin compounder it would have the same role as the zest of imported lemon and lime found in most modern botanical grists. It only sounds unwholesome when you call it "turpentine," which evokes today's entirely synthetic product. Give a dog a bad name...

Sulfuric acid though, doesn't sound wholesome whatever you call it. But the half-ounce (to 120 gallons, remember!) recommended here is in a perfectly safe concentration and is no more than a process aid near-ubiquitous at the time and for decades after, used in this case to neutralize the gallon of alkaline slaked lime[100] and also creating ether, a common and slightly sweet-tasting analgesic that was used to relieve anxiety and produce a mild high. Slaked lime (no, not the citrus fruit!) was used in bulk to thicken and stiffen bricks and plaster; in small quantities, as here, it had a similar role, coagulating and precipitating fine particles of protein and other haze-forming impurities. If it didn't work first time, a few ounces of alum (a flocculent that was also a mild sweetener) came in as back-up. Spirits of wine (unwatered *eau de vie*) was made into a paste with sugar and any particularly oily aromatics to emulsify the lipids and stop them floating on the surface. And finally, the two "poisons," bitter almonds and *Cocculus indicus* (or India berry) were both used medicinally in trace quantities at the time, the former as a mild sedative and analgesic, the latter against nausea, dizziness and cramps. Their use had no nefarious purpose or injurious effect and reminds us, as noted above, that spirits were first used as solvents for medicinal herbs and spices, and especially to activate water-insoluble plant alkaloids such as quinine sulphate. In fact there is nothing you can say about either bitter almonds or *Cocculus indicus* that you cannot also say of quinine. That is not to say that these and other substances equally noxious in any quantity were not commonly used at this time and well into the 19th century, generally to disguise the fact that the commodity in question had either been heavily diluted or was masquerading as something else — cider sold as hock, for example. But not in this case. Here they are process aids and botanicals just as are used today.

There never was a gin craze. Yes, there was a boom driven partly by the landowners and distillers and partly by the huge increase in London in the number of reasonably paid people of working age, because the "demographic deficit" was not the consequence of gin's popularity but its cause. There was certainly no "orgy of spirit-drinking" when, even in gin's peak year and even among its target demographic, average personal consumption was below danger levels. Every blast that came from the clique of middle-class evangelists expressed not truth, but anger, fear and disgust at the presumption and indiscipline of the lower orders seeking pleasure and, in the case of retailers, advancement. Their denunciation of the existential threat presented by a free London turned out to be misleading, untrue, and often contradictory. Even the most simple and direct of attacks — that gin was nasty, toxic muck concocted from dangerous chemicals by compounders no better than poisoners — doesn't stand up to scrutiny. Crime waves caused by gin? Or perhaps by unemployment and a stifling lack of opportunity for advancement? Enfeebled workforce and soldiery? Yet the industrial revolution happened in London just as much as in Coalbrookdale and Manchester, and the workforce was not noticeably "enfeebled," whatever that might mean;

nor was Britain unable to find sufficient soldiers and sailors to sustain an almost permanent and largely successful state of war against the French and their proxies and allies in three continents. Infant mortality? Disease to blame, not drams. The list goes on. But London by the 1720s was a blast furnace in which that familiar substance, the working class, changed its nature. Robbery and riot were commonplace. Working-class women were emancipated, to their shame. Atheism and sexual license undermined Christian authority. Alehouses, low taverns, dram-shops, gaming houses, theatres and pleasure gardens were ungoverned spaces where the common people could mix and mingle to their own perdition and society's, if they chose. And gin was traduced as both lubricant and corrosive, destroying the very souls of the common people; causing them to murder their children, or at very least starve and neglect them; weakening them so they could neither fight nor work. The hysteria, the propaganda, and the clamor for repressive action were class war in action. And it was seen as such by many who might have been in sympathy had not the ruling classes continued their abandoned and dissolute lifestyles completely unaffected by the reproaches leveled at the workers.

> There was, from the start, a strong sense that the [1736 Gin Act] was a class measure. One writer declared that "getting drunk will for the future be a great sign of a man's riches; the generality of the people will think themselves oppressed." There was a long-standing hatred of the arbitrary activities of the excise. There was a belief that the London justices were exceeding their powers, trying not only hawkers but "housekeepers and people of credit": not just the poor but respectable citizens were being ruined. In 1737 an attorney declared to a mob… that it was "a great hardship upon the subject that people should be convicted for such offences."[101]

But it was a class war waged only by the middle class, and not even the whole middle class. The bourgeoisie and the squirearchy could be quite as self-indulgent, on occasion, as the notoriously profligate aristocracy; and far more so than the gin-swilling workers the moral reformers sought to put down. Here is the record, quite severely abridged, of the surgeon and diarist John Knyveton's dinner with Dr. Johnson and his friends at the Devil's Tavern on December 11th, 1751[102]:

> The waiters did bring in the supper, such a profusion of dishes as I have never seen before, the company being a large one of some twenty souls or more… Amongst those dishes I remember were:
>
> A dish of rabbits all smothered with onions
> A leg of mutton boiled with capers
> A side of beef with frizzled potatoes
> A roasted goose with some chickens and other game
> A roasted lobster
> A dish of fish stuffed with pudding
> A currant pudding and a vast apple pie, this last especially ordered by the Doctor.
>
> We did drink ale and wine according to our taste… About eleven of the clock… nuts and fruits were set out and coffee served; some of the gentlemen being overcome with the heat of the room and the potency of the wines. I did feel somewhat foxed myself and on looking round did see that Mr. Pope had already left, but did later find him beneath the table… And so feeling infernally sleepy and fuddled did awake George Blumenfield who had gone to sleep with his feet on the table and out with him into the street. The inn all dark, mine host and his servants all gone to bed… I heard from Mr. Pope that the supper party lasted until the dawn… but the company much diminished

> and those still present with difficulty keeping their feet and their wits... it was eight in the morning when the last guest left.

And here, too, is a list of the liquor brought aboard HMS Argo in an Italian port by Captain Clements in 1761 to replenish his personal cabin stories:

> Messina; 1 butt and 3 kegs of 40 gallons
> Port: 2 hogsheads
> Cyprus: 2 kegs, 1 demijohn, 2 bottles
> Champagne: 6 dozen bottles
> Burgundy: 12 dozen bottles
> Claret: 12 dozen and 7 bottles
> Frontenac: 6 bottles
> Montepulciano: 1 chest
> Florence: 8 chests and a half
> Malvasia: 2 chests
> Rum: 1 dozen and 9 bottles
> Beer: 3 dozen and 6 bottles[103]

Meanwhile Pitt the Younger drank three or four bottles of Port a night.

Professionals and businesspeople whose own lives included such pleasant excesses could hardly welcome the thin end of the wedge that the moral reformers wanted to hammer home, even if they felt no sense of shame that just beyond their windows lurked want, disease and degradation. As for the ruling class — the real ruling class — it may have bowed to the pressure in 1736 for action based on social and moral concerns, but in the 1740s it reverted to type and put the revenue first.

The myth of the gin craze is perhaps best summarized by Hogarth's twin prints, Gin Lane and Beer Street. Not only are they shamelessly exaggerated at a time when gin consumption, as Hogarth knew or should have known, had been falling for some years; but they present such a gaping false dichotomy that is a wonder that anyone ever gave them credit: gin-drinkers, as Jessica Warner points out, also drank beer,[104] and beer-drinkers also drank gin.[105] (It's also worth noting that the Swiss commentator César de Saussure, who spent the years 1725–1730 visiting, observing and describing London has plenty to say about drink but nothing to say about gin: "The taverns are almost always filled with men and women and sometimes even children who drink with so much enjoyment that they find it difficult to walk on going away."[106]) Perhaps if one contrived to superimpose the two prints and then retitled them simply "London," they might convey a truth that Hogarth could have perceived every day by the simple expedient of looking out of his window.

To add insult to injury, Hogarth has inscribed over the doorway of the cellar that we assume is intended to be a gin-shop the famous slogan "drunk for a penny, dead drunk for twopence, clean straw for nothing," a slogan expounded upon by Tobias Smollett in his contribution to A History of England (compiled by various authors between 1757 and 1765):

> The retailers of this poisonous compound set up painted boards in public, inviting people to be drunk for the small expense of one penny, assuring them they might be dead drunk for twopence, and have straw for nothing. They accordingly provided cellars and places strewed with straw, to which they conveyed those wretches who were overwhelmed with intoxication. In these dismal caverns they lay until they recovered some use of their faculties, and then they had recourse to the same mischievous potion.

This has been repeated so often that it has become accepted fact that the slogan was plastered all over London as rallying-cry for a recklessly debauched proletariat. In fact, more recent research[107] has established that Hogarth saw it used to advertise a gin-shop in Southwark. Once.

Technocrats, Technology, Techniques: The Science and Business of Gin

The 1751 Act established gin retailing as a mainstream concern, reducing the license fee to a level which pretty much any trader with a fixed premises and a stable business could live with, but which street hawkers and market traders couldn't. A series of prosecutions quickly persuaded the latter to give up any idea of continuing as before and of course, all their custom was transferred to the licensed traders. With only a few last lashes of its worn-out tail, the prohibitionist movement collapsed; the scaremongering stopped; and gin was free to find its own level.

Meanwhile higher duty coupled with generally falling wages and a phenomenal rise in tea-drinking saw consumption continue to decline, and a two-year ban on distilling with grain following the failed harvests of 1757–1758 drove prices even higher and consumption even lower. Malt distillers turned to using molasses instead, but spirit sales were much reduced and, crucially, many compounders went out of business. But perhaps the profoundest change arising from the Act was the clause forbidding compounders and rectifiers to operate gin-shops of their own. This was coupled with the introduction of a minimum still capacity of 100 gallons; and given the choice between making gin on such a large scale and retailing it, most of them chose the latter.

As a result of all these changes the malt distillers were snapping up many of the larger rectifiers, and by 1794 Kent's Directory covering the Cities of London (including Wapping and Whitechapel) and Westminster and the Borough of Southwark listed a mere 10 malt distilleries, some of them still familiar names today[108]; 56 "distillers" (i.e., compounders and/or rectifiers), compared to the estimated 1,500 of the mid-century; and 173 "brandy merchants," or wholesalers distributing to the various retail trades. Being a trade or in modern terms a B2B directory, Kent's excluded all retailers whether inns, pubs (a term just then gaining currency), taverns, chophouses, gaming houses and other licensed premises where spirits were sold alongside beer (and in some cases wine) mainly for consumption on the premises or chandlers and grocers where spirits were part of a much wider sales mix and were sold mainly to take away. But a pattern of trade which was already becoming familiar in the brewing industry was beginning to emerge in distilling too: the growth of the best-capitalized producers through concentration in the market and investment in technology, with the disappearance both of compounder/retailers and of pubs that brewed their own beer.

Falling consumption — due to low wages in the later 1740s, the duty increase contained in the 1751 Act and finally the pause of the late 1750s, when distillers had to brew their wash with molasses for lack of grain — cut a swathe through the ranks of London's malt distillers and applied a sharp brake to the spread of distilling outside the capital. In 1736 there were 28 of them, rising to 30 in London and 10 in the rest of England by 1750. In 1760 there were only 12 left in London, and none outside. By 1780 the number had fallen to a mere eight,[109] although it then started to recover.[110] One result of concentration was a great increase in the wealth and hence social standing of the survivors. Some of those listed in the 1794 directory founded long-lived dynasties; and while others had all too short a date, as a cohort that had weathered the political storms of 1720–1751 and the economic vicissitudes that followed, they represent the foundation stones of the modern gin-distilling industry. Geographically they fall into three fairly tight clusters, all dictated in different ways by the availability of water: Clerkenwell and Finsbury, where deep wells tapped into an aquifer of marvelously pure and plentiful water for both brewing and temperature control; West Ham, where the River Lea and Bow Creek also provided water-power to drive mills; and Battersea/Vauxhall, with an outlier in Bermondsey, where the Thames made light work of transporting grain in and gin out.

Two of the best-known and longest-lived dynasties, those of Gordon's and Booth's, were established in Clerkenwell, Booth's in Cowcross Street as early as 1740 and Gordon's in St. John's Street in 1786, having moved from Bermondsey where it was founded in 1769. The story of Booth's is one of the better known in the anthology of gin distillers: John Booth was a scion of the cadet branch of a very old-established Lancashire family whose senior branch had been ennobled as Earls of Warrington. The junior Booths migrated to Lincolnshire where they are reported as having been prosperous wine-shippers as early as 1569. John Booth moved to London at the age of 29 to start the distillery at 55 Cowcross Street (according to Patrick Dillon, Booth set up as brewer and wine merchant in Turnmill Street in the 1540s and only built the distillery after 1751); his son Philip joined the firm in 1760 at the even more tender age of 15; the third generation, Felix, was born in 1775 and became famous (and earned himself a baronetcy) as an avid sponsor of voyages of exploration in both the Arctic and Antarctic. He bought a brewery, Hazard's, next door to the distillery, presumably to expand production of wash, and renamed it the Red Lion Brewery from which Booth's took its trademark.

John Booth's is a fairly straightforward Dick Whittington story: ambitious young man comes to London from the sticks to make his fortune; turns out he's actually quite well-connected; makes fortune; founds dynasty; dies rich and laden with honors.

(A more intriguing and romantic story has recently been revealed by blogger Solomon Cohen on www.ourjewishagenda.weebly.com. The Booths, he says, were originally Sephardic Jews exiled from Portugal during the mass expulsion of 1497. They settled in the Netherlands along with many others, taking the surname Botha and exporting wine to the northern ports of England. One scion, Ricardo, born 1675, migrated to England and Anglicized his name; it was his great-grandson who founded the distillery. Cohen cites no sources for this great family saga, but *se non e vero....*)

Alexander Gordon's early life is equally vague. He was supposedly born in Wapping, although no one seems to know when; he was raised by his grandfather in Scotland, although no one seems to know why; he returned to London as grown man with sufficient capital to open a distillery, as above. But we have a pretty clear idea of where he came by the money: his partner as listed in the 1794 Kelly's was the delightfully named Malachi Foott, who was the commander during the Seven Years' War (1756–1763) of a 10-gun privateer, the *Charming Mary*, and doubtless came out of it with a few hatfuls of prize-money to invest. The partnership was dissolved in 1797 when Foott retired and a new investor, Henry Knight, was quickly found to help fund Gordon's ambitions. The company is listed as Gordon, Knight in a newspaper report of the murder of their clerk John Pamplin in a street robbery in 1802; and in various registrations of partnership changes as Gordon Son & Knight in 1803 when young Charles Gordon completed the seven-year apprenticeship on which his father had insisted; Gordon, Knight again when Alexander Gordon retired; Gordon, Knight & Buggs in 1823; and just plain Gordon, Knight yet again in 1843. No one seems to know who Buggs was, nor what became of him.

The last of our Clerkenwell trio also founded a dynasty — the only one, in fact, that is still represented on the gin scene today. The Finsbury distillery in Ropemaker Street, Moorgate, was founded in 1740 by Joseph Bishop, member of a family of rectifiers since at least the 1680s, and was originally located in either Holborn Bridge or Aldersgate. In the 19th century it joined forces with a local grocer, Joseph Stone, to make the ginger wine that bears his name to this day; and it remained independent until the 1960s when it merged with the wholesaler Matthew Clark. In the mid-19th century the distillery moved north a couple of miles to Moreland Street and didn't finally close until 1992 (at the same time as the much bigger 1950s Gordon's rectifying plant next door) and the highly regarded Finsbury Gin brand was bought by a German drinks company. The last managing director, Charles Maxwell, was the 11th generation of the family to run the place and went on to found Thames Distillers in Clapham in 1997. As a contract distillery selling ethanol to craft distillers and crafting brands for myriad clients, Maxwell can boast that the craft distilling revolution might never have happened without him. It's only sad that Finsbury is made by one of his competitors, Langley Distillery in Birmingham — although happily Thames Distillers does make Nicholson's.

The East London cluster has left no survivors from the 18th century, but in the remarkable Three Mills complex at West Ham it has left London's only tangible heritage site from what was once such a large and flourishing industry.[111] The complex, which was spread over more than 15 acres on a spit between the Lea and Bow Creek, comprised at its height two water mills, a windmill, two distilleries, a rectifying plant, a brewery, a maltings, granaries and other warehousing, an alehouse, five dwelling-houses, grazing for thousands of pigs (whose diet was richly supplemented not only by the spent malt itself but also by hay soaked in the pot ale left after distillation), and a slaughterhouse and curing shed where bacon was made. This was a very important sideline for distillers and brewers whose locations on the edge of the city allowed enough space for livestock: in the mid-18th century it was reckoned that between them they fattened 100,000 hogs a year.[112] Three Mills had been producing flour for centuries: before the Dissolution it had been the jewel in the crown of Langthorne Abbey's extensive holdings. In the 17th century it changed hands frequently and was greatly extended until in 1728 it was bought by a baker and miller and the son of a Huguenot immigrant, Peter Lefevre, for £5,000. As well as silk-weavers the Huguenots were also known as ale-brewers and one of the first investments Lefevre made was to build a brewery — presumably, to supply wash to the distilleries. A measure of his success was that its value had increased to £7,200 by the time it was next sold in 1756; and although there was never any stability of ownership it was reckoned to be Britain's second biggest distillery by 1795, leapfrogging from fifth in 1792 possibly due to its then owner Philip Metcalfe's success in landing navy contracts (the Revolutionary War with France having broken out in 1793). Still visible on the site are the picturesque Clock Mill with its arched windows, two great kilns, brick clock tower, and white-painted wooden lantern, and the magnificent if somewhat austere House Mill of 1776, said to be the world's biggest tidal mill. Three Mills was bought by Nicholson's in 1872 to make its Lamplighter brand; later all production was transferred there until 1941, when shortages forced its closure. Nicholson's finally sold the site in the late 1980s. House Mill itself was still working until the Blitz; after the war it was repaired, but not to working condition. It is now slowly being restored by the River Lea Tidal Mill Trust, and guided tours are available. Other original buildings on the site include a distillery warehouse converted into flats and Three Mills film and TV studios, London's biggest.[113]

The great East London distilleries may not have left us any dynasties to compare with the Scotch whiskey aristocrats of the following century, but some of the characters they threw up were just as colorful. John Liptrap, for instance, whose distillery covered seven acres off what is now Durward Street but was then Ducking Pond Row off Whitechapel Road, achieved notoriety in 1796 when he invited the Prince of Wales to dinner. When the ladies withdrew, the Prince followed them — a breach of protocol, perhaps, but then a prince is a prince. When he didn't return after some considerable passage of time, however, a rather anxious host set off to look for him — and found him in bed with Mrs. Liptrap. The enraged distiller promptly chased "Prinnie" out of the house and into a cesspit in the distillery yard.[114] Liptrap didn't suffer as a result, but he did a few years later when he fell foul of a corrupt magistrate named Joseph Merceron, who ruled the East London pub trade from his house in Brick Lane.[115] Merceron's racket was to refuse licenses to publicans in his manor who displeased him, which now included any who stocked Liptrap's gin. In 1812 Liptrap was declared bankrupt with debts of £100,000. His house and all its contents as well as the distillery's supplies of consumables were auctioned off, and Liptrap died a few years later. The distillery, which had been founded by his father in 1767, soldiered on under his younger brother, who sold it for £40,000 in 1821. It finally closed 40 years later.

Cooke's of Bow Bridge in Stratford, whose founder we have already encountered as an early adopter of both the thermometer and the hydrometer, was meanwhile carrying on in the same vein by installing a Boulton & Watt steam engine, the first in London and the third in the entire country. Cooke's was also one of the capital's biggest hog-rearing concerns[116] and was the second-biggest distillery until overtaken by Metcalfe's Three Mills. At its peak its output averaged 500,000 gallons a year.[117] Finally Hatch Smith & Currie, in which William Currie was the principal partner, suffered from being just downstream of Three Mills. Consequently there were constant disputes over water rights, so when the plant was rebuilt after a fire in 1789 it was equipped with steam-power and became the biggest in London, leaving both Cooke's and Three Mills behind before eventually becoming part of Tanqueray Gordon & Co, which was created in 1898 by the merger of the two companies.

During the course of the 18th century the whole of the South Bank or Surrey Side of the Thames became one long skein of industrial development interspersed with slum streets and the odd historic monument (including Old London Bridge, although the shops and houses for which it was famed were all demolished between 1758 and 1760). Among the breweries, vinegar factories, chemical works, sugar refineries, and flour mills there were of course a number of distilleries; and as all these concerns started thriving, expanding and redeveloping, there was hot competition for space. Some of the factories of Bermondsey and Battersea were therefore quite short-lived however well they traded — Johnson's of Vauxhall for instance, mainly noted for having the original Vaux Hall (or Copt Hall) in its grounds. William Johnson is a rather shadowy figure: probably from Liverpool, he either set up the distillery or took over an existing one in the 1780s (perhaps) and sold it about 25 years later to buy the Heybridge saltworks on the Blackwater in Essex, where in 1814 he patented an improved process that may have owed a great deal to his knowledge of distillation. His two sons Cuthbert and George both trained as lawyers but became widely respected writers on agriculture and gardening; neither of them proved remotely interested either in gin or in salt — or, for that matter, the law.

Almost adjoining Johnson's distillery and on a much bigger site was Fassett, Burnett & Sons, whose name has come down to us mainly thanks to its Burnett's White Satin brand. John Fassett and Robert Burnett had previously had neighboring works in Horsleydown Lane, Bermondsey, where Fassett was a distiller mainly (like many distillers on the Surrey side) making vinegar while Burnett was a grain factor. It was a match made in heaven, and supposedly in 1770 (the date on the label) but certainly by 1779 (the first record of their partnership in the London Directory) they had upped sticks and moved into a bigger distillery some way across town — right underneath what is now the MI6 building, in fact. This had previously been Pratt's Vinegar Distillery and had been run for 20 years by the founder's nephew, Thomas Mawbey, who was by now an active radical MP, a judge, and a knight of the realm. Burnett himself was also knighted in 1795 when he was Sherriff of London — both honors going to show how high an ambitious and successful distiller could rise in the world.

Underlying the success of the surviving malt distillers were the concentration we have noted, giving them bigger shares of a smaller market, and advances in technology that made the various processes of distilling more efficient and therefore more profitable. These innovations included, as well as steam engines and laboratory equipment, energy-saving devices such as the Pontifex Box, which recycled steam before it could condense, and innovative wrinkles such as drying coal thoroughly before using it, which improved its performance by 7–8%.[118] Advances in metallurgy allowed the gin distillers of the 1790s to install 10,000-gallon pot stills compared to the 5,000 gallons possible in the 1750s; and thanks to the fact that in the 1840s the Glenmorangie distillery in Scotland was fitted with second-hand gin stills which have been replaced as necessary with more or less faithful replicas ever since, we have a good idea of what they were like and what they produced. The original Glenmorangie stills were unusually tall at 16 feet 10 inches so that some of the vapor cooled and condensed in the neck, rolled back down, and was vaporized afresh. During this process, which is known as reflux, the surface of the copper collects and extracts much of the congener content — the various heavier compounds that rise with the vapor — so that the resulting spirit is lighter and cleaner.[119] Reflux bowls fitted at the top of the neck enhance the extraction and collection, making the spirit even lighter and more pure; but just around the corner was the invention that would make the distiller's dream of an almost completely pure spirit a reality.

At this point, the story of Britain's three distilling industries — whiskey in Scotland and Ireland and gin in England — were beginning to converge. The English gin industry had been though its baptism of fire in the form of the bogus gin scares of 1720–1751, which as we have established were an entirely put-up job perpetrated by a small clique of desperate evangelists who sporadically managed to tug an abstracted government's sleeve just hard enough to extort a series of poorly judged and poorly enforced regulatory measures until sense finally prevailed. In Scotland there had been a running battle for even longer than that — for more than a century, in fact, as attempts at enforcing excise regulations following the Act of Union in 1707 gradually drove a long tradition of farm distilling underground and led to a five-cornered political battle between excisemen, distillers, Highland lairds, Lowland lairds and English landed proprietors, finally settled by a compromise Excise Act in 1823. Ireland was late to the fray: its distilling industry was theoretically regulated by a registration and licensing system which was completely unenforced until Acts of 1759 and 1779 drove it too underground, the 1,228 registered distillers of 1779 becoming a mere 32 by 1821 with, according to an excise officer named Aeneas Coffey, 800 bothies in Donegal alone.[120] Here too sense prevailed, with a tax-cutting Excise Act that, like Scotland's, and like England's 1751 Gin Act, made it possible for respectable traders to trade.

More settled market conditions made it possible for proprietors in all three countries to invest in heavier and more advanced capital equipment, and it was Ireland that led the way. Before 1823 the biggest still permitted in Ireland had been 750 gallons, but in 1825 the world's largest-ever pot still at an astonishing 31,600 gallons was installed at Old Middleton — if "installed" is the right word, as the still-house had to be built round it. It's still there, and although it is no longer operational you are welcome to visit it whenever you're in Cork. But even as the coppersmiths of Ireland were working on this leviathan of stills, another Irishman was quietly beavering away perfecting another design altogether, one that many had struggled to improve but none had brought to fruition. And the continuous or column still as patented in 1830 by the exciseman Aeneas Coffey, who retired from public service in 1824 and was now part-owner and manager of three Dublin distilleries, was perhaps the last really major advance in distilling to date.

The first patent for a continuous still was taken out by a chemistry student from Rouen, Edouard Adam, only in 1801. The idea was to replace the pot still, which distils in single batches, with a heat-exchanging loop to take in a continuous flow of wash, vaporize it with a blast of steam, then automatically re-condense the result into its constituent compounds by means of a column with a series of cooling and collecting plates at the appropriate junctures. One advantage of the continuous still was that the spirit it produced was absolutely free of the methyl alcohol, aldehyde and acetone that make up the "foreshots" in pot-distilled spirits and the various butyls that make up the "feints." These are in varying degrees toxic and in a traditional pot still have to be collected separately from the ethanol which is by far the largest fraction, either to be discarded or redistilled. The master distiller has to identify them by eye as they emerge from the condenser, but the ingenious continuous still can work almost unattended, its ethanol being at or near its azeotrope[121] of 95.63% after an operation that is much quicker and more thorough and requires less energy and less labor than a pot still.

Adam's apparatus didn't catch on, but many more qualified chemists and distillers took up where he left off and for the next 30 years there was a scramble to produce and patent a version whose commercial and operational viability lived up to its promise. The winners in the short term were a still designed by a German brewer, Johannes Pistorius, primarily to make potato spirit for vodka and schnapps, which remained in use throughout Germany and Scandinavia until the end of the 19th century; another rather cumbersome variant by the Scottish distiller Robert Stein, which was installed in many of the Lowland plants owned by the Stein and Haig families; and Aeneas Coffey's, which was an improved version of a type patented in 1822 by another Irish distiller, Anthony Perrier. Coffey's continuous still, however, proved too efficient for the whiskey distillers, who complained that the near-pure spirit it produced was bland and tasteless; only a few were installed in either Ireland or Scotland until very much later. Coffey therefore moved to London, founded the unsuccessful Lambeth gin distillery, and then turned full-time still manufacturer. Gin distillers by and large loved his invention: purity was exactly what they were after, and they were especially enamored of the fact that continuously distilled spirit came in at half or even less of the cost of the pot-distilled product. Always early adopters, the gin makers were for the most part willing converts; hence the availability of used gin-stills for Glenmorangie in the 1840s. Coffey himself died in 1852, but the business flourished under his son and flourishes to this very day under the name John Dore & Co of Guildford.

The efficiency of the new equipment allowed distillers to produce new kinds of gin and whiskey so different from the old that they could hardly be classified as gin and whiskey at all — in fact many whiskey traditionalists, including the Irish distillers, rejected the description of grain spirit as whiskey for nearly a century until 1908, when a Royal Commission decided that both pot and column-distilled varieties might legitimately call themselves whiskey. The new, much purer, and unsweetened column-distilled gin attracted the name it still bears, London Dry. The old-style gin, less efficiently distilled and therefore carrying a much higher content of congeners (the flavor components derived from the grain, unfairly dismissed as "impurities"), and often slightly sweetened, came to be called Old Tom and long retained a significant following among drinkers. The derivation of the term is uncertain, but for some reason there has long been an association between gin and cats (remember the puss and mew houses of the 1730s), particularly tomcats. It is possibly a humorous evocation of their spray, of which more below; but more significantly the descriptor "old" in this context perhaps implies not "aged" but "old-style," just as the "oud" in Oud Genever does.

Old Tom co-existed with London Dry for decades; many British distillers also made "Hollands," an attempt to copy Dutch gin; and in Plymouth the distillery made a style of its own, darker, fuller and rootsier than London Dry and popular with naval officers. It all goes to show that although the gin distilling industry as a whole was one of early adopters, it was also one of pragmatists which continued even after the arrival of the new technology to develop and improve upon the old.

Flaring and Glaring: Gas, Glass and Gilt

As the last volleys of musket-fire died away over the shambles of Waterloo, a new world took shape; a world in which the old Continental powers had bled themselves to death in more than 20 years of warfare; a world in which a new power, the second British Empire, had achieved a dominance it was to maintain for a century. Britain might have lost its first empire in 1781 when its troops surrendered to George Washington at Yorktown. But even as the Americans gained their freedom, the kings and princes of India were losing theirs. The French may have helped Washington win America, but in India they could help neither themselves nor their allies as the mercenary armies of the British East India Company, sustained by the global reach of the Royal Navy, remorselessly chewed them away. On the morning of Waterloo Britain was already the most formidable imperialist power in the east; that evening, it was the most formidable power in the west as well.

Victory transformed London, too, into a world city: not just the capital of a great trading and industrial nation, but the seat of empire. The very geography changed: Waterloo Bridge was opened in 1817 and the Parish of Waterloo was hacked out of Lambeth in 1822. Work started on clearing the site of the former King's Mews to create Trafalgar Square in 1826; Nelson's Column, its principal adornment, was completed in 1843. Meanwhile a few miles to the northwest, a smart new suburb of respectable middle-class housing, Maida Vale, took its name from an obscure British victory over the French in Italy in 1806. And all the time, even during the lean years that immediately followed the end of the war, money flowed in until even if the streets weren't actually paved with gold they shone as brightly as if they were; for by 1816 all the city's main thoroughfares were, to the marvel and envy of the rest of Europe, lit by gas. And the newly laid gas mains that supplied the flaring streetlights could also supply light of unimagined brilliance to shops and pubs whose owners, brimming with confidence and eager to invest, were also now installing windows of plate-glass in sheets of previously impossible size, steam-polished by the newly invented Ravenhead grinder to perfect smoothness and clarity, etched and gilded as the showiest imaginable advertisements for their ever bigger, brighter and more fantastical architectural extravaganzas.

Among these, in the first half of the 19th century, were many descendants — thousands, according to some — of the dram shops of an earlier period, still purveying the familiar quarterns to society's less genteel but doing it in style, their gas-flares reflected and amplified by huge mirrors, brightly polished bar counters, gantries and galleries of oak and mahogany, gleaming china spirit-barrels, counter-tops of marble, and taps of twinkling brass. Gin-palaces they were nicknamed by customers used to much plainer and more utilitarian surroundings: as grand as any palace, but palaces for the people; and the first of them — or so it is always said — was Thompson & Fearon at 94 Holborn Hill.

The expression "gin-palace" itself is vernacular and its origin is therefore necessarily vague; it is not known when it was coined but by 1834, when it was used at the Commons Select Committee on Drunkenness both by one of the witnesses and by the chairman, it was evidently in common currency, describing, or attempting to describe, a dram shop remodeled to incorporate all the design features described above in as flashy a way as possible. It's often remarked, perhaps following Dickens (below) that these establishments tended to be located as close as possible to a slum quarter in a deliberate attempt to entice its denizens out of their rats' nests and into the warm and addictive arms of Mother Gin. The claim doesn't really stand up to scrutiny, though. For a start, almost every primary location in late Georgian London was within a stone's throw of a "rookery," as the packed slum courts came to be known; secondly, it didn't take £10,000 or £15,000 in plate glass, stucco, and brass to entice the poor; thirdly, the poor, by virtue of being poor, weren't much of a target demographic anyway. The truth is that the most free-spending of the proprietors were competing primarily for middle-class or upper working-class money, and that they redesigned their establishments to appeal to the appropriate tastes and aspirations (or perhaps pretensions). This is particularly relevant in the light of the halving of spirit duty in 1825, which killed the smuggling industry stone dead overnight and drove the middle-class households who had been the smugglers' best customers back into the arms of the legal trade, of which much more below. Of course the few pennies that a starveling alcoholic might spare for a quartern or even a single dram were always welcome — but not if the starveling alcoholics drove away the more respectable custom. There were plenty of unimproved slum pubs down backstreets and alleyways where the poor and disreputable could get their gin, like the Three Cripples in Saffron Hill, Fagin and Bill Sikes's local, where:

> The room was illuminated by two gas-lights, the glare of which was prevented by the barred shutters and closely-drawn curtains of faded red from being visible outside. The ceiling was blackened... and the place was full of dense tobacco smoke.

Hardly palatial!

The drink in this excerpt from *Oliver Twist* (1838) is gin and water, and gin runs through the whole novel like veins through marble as a metaphor for various stages of degradation from the accident of Oliver's being baptized in it to his being sedated with it once he has joined Fagin's gang of dippers, skinners and natty lads (all of whom enjoy regular doses too, despite their tender years). The Three Cripples, however, is nothing like a gin palace: for that, we turn to Dickens again and his description of various elements of the unnamed gin-palace in *Sketches by Boz* (1836):

> The extensive scale on which these places are established, and the ostentatious manner in which the business of even the smallest among them is divided into branches, is amusing. A handsome plate of ground glass in one door directs you "To the Counting-house;" another to the Bottle Department; a third to the Wholesale Department; a fourth to The Wine Promenade; and so forth, until we are in daily expectation of meeting with a Brandy Bell, or a Whiskey Entrance. Then ingenuity is exhausted in devising attractive titles for the different descriptions of gin; and the dram-drinking portion of the community as they gaze upon the gigantic black and white announcements, which are only to be equalled in size by the figures beneath them, are left in a state of pleasing hesitation between The Cream of the Valley, The Out and Out, The No Mistake, The Good for Mixing, The Real Knock-me-down, The celebrated Butter Gin, the Regular Flare-up, and a dozen other equally inviting and wholesome liqueurs. Although places of this description are to be met with in every second street, they are invariably numerous and splendid in precise pro-

portion to the dirt and poverty of the surrounding neighborhood. The gin-shops in and near Drury-Lane, Holborn, St. Giles's, Covent-garden, and Clare-market, are the handsomest in London. There is more of filth and squalid misery near those great thoroughfares than in any part of this mighty city. We will endeavor to sketch the bar of a large gin-shop, and its ordinary customers, for the edification of such of our readers as may not have had opportunities of observing such scenes; and on the chance of finding one well suited to our purpose, we will make for Drury-Lane… All is light and brilliancy; and the gay building with the fantastically ornamented parapet, the illuminated clock, the plate-glass windows surrounded by stucco rosettes, and its profusion of gas-lights in richly-gilt burners, is perfectly dazzling when contrasted with the darkness and dirt we have just left. The interior is even gayer than the exterior. A bar of French-polished mahogany, elegantly carved, extends the whole width of the place; and there are two side-aisles of great casks, painted green and gold, enclosed within a light brass rail, and bearing such inscriptions, as Old Tom, 549; Young Tom, 360; Samson, 1421 — the figures agreeing, we presume, with gallons[122]. Beyond the bar is a lofty and spacious saloon, full of the same enticing vessels, with a gallery running round it, equally well furnished ... Behind (the counter) are two showily-dressed damsels with large necklaces, dispensing the spirits and compounds. The two old washerwomen seated on the little bench to the left of the bar are rather overcome by the head-dresses and haughty demeanour of the young ladies who officiate. They receive their half-quartern of gin and peppermint with considerable deference, prefacing a request for "one of them soft biscuits" with a "Jist be good enough, ma'am."

Those two old men who came in "just to have a dram" finished their third quartern a few seconds ago; they have made themselves crying drunk; and the fat comfortable-looking elderly women, who had "a glass of rum-shrub" each, having chimed in with their complaints on the hardness of the times, one of the women has agreed to stand a glass round, jocularly observing that "grief never mended no broken bones, and as good people's wery scarce, what I says is, make the most on 'em, and that's all about it!" a sentiment which appears to afford unlimited satisfaction to those who have nothing to pay.

The knot of Irish labourers at the lower end of the place, who have been alternately shaking hands with, and threatening the life of each other, for the last hour become furious in their disputes, and finding it impossible to silence one man who is particularly anxious to adjust the difference, they resort to the expedient of knocking him down and jumping on him afterwards.

George Augustus Sala's account of a gin-palace in *Gaslight & Daylight*, 23 years on, is very similar to Dickens's, other than the addition of whiskey — both Irish and Scotch — to the array of advertising placards which have succeeded the decorative china spirit casks on the gantry, and the greater prominence of beer. We are also witnessing here the beginnings of the later habit of dividing up huge and impersonal interiors into much smaller and more intimate spaces, partly because the latter are more comfortable and so tempt the drinker into lingering longer, and partly because if trouble breaks out in one compartment it tends not to spread.

This ginnery has not only a bar public, but divers minor cabinets, bibulous loose boxes, which are partitioned off from the general area, and the entrances to which are described in flowery, but somewhat ambiguous language. There is the Jug and Bottle Entrance, and the entrance For Bottles Only. There is the Wholesale Bar, and the Retail Bar; but wholesale or retail, jug or bottle, the different bars all mean Gin! The long pewter counter[123] is common to all. A counter perforated in elaborately-pricked patterns, like a convivial shroud, apparently for ornament, but really for the purpose of allowing the drainings, overflowings, and outspillings of the gin-glasses to drop through, which, being collected with sundry washings, and a dash, perhaps, of fresh material, is, by the thrifty landlord, dispensed to his customers under the title of "all sorts." Your dram-drinker, look you, is not unfrequently paralytic, woefully shaky in the hand; and the liquor he wastes, combined with that accidentally spilt, tells up wonderfully at the close of the year… Besides what I have described, if you will add some of my old friends the gold-blazoned boards, bearing the eulogies of various brewers, together with sundry little placards, framed and glazed, and printed in colours, telling, in seductive language, of Choice Compounds, Old Tom, Cream of the Valley, Superior Cream Gin, The Right Sort, Kinahan's LL, The Dew off Ben Nevis, the Celebrated Balmoral Mixture, "patronized by his Royal Highness Prince Albert" (the illustrious personage, clad in full Highland costume, with an extensive herd of red deer in the distance, is represented taking a glass of the Mixture with great apparent gusto); besides these, I repeat, you will need nothing to 'complete the costume,' as the romancers have it, of a Gin Palace.

One word about the customers. Thieves, beggars, costermongers, hoary-headed old men, stunted, ragged, shock-haired children, blowzy, slatternly women, hulking bricklayers, gaunt, sickly hobbledehoys, with long greasy hair… Is it not the same everywhere! The same pipes, dirt, howling, maundering, fighting, staggering gin fever. Like plates multiplied by the electro-process — like the printer's stereo — like the reporter's manifold — you will find duplicates, triplicates of these forlorn beings everywhere. The same woman giving her baby gin; the same haggard, dishevelled woman trying to coax her drunken husband home; the same mild girl, too timid even to importune her ruffian partner to leave off drinking the week's earnings, who sits meekly in a corner, with two discoloured eyes, one freshly blacked, one of a week's standing. The same weary little man, who comes in early, crouches in a corner, and takes standing naps during the day, waking up periodically for "fresh drops." The same red-nosed, ragged object who disgusts you at one moment by the force and fluency of his Billingsgate, and surprises you the next by bursting out in Greek and Latin quotations. The same thin, spectral man who has no money, and with his hands piteously laid one over the other, stands for hours gazing with fishy eyes at the beloved liquor — smelling, thinking of, hopelessly desiring it. And lastly, the same

> miserable girl, sixteen in years, and a hundred in misery; with foul, matted hair, and death in her face; with a tattered plaid shawl, and ragged hoots, a gin-and-fog voice, and a hopeless eye.

Well, Sala was certainly a greater moralizer than Dickens, if not perhaps as great a moralist. Surely the objects of his contempt listed in the final paragraph belong more to the Three Cripples than to the grander establishment he describes; indeed, they bear an uncanny, not to say plagiaristic, resemblance to the creatures encountered by Dickens on his police-escorted tour of the slums of St. Giles.[124] But by his time gin was already well on its way to losing its pariah status anyway. A rather more measured account of the gin-palace by the Lincolnshire writer, basket-maker and peasant poet Thomas Miller (he was a contemporary of John Clare's) in the Illustrated London News of 6th May 1848 draws a (slightly) less judgmental picture of a clientele that is rather more mixed and somewhat less degraded than Dickens or Sala would allow (although there is still more than a whiff of the bourgeoisie's disgust at the working class), while testifying to the insensible merger of gin-shop and public house:

> There are few places in London where so great a variety of characters may be seen popping in and out in a short space of time, as at the bars of our modern gin-palaces. Even respectable men who meet each other by chance, after a long absence, must drop in at the nearest tavern, although they have scarcely a minute to spare, to drink a glass together at the bar, and enquire about old friends. Married women, we are sorry to say, many of them the wives of clever mechanics, also congregate when they ought to be providing the dinner for their families. Such things are thought but little of among those who are far from being num-

> bered with the lowest orders of society. Then there are young itinerant vendors of almost every imaginable thing — these are, also, constant members of the bar, confining themselves generally to pennyworths of gin. The costermongers, who come wheeling and shouting from opposite directions, with their barrows, if they chance to meet near the door of a tavern must, after a little gossip, go in and have their "drain." Added to these, there are the poor, the old, and the miserable, who look and feel "half-dead," as they themselves express it, unless they are "lighted up" every two or three hours with a glass of spirits. Many of these have become so habituated to drink that they care but little for food, and very rarely partake of a substantial meal; a pennyworth of boiled shell-fish, such as whelks or mussels, an oyster or two, or a trotter, or sometimes a fried fish — all of which are borne into these places by hawkers every hour of the day — may be taken as fair samples of the food consumed by these regular drinkers.

Nor is it at the front of the gaudily fitted-up bars alone where such quantities of spirits are consumed. Women and children even are coming in with bottles; some of the latter so little, that... they are scarcely able to reach up and place the bottle upon the zinc-covered bar. If the weather is cold they are generally sent out in their mothers' shawls and bonnets, the one trailing upon the ground, and the other completely burying their little dirty faces. Even these young miserable creatures are fond of drink, and may sometimes be seen slyly drawing the cork outside the door, and lifting the poisonous potion to their white withered lips. They have already found that gin numbs and destroys for a time the gnawing pangs of hunger, and they can drink the fiery mixture in its raw state.

A more dispassionate view still comes from George Dodd, the journalist, writer, and associate of Charles Dickens, in his monumental *The Food of London* (1856).

> The Public-Houses of London, as distinguished from hotels, inns, chop-houses, eating-houses, and coffee-rooms, have undergone great changes within the last few years. They have been transformed from dingy pot-houses into splendid gin-palaces, from painted deal to polished mahogany, from small crooked panes of glass to magnificent crystal sheets, from plain useful fittings to costly luxurious adornments. The old Boniface, with his red nose and his white apron, has made way for the smart damsels who prepare at their toilettes to shine at the bar. The comfortable old landlady is less seen than formerly, ensconced behind and amongst her rich store of cordials and compounds and liqueurs; she, too, must pass under the hands of the milliner before making her daily appearance in public. Even the pot-boy is not the pot-boy of other days; there is a dash of something about him that may almost be called gentility; his apron is cleaner than were the aprons of pot-boys twenty years ago; and the tray filled with quarts and pints of dinner-beer, carried out to the houses of the customers, seems to have undergone some change, for it is less frequently seen than "in days of yore."

Better-off women, not normally seen on their own in licensed premises, were also welcome in some mid-century gin palaces — although they were not expected to rub shoulders with the hoi-polloi in the public rooms. As the American travel writer William O'Daniel observed[125]: "In the gin palaces, bars are put up always for ladies' use. The common girls of the city are by no means admitted to the ladies' bar; they must stand at the common bar among crowds of men." The ladies' bar, O'Daniel noted, doubled as the jug and bottle or take-home counter, where off-sales far outnumbered drams.

As well as noting the increasing gentility of the gin-palace O'Daniel, like Sala and Miller, noted its merger into the mainstream of the licensed trade: "Next to gin, the people drink ale and stout," he wrote; and in less than 30 years the gin palace had travelled a long way from the business model of the celebrated pioneer, Thompson & Fearon of Holborn Hill. For the truth, indeed the most important thing, about Thompson & Fearon was that it wasn't really a gin-palace at all in the generally accepted sense: in fact it wasn't even a bar. It was a wine and spirit merchant mainly distributing to the various branches of the retail trade, although its Holborn Hill branch (there was a second in Bond Street) also retailed a little, mostly in small barrels delivered to private family cellars. It was founded in 1807 by a fascinating character, the hyper-religious Samuel Thompson (1766–1837), son of a Houndsditch publican and apprenticed to a watchmaker before joining the liquor trade. After his first wife died tragically young he turned to religion and in 1798 founded the Freethinking Christians, which over the years took up more and more of his energies. He therefore left much of the running of the business to his sons-in-law William Coates, who seceded after a family row and set up for himself in Whitechapel, and Henry Fearon, who soon became, in modern terms, Thompson's chief operating officer. Both Coates and Fearon were God-fearing men and if temperance campaigners saw them as just two more missionaries from Hell, that's not how they saw themselves. In their own eyes they were upmarket retailers like any other, selling top-quality products to a clientèle as upright[126] and as legitimate as themselves. Having said that, most of what they sold was gin.

In March 1830, Henry Fearon, while giving evidence to the Commons Select Committee on the forthcoming Beer Act, revealed that his firm was just about to spend the then eye-watering sum of £15,000 on its Holborn Hill premises in the rebuilding exercise that was to give it its spurious renown as the first of the gin palaces. The committee was actually discussing abolishing beer duty and opening beer retail to all on payment of a two-guinea excise license. The measure was partly aimed at curbing gin consumption, which had doubled to more than 10 gallons per head per annum in the preceding decade, by opening up competition and increasing spirit duty by 6 pence a gallon. Fearon took the stand along with many others from different branches of the liquor trade to explain why this might not be such a good idea. The firm's primary business, as we have seen, was wholesale distribution. The second biggest department was what Fearon described as "large division" retail — that is, delivering wines and spirits in bulk to private cellars. This was the trade that had benefited most from the 1825 near-halving of duty on spirits from 10 shillings 6 pence a gallon to 5 shillings 10 pence, or 7 shillings on the newly introduced imperial gallon of eight 20-ounce pints. This was largely intended as a measure to prevent smuggling, which had reduced parts of the south coast almost to a state of guerrilla war and was costing the Treasury more than £300,000 a year in prevention. It was spectacularly successful, so much so that officially recorded per capita gin consumption returned to 1740s levels. The middle classes had previously been the smugglers' biggest customers and, like cocaine users today, scarcely thought of it as a criminal enterprise despite the trail of blood it left in its wake: in October 1792 the good-hearted Parson Woodforde of Weston, Norfolk, records with some relief in his diary that John Buck, the village blacksmith and bootlegger, had been caught with a tub of gin in his house but "was pretty easy fined." Perhaps the magistrate was also a customer? Two weeks later, says the parson, "Had a tub of brandy and a tub of rum brought this evening. Gave one of the men that brought it 1s." On another occasion: "Had another tub of gin and another of the best Coniac brandy brought me this evening about 9. We heard a thump at the front door about that time, but did not know what it was till I went out and found the two tubs — but nobody there."

The clear implication is that malt distillers were as complicit in the illegal trade as any complaisant magistrate: Parson Woodforde's tax-free tub of gin was smuggled not from France but from the back door of a distiller's warehouse. It was the Parson Woodfordes of the world who, once they could afford duty-paid spirits, flocked back in droves to respectable merchants like Thompson & Fearon; in consequence, the firm strongly discouraged the practice for which it was most criticized. Its "small division" sold bottles and jugs of gin for children and servants to take home to their parents or masters, the customers supplying their own vessels; but the same counter also sold single glasses for passers-by to down as the fancy took them. Fearon estimated that while the large retail division took £2,500 a month, the small division took only £1,800, mostly in takeaway form. There was no seating, and no one was allowed more than the single measure: sales by the glass were finally dropped in 1836 as being more trouble than they were worth.

William Coates, now in business on his own account in Whitechapel High Street, went into more detail on the lack of seating, asserting beyond doubt that it was not a ploy to get the poor to drink more and more and faster and faster, but rather the opposite:

> We find that (seating) is an intolerable evil where there is a large trade. They want another glass; a friend comes in, and they hold a little conversation and call for glass after glass, which it is not our custom to allow. It leads to the congregation of idle persons, who drive away respectable persons... and it is not to be endured that respectable persons who send their and daughters with their orders should pass [sic] through a tap-room where coal-heavers are drinking and smoking.

Coates, Fearon, and other spirit merchants of the time were well aware of the fragility of their good name and the importance of their reputation with the licensing authorities. There were plenty of people set against them, from the swelling ranks of the temperance lobby (who, unlike the reformers of a century before, did not focus particularly on gin but were opposed to drink in all its forms) to publicans like Thomas Spring of the Macclesfield Arms in City Road, a beer-seller whose pub was, he said, "not a spirit house." Spring claimed to have lost two-thirds of his trade to his gin-selling neighbours in the preceding three or four years and rued the day when a thirsty coalheaver first asked for a quartern of gin with a pint of water at 3 1/2 pence instead of a pot of beer at 5 pence. He told the committee:

> I have been here 26 years this June and I believe that every one of the houses in our parish which are, to use the magistrate's own expression, flaring and glaring gin shops, has been established within the last 15 or 16 years, [i.e., since the end of the war]. We have got a gin-spinner in our parish that drives his carriage and four in as great a style as almost His Majesty. He has built a place which I understand has cost him above £10,000; Edward Weller, his name is. It opened in the first week of last October… there was such a scene there as never took place before. There was 60 pipes of gin brought through in one day. He is doing £16–17,000 a year in gin, while I do £4,000 in beer; my expenses are £400, his are ninety.

Investigative journalists and temperance campaigners often tried to keep a count of customers entering and leaving these great establishments, not always accurately. When the Times estimated that Thompson & Fearon carried out 360 transactions an hour, Fearon retorted that at peak times it was more like 480; but he was a little less sanguine when the newly formed Temperance Society counted purchasers of soda water and ginger beer — an innovation of which he was very proud — among the "intoxicated" to be found on his premises.

It is indicative of Thompson & Fearon's sense of their status in the commercial world that they chose as the designer of their enlarged and glorified Holborn Hill premises one of the most prominent commercial architects of the day. Now at the height of a very distinguished career, J.B. Papworth had laid out the elegant Montpelier Estate in Cheltenham with its fine Regency shops and villas; designed the elaborate chinoiserie decoration on the frontage of F&R Sparrow, superior tea merchants of Ludgate Hill; and enlarged Butterworth's, the noted legal booksellers of Fleet Street, in appropriately grand style. Thompson & Fearon was his only licensed premises,[127] emphasizing that the firm did not position itself as a run-of-the-mill gin-shop, let alone as a pub, but as a high-status retailer of top-quality goods to affluent and respectable families. For the first mention of the expression "gin-palace," in a context suggesting its present meaning of opulently decorated urban pub, we have to look four years into the future and another Commons Select Committee, this time on drunkenness. Asked about public drunkenness in his parish George Wilson, a grocer of Tothill Street, replied:

> Drunkenness always was the master evil in this neighborhood, but it has increased very much lately. I am induced to think that this has been caused by the great excitement of the gin-palaces, as they are termed, of which we have abundance. I am induced to think so from the following circumstance: a public house nearly opposite my residence, where the consumption of spirits was very trifling, was taken for a gin-palace. It was converted into the very opposite of what it had been, a low dirty public house with only one door-

> way, into a splendid edifice, the front ornamented with pilasters, supporting a handsome cornice and entablature and balustrades... remarkably striking and handsome; the doorways were increased in number from one, and that only a small one... to three, and each of those three eight to 10 feet wide... and the doors and windows glazed with very large single squares of plate glass, and gas fittings of the most costly description... certainly from the boldness of the design and the elegance of its execution justifying the term palace...

A tour of inspection, along with a Mr. Green and a posse of like-minded neighbors, of the other gin-palaces in the district revealed that they had lost no custom to the newcomer, or so it seemed to Mr. Wilson; their response had been to lower their prices, and as a consequence:

> All the gin-palaces were equally as crowded as before... each gin-shop, in fact, was as full as it was possible to be, and from that circumstance, I think that the addition of houses only increases the demand for gin... there are other palaces in a state of forwardness in the neighborhood, the proprietors having been induced, no doubt, to make the alteration by the great success of those that already exist.

The grandeur of the décor apart, the type of establishment Wilson described shared almost nothing with the mainly take-home operations run by Fearon, Coates and their like. There is certainly no suggestion of rationing customers to a single glass at the kind of gin-shops described by Dickens and Sala.

Nevertheless, as Coates told the 1830 Select Committee: "Gin is the weakest and most innocent spirit that is consumed." It was watered down before it reached the public and then watered down again, often with a peppermint or fruit-flavored cordial, by the customers themselves. Not only was it weaker than brandy, whiskey, or rum, it was cheaper too, and since the halving of duty five years earlier it had displaced rum and wine in the "two-gallon trade," which had quadrupled in volume. Gin still had its old following of heavy drinkers, said Coates, including the Irish who "talk a great deal about whiskey but prefer gin," but it had also "got among another class." Respectable women no longer felt any pressure to conceal the fact that they frequented licensed premises, although perhaps not on their own. "All that secrecy is out of the question," he said. "A man and his wife will come in and take their glass and drink their good wishes to each other; the supposed secrecy exists only in the imagination of the magistrates, and not in fact." Another wine and spirit merchant, John Watchorn of the Dover Castle in Marsh Gate, Surrey, noted in his evidence to the committee: "There has been so much puritanical cant about the subject of gin-drinking lately that the magistrates have felt themselves bound to take it up," but added, "Gin has found its way latterly among all classes of society from the very superior quality of the article."

The same was true of the gin-palace. The fashion for opulence, for extravagance, for what we would call high-end design persisted and intensified throughout the 19th century in commercial architecture generally: department stores, upmarket shops of all kinds, especially those in select shopping streets and arcades, and urban pubs were far from immune, and the capital required to fit out a new one or refit an old one grew and grew until many pub-owners went bust trying to keep up. By the 1890s, the most mundane of pubs merited the attentions of the finest decorative artists in London. These grandiose piles somehow acquired the name "gin-palace," and when we think of, say, the Salisbury in St. Martin's Lane or the Princess Louise in High Holborn, that's the descriptor we reach for. But although these are indeed palaces, they never had any connection with gin beyond stocking it alongside every other nectar known to humanity. Over the course of the century the different categories of on-licensed premises gradually lost their individual identities as every licensee sought to outdo their neighbors and, like Tesco, to sell everything to everybody. But it is not evident that — as is so often argued — the gin palaces appeared in response to the threat of competition from unlicensed beerhouses, for men like Coates knew they could far outcompete any grubby cottage parlor. As Coates put it when contemplating the harm that the Beer Act might do to his business:

> How are we to be compensated? By going more largely into the beer trade. Our premises, our shops, our knowledge of the business, all fit us to do this… There are gentlemen in our line who afford no accommodations at all and yet are largest venders of beer in the metropolis; there are gentlemen selling 30 butts of beer a month without a form or a seat of any kind to sit down upon.

He was, of course, quite right: the unlicensed beerhouses opened by the thousand as a consequence of the 1830 Beer Act throve for a while but before long were all applying for full on-licenses while the better-capitalized operators, whether independent or brewery-owned, trumped them through widening their appeal and raising their standards. By 1900 the centers and suburban high streets of London and all the major provincial cities boasted great and magnificent pubs that were not and never had been gin-palaces. Nevertheless if pubs had come up in the world, so had gin.

It Ain't Tea

The officially recorded increase in sales following the 1825 duty cut, even if in reality it represented displacement rather than increment, provoked a fluttering resurgence of the moral crusade against gin; but as noted the 19th-century temperance movement was much broader in its outlook than its mid-18th century predecessors and regarded gin as no more than one among a whole host of liquid demons. Temperance crusaders might also have been sensible of Mr. Watchorn's dictum in 1830 that gin had latterly found favor with all classes "from the very superior quality of the article." That is not to say that gin had become respectable; merely that it had joined the mainstream, exactly as gin-palaces merged into the mainstream of pubs, and was no longer regarded as egregiously dangerous.

But where the improvement in quality noted by Watchorn and others that helped give gin its leg-up into the mainstream came from is not as straightforward as it seems. It is always said that the purer spirit that flowed from the two patented column stills, the Stein and the Coffey, made for a cleaner, drier, more acceptable drink; but the former was patented in 1828 and was only used within the Stein/Haig family combine, and the latter was patented in 1830 and was slow to catch on. Watchorn's assertion therefore predates the availability of column-distilled gin, so the "superior quality" he commends can only refer to gin made in pot-stills by the traditional batch method. We have seen that the second-hand gin-stills used to equip Glenmorangie in 1843 were unusually tall and generated a high level of reflux, making for a smoother spirit; perhaps it was developments in still design such as this, as well as the temperature control systems already mentioned, that created the "superior article?" Furthermore it should not be assumed that column-distilled spirit was necessarily of better quality than the output of pot stills lovingly tended by experts: you would never say the same of Cognac or single malt whiskey! Column-distilled spirit may be azeotropically close to neutral, with all the natural flavors and aromas of the original grain-bill stripped out; but modern commentators who describe batch-distilled gin as "rough" without ever having tried it are merely repeating the language of gin's detractors. Parson Woodforde evidently didn't find it so! Indeed the possibility that the new-fangled column-distilled gin was regarded by at least some contemporaries as bland — much as lager is seen by cask ale enthusiasts — is suggested by the persistence of the sweeter style.

Batch or pot-distilled gin was generally quite heavily sweetened — with, according to one early 19th-century recipe, 35 lbs of sugar dissolved in nine gallons of water and added to 100 gallons of spirit.[128] At about the same time a new name, Old Tom, appeared for a type or variant of gin which was always described as sweet. Various charter myths have been conjured up for the name: one is that it was named for a distiller's cat that fell into the washback and drowned; another is that Tom Norris, a distiller turned gin-palace owner of Great Russell Street, Covent Garden, named one the gins he stocked after Tom Chamberlain, his old apprentice-master at Hodge's distillery where they had been known as Young Tom and Old Tom. This story first surfaced in 1849 when Boord's distillery trademarked its brand of Old Tom, which it called Cat & Barrel. The earliest solid citations of the name Old Tom come from David Wondrich,[129] reporting a mention in an issue of the New

Statesman in 1810, in newspaper advertisements from 1812 and after, and in a commendation from an unnamed vintner in 1830 that it was only the "best and strongest cordial gin" that was "sold under the general name of Old Tom." Wondrich's chronology rules out the origin of the name as a convenient contrast between the old-fashioned batch-distilled version and the new-fangled column-distilled London Dry; if one discards the charter myths (which is normally wisest) one is left with the probability that Old Tom was not only sweetened but also barrel-aged to some extent before going on sale, which would have mellowed it a great deal and colored it a little. Some distillers boasted of aging their gin for as long a year, in which case it would have been a third of the way to being whiskey!

The "tom" component is interesting in itself because for some reason in the 18th-century mind cats and gin seemed to have become entwined. And there may be a very good reason for that. As London expanded higgledy-piggledy in the 16th and 17th centuries it was equipped piecemeal, district by district, with local networks of storm drains which emptied into the city's many rivers. These were not intended as sewers but as flood defenses, but inevitably much of the waste generated by the inhabitants ended up in them. (Although by no means all: older houses retained their basement cesspools: on 20th October 1660 Pepys famously stepped in "a great heap of turds" that had leaked into his cellar from his neighbor's. In slum courts and alleys human ordure simply lay on the ground until eventually a contractor scooped it up and hauled it away for fertilizer). Since the drains couldn't cope, an Act of 1662 ordered that householders should periodically put out their refuse, of whatever sort, "in baskets, tubs, or other vessels ready for the raker or scavenger." The liquid that settled out of the contents of these tubs went to the tanneries of Smithfield which were later, when the stench had become too much for even the most habituated of residents, exiled to Bermondsey. Here their ammonia content could concentrate without causing too much of a public nuisance into the strong caustic in which freshly flayed animal hides were softened before being shaved of hair and flesh. These tubs of maturing ammonia, left open to permit the necessary evaporation, stank to high heaven, and if you have ever encountered the spray of a rutting tom cat you will know exactly what they smelled of. Hence, perhaps, Old Tom as one of gin's many vulgar but jocular nicknames; very like "a pint of diesel" today, and not be taken as a serious reflection on the quality of the drink; and hence perhaps the frequent depiction of rather smug-looking cat sitting on a barrel. And there's another cat connection too: Jacob Larwood in English Inn Signs (1866) gives "How-d'ye-do and spew" as a demotic alternative to Salutation & Cat, reminding us that "to cat" was slang for to vomit — a sense that has only recently become obsolete. The Cat & Barrel trademark applied by Boord's to its brand of Old Tom is supposed to have commemorated an old city tavern, but no such tavern-name is recorded; not by Larwood, at least, and he was an avid collector. Perhaps Old Tom was originally an abbreviation of tom cat's pee or spray, and "cat and barrel" described, albeit in jest, not the cat *on* the barrel but the cat *in* the barrel. It's not as unlikely a suggestion as it might seem, for this kind of cheerful scatology was not at all uncommon in London vernacular. One of the many gin substitutes concocted after the 1736 Act, for instance, was nicknamed tow-row — slang for vagina.[130]

These euphuisms, though, belong to the Georgian era, and the early Georgian era at that, when life was lived in the open and on the surface, and people were apt to say more than they meant. By the end of the Georgian era public manners had altered beyond recognition. Euphemism had succeeded euphuism; sly hints had evicted streams of oaths; meanings were concealed, appearances kept up. For Dickens, as we have seen, gin was often a metaphorical measure of human degradation from the outright wickedness of Bill Sikes to the peccadilloes of Mrs. Mann, the object of Mr. Bumble's fatal affections in *Oliver Twist* (1838), and Sarah Gamp, the *tour de force* of comic invention in *Martin Chuzzlewit* (1844). Offering the love-struck beadle a "leetle drop" of daffy or laudanum tincture (the universal painkiller of the day) Mrs. Mann finally admits: "It's gin. I'll not deceive you, Mr. B. It's gin." Likewise Sarah Gamp, distraught after her falling-out with Betsey Prig, is offered a cheering cup from her own teapot by a solicitous John Westlock.

> "Have a little..." John was at a loss what to call it.
> "Tea," suggested Martin.
> "It ain't tea," said Mrs. Gamp.[131]

Doubtless it was Old Tom or some other sweet and full-bodied variant of gin — Cream of the Valley, perhaps — that Mrs. Mann and Mrs. Gamp concealed under the guises of daffy and tea.[132] But it could quite easily have been tea. Since the early 18th century the duty on tea had been progressively reduced to encourage its evident popularity, and gradually but steadily national consumption increased from less than 100,000 pounds in 1700 to 15 million pounds in 1800.[133] Originally an exotic luxury, by Mrs. Gamp's time it had to a great extent succeeded beer as the ordinary everyday beverage of the masses: heavily sweetened, it was as calorific as beer; made with boiled water, it was as safe as beer; in the form of dried and fermented leaves (not all of which, in that age of adulteration, were tea-leaves!) it was far less perishable than beer; it was much, much cheaper than beer; and it didn't make you drunk. Pace Mrs. Gamp, tea-drinking also replaced gin-drinking at work and on most other daytime occasions and gin consumption, at 8 million gallons in the mid-1740s, was down to less than 2 million gallons (shared among a very much larger population) by the end of the century.

By Dickens's prime in the 1840s and 1850s, column-distilled London Dry gin was beginning to compete with batch-distilled sweet styles[134] in large part because it was 50–70% cheaper to make,[135] a fact that undoubtedly endeared it to distillers, wholesalers, and retailers because it could be sold at the same price. From the drinker's point of view, dry gins — so-called because they were sold unsweetened — offered greater flexibility. Sweet gins could be and were drunk with fruit or herbal syrups, often as ad hoc curatives: peppermint was a favorite additive as an antacid and hangover remedy, as indeed it still is, and Ambrose Cooper's *Complete Distiller* (1757, reprinted 1800) contains recipes for more than 100 spirit-based vegetal compounds clearly intended as medicines since he gives quantities of a single gallon (for home preparation) and 10 gallons (for preparation by druggists). The habit of adding sweet cordials or syrups — or just sugar and water — to spirits of all varieties[136] is an indicator of popular taste at the time: as one historian put it, sugar was "a rarity in 1650, a luxury in 1750... a virtual necessity by 1850."[137] Many have remarked that one characteristic of such a clean spirit as column-distilled dry gin was that it didn't need to be sweetened, but the customer didn't necessarily agree and although dry gin might have reached the glass unsweetened, it wasn't always consumed that way. You could take your Old Tom or your Hollands with only a little water or even neat; but nobody drank London Dry straight up.

Not that the habit of mixing drinks was anything new. Back in 1736 the only two Gin Act licenses ever issued were taken out by two self-identifying "punch houses," and Dickens himself had a passion for making (and describing) many and varied punches which he clearly regarded not as a novelty but as a revered tradition redolent of the simple conviviality of a lost age. What was novel was that the new technology made it both practical and profitable to start producing proprietary brands on a large scale. One such brand is still a household name today: Pimm's No. 1 Cup. A theology graduate, James Pimm had an early change of career and in 1823 opened his own oyster bar in London (either in St. James's or the City, depending on which unsupported assertion you prefer to believe) at the age of just 25. Oysters were enormously popular in Regency London and Pimm's affairs flourished, until after 10 years he had a chain of five restaurants serving a specialty drink of his own devising: a little tankard (hence the name) containing an infusion of gin and various healing herbs and sold probably without much resistance to distended and doubtless slightly foxed diners as a digestif. It is uncertain whether Pimm compounded the mixture himself or had it made under license: the Royal Warrant naming Pimm's as "Distillers and Compounders to Her Majesty" dates only to 2011. Nonetheless, the brand was a great success and in 1851 he launched the scotch-based No. 2 Cup and brandy-based No. 3 Cup; he sold up in 1865 and died the following year. Since then there have been a No. 4 Cup (rum), a No. 5 Cup (rye), and a No. 6 Cup (vodka); but only the original is still in regular production.

Perhaps more significant in the longer term, although now largely forgotten, was Warburg's Tincture, a powerful antipyretic concocted in 1834 by a German doctor, Carl Warburg of Mainz, who spent part of his early career in the British West Indies developing treatments for yellow fever and malaria. His proprietary Tincture, made to a secret recipe not published until 1875, was considered by many to be superior to quinine. Launched in 1839, it quickly gained official recognition in Austria-Hungary and won testimonials from many of the British physicians whom Warburg bombarded with free samples. It was also very well received by British generals and explorers including Dr. Livingstone for its utility in the various tropical colonies where its efficacy and ease of administration — it came in single-dose bottles, with which the forest floors of India and Africa are presumably now littered — was somewhat marred only by an inconvenient purgative effect. Nevertheless the British Government bought it in huge quantities; only when the recipe was published was it discovered that the main ingredient (contrary to Warburg's own claims) was indeed quinine sulfate dissolved in pure spirit, along with a whole pharmacopeia of much more traditional ingredients including rhubarb and aloes (hence the purgative effect).

Warburg's Tincture remained in production until the end of the century, although it fell out of favor in its inventor's old age and he died in extreme poverty in 1892, having seen the failure and demolition of his Surrey laboratory and being supported only by public subscription. By then an easier way of taking quinine, and one without the unfortunate side effect, had been discovered. Quinine sulfate was one of the vegetal alkaloids isolated by the French chemists Pierre Pelletier and Joseph Caventou, along with caffeine and strychnine. For these and other discoveries, and for their refusal to profit from them by patenting them, a monument was erected to them in Paris. They isolated quinine sulfate in 1820 by washing the standard malaria remedy, powdered cinchona bark, in sulfuric acid to produce that yellowish resin whose antipyretic qualities have probably saved more lives than any other drug in human history, antibiotics included. Cinchona bark, introduced from Peru as recently as 1639, had hitherto been administered as a powder suspended in wine and flavored with rosewater and lemon to moderate its bitterness. It had saved the lives of — among many, many others — Charles II and his French contemporary, le Grand Dauphin (but not Oliver Cromwell. He spurned it because of its Papist origins and paid the price). France still has a famous branded wine containing quinine, Dubonnet, formulated in 1846 and, like Warburg's Tincture, favored by the military in the swampier parts of the French empire. Italy has a classier version, Barolo Chinato, which is probably rather too expensive for most squaddies. But in its unprocessed state the active ingredient was only weakly soluble in alcohol; as a sulfate, however, and compounded with the pure ethanol only the column still could produce, it was one of the most efficacious drugs ever known.

But there were still concerns that the medicine had to be taken in alcohol, especially in some quarters of the military among which quinine was in constant use — and, indeed, with some of the more abstemious missionary-explorers who opened the African interior to white (and particularly British) imperialism. Then in 1858 a soda-water maker from West London, Erasmus Bond, made a breakthrough. Little is known of Bond except that he had close links with J & J Vickers' distillery in

Southwark and that thanks to his invention of tonic water he left the world a considerably wealthier man than he entered it.[138] By the time he came on the scene the carbonated (or, as he would have put it, aerated) mineral water industry was well established, with ginger beer a firm favorite. Joseph Priestly had discovered in 1772 that combining hydrochloric acid, marble dust or chippings, and water created a pleasant drink fizzing with "fixed air" or CO2; and it was soon found that in a strong and well-sealed container the natural pressure would retain the gas in suspension, effervescing only when the seal was released. At first these mineral waters were sold as artificial versions of naturally carbonated spa waters such as Pyrmont and Seltzer (hock and seltzer was Byron's favorite restorative); but it wasn't long before they were being sweetened and flavored as well. Bond's breakthrough seems to have been to add his powdered cinchona bark while the CO2-generating reaction was still in train, thereby producing water-soluble quinine hydrochloride rather than ethanol-soluble quinine sulfate. Adding enough sugar to subdue the taste of quinine gave Bond a medicinal soft drink that wasn't too sweet for the masculine palate and that also blended perfectly with the cleaner notes of dry gin. With his connections in the distilling industry and a stand at the 1861 International Exhibition he was able to make a great success of his invention and died in 1866 leaving to his widow and four children the considerable sum of £4,000 and to the world, the gift of gin and tonic.

Gin and tonic soon supplanted Warburg's Tincture as the army's favorite carrier of quinine because it was pleasant, a good deal less alcoholic, and lacking the unfortunate aperient side-effect. But gin was popular with naval officers as well: it was shipped by the barrel among the other wardroom stores at proof or even cask strength in order to save space — always at a premium on a warship: the rum which sailors were allotted when their beer rations ran out was also carried at high strength and diluted by a factor of five, with lemon or lime juice and sugar added before being doled out in the familiar quartern at five bells and eight bells.[139] The officers likewise took their gin with lime juice, sugar and plenty of water,[140] or with a drop or two of a strong medicinal bitters perfected by Simon Bolivar's surgeon-general (and Waterloo veteran) Johann Siegert. Siegert ran the military hospital at Bolivar's capital, Angostura (now Ciudad Bolivar) and developed his bitters in 1830 as an anti-malarial and antipyretic to aid an army racked with every type of fever imaginable. Like all such preparations — and there were many — it was basically ethanol infused with any efficacious herbs, spices and barks the compounder could lay hands on. The main active component of Dr. Siegert's Angostura Bitters was not quinine nor even the native Angostura bark but gentian, familiar to him from his native Silesia, also indigenous to the Andes, and the principal therapeutic ingredient in the eponymous liqueur, in Suze, in Aperol and in Underberg.

Gin was probably favored by army and naval officers over rum or brandy partly for reasons of social standing (dearer than the former, cheaper than the latter; just right for middle-ranking officers!) and partly because in the hot climates where so much of their military service was be passed it was lighter-bodied, fresher-flavored and more thirst-quenching, especially when taken long with tonic water, or with Angostura bitters or lime juice and plenty of water.[141] In society at large gin's association with the armed forces, and especially the officer class, not only wiped away much of the social tarnish of earlier times but also gave it more of a masculine image. Gin was no longer the half-kept secret of Mrs. Gamp's teapot: it was manly; it was middle-class; it was metropolitan. From the officers' messes and wardrooms of the British Empire's garrisons and warships, gin prepared to conquer the world. But before it could do that, it needed a secure home base.

Today the Suburbs

The story of gin, like the story of beer, is as we have seen very closely tied up with the story of its retailers. Gin has no romantic legend like the South Coast smugglers and their darkling convoys of pack-ponies laden with brandy for the parson and baccy for the clerk, nor the Highland bothie-men forever fooling the hapless gaugers. It doesn't have much to do with cozy country alehouses or grand coaching inns, either. Gin's legend, fabricated and embellished by its detractors — a rare, perhaps even unique, occasion when history was written by the losers — is predicated upon what they saw, or rather imagined they saw: in the 18th century, squalid and degenerate dram-shops, proliferating beyond all limit or control, where an entire class was turned into addicts by the lure of clean straw on which to dream away their misery in a haze of cheap narcosis; and in the 19th, those same abject brutes led into temptation and beyond in a hell of gilt and glass, its infernal fires fuelled by coal gas.

If the crusades against gin from 1720–1751 and in the 1830s were prompted by new and, to some, alarming developments in retailing, its slow retreat into the background was similarly driven. While temperance campaigners widened their attack from gin to alcohol in all its forms, so the retail trade was becoming less specialized: in 1830 Thompson & Fearon needed separate licenses for every type of liquor it sold; by the end of the century a single full license covered beers, wines and spirits indiscriminately, for consumption both on and off the premises. But at the Beer Act select committee to which Fearon gave evidence, things looked as if they were going in precisely the opposite direction. The Beer Act was intended to undermine both the brewers and the distillers by throwing open beer and cider retailing to any ratepayer of good character for an annual £2 excise license. As well as cutting out the magistrates, the act abolished beer duty (although not the malt tax). The idea was to create a class of beerhouse-keepers who would mostly brew their own beer, thus checking the gradual extension of brewers' tied estates and offering the public a cheaper and healthier alternative to poisonous gin. The brewers who gave evidence to the committee asserted that they could brew cheaper and more consistent beer than any small and inexperienced owner-operator, in which they turned out to be right; and all that happened — to the casual observer, at least — was that over the next few years some 45,000 householders across the land laid in some stock, some tankards, and a cash-box and invited the neighbors in. Some flourished, some failed, but there was no great resurgence in home-brew houses; in fact the beerhouses were for the most part supplied by existing brewers; and after a dip in liquor sales generally in the later 1830s and 1840s due to economic stagnation, the mainstream brewers resumed their inexorable progress towards dominance over the pub trade.

Beneath the surface, though, the 1830 Beer Act had a very profound effect indeed, and one that had great consequences for the progress of the distilling industry in general. A determination set in among the magistracy not to surrender control; and paradoxically, they manifested their determination by handing out full licenses to almost anyone who wanted one. Rather than allow unlicensed and uncontrollable beer-only houses to swarm all over their neighborhoods unopposed, they reasoned, they would erect a defensive wall of well-ordered, properly conducted licensed victuallers catering for a broadly based market of decent working people. Quality, it was hoped, would triumph over quantity.

It was the right time, as far as the distillers were concerned, for the magistrates to abandon their austere attitude towards the granting of new licenses. From the late 1840s onwards, London underwent yet another of its periodic transformations, lunging outwards in all directions at once along a spreading armature of railway and, from 1863, underground lines until by the outbreak of World War I the city could be characterized not by the City itself, not by the West End nor by the East, not by palaces and mansions nor by factories and docks, but by suburbs, mile upon brown-brick mile of them. And on every street corner in every new district, whether of the spacious townhouses of Ladbroke Grove, the solid villas of Tufnell Park, or the three-and-a-half bed terraces of Bow and Stoke Newington, the developers — mostly small or middling concerns — first planted a pub. These everyday suburban locals — and since they were often spaced at intervals of less than 300 yards, thousands were built and hundreds survive — were not the grand glaring and flaring glass and gilt palaces of central London, but their role was critical both to the development process itself and to the subsequent characters of the new suburbs. During the building operations they acted as canteen and pay office for the laborers and as a saleable surety in case cash-flow dried up; and as the residents gradually moved in, the pubs were both comparatively high-rent leases to tide the developers over and nuclei where new neighbors could meet and, with luck, bond. (In the grander quarters the pubs tended to occupy discreet sites in mews courts and down side streets, and were intended for the custom of servants and tradesmen; but they were there nonetheless.) And because they were fully licensed they were able to stock wines, beers... and spirits.

The appearance of these suburban locals also finally winkled gin out of its London ghetto and gave it a legitimate, even respectable, home on the back fittings of public and saloon bars across the entire country. For every single town and city center in Britain, whatever its scale or provenance, grew its crust of Victorian terraces; every such district had its quota of fully licensed street-corner pubs; and every single one of them sold spirits. And in 1869, when a reform of licensing law required the unregulated Beer Act houses to acquire justices' licenses, most but not all of them went the whole hog and applied for full licenses so that they, too, could stock whiskey, brandy, rum and gin.

While the nation's fast-growing suburbs were liberally speckled with recognizably modern pubs selling liquor of all kinds, the wider leisure industry was also finding new shapes and creating new opportunities. Londoners and provincials alike were being offered and were flocking eagerly to new diversions where liquor was a less prominent feature of the sales mix — eating-houses, music halls, organized professional sports, billiard halls (often unlicensed) and more — while older styles of drinking venue were disappearing. Among the most obvious casualties were London's many pleasure gardens, great and small, every last one of which disappeared before the tsunami of drab London brick. The gin-shops went too, or at any rate were transformed. The gin itself stepped into the background, and the high gantries and their giant decorative barrels were consigned to the lumber room to be replaced at first by smaller kegs or rows of bottles on the shelving behind the bar; then by elegant glass "spirit urns," often acid-etched and wound about with filigree, mounted on the bar-counter itself; and from the early 20th century by bottles plugged into Optic measured dispensers, their upside-down labels legible only with a squint, upstaged by the hand pumps in the foreground. For beer and brewing had reasserted their dominance and gin — like whiskey, brandy, rum, and cider — had plumped instead for a ride on the brewer's dray. Just as William Coates had warned in 1830, if the Beer Act were passed then big gin-shop owners like him would diversify, and diversify they did. Symbolically, perhaps, Thompson & Fearon itself was pulled down in 1866 to make way for Holborn Viaduct, but the company Coates founded batted on as a straightforward pub chain until 1959, when it was bought out by the wine merchant Corney & Barrow as a foundation on which to build its chain of wine bars.

These new patterns of trading, whether through the misnamed but increasingly grandiose gin-palaces that lined the great urban thoroughfares or the numberless new pubs in the burgeoning suburbs, brought both the makers and the retailers of gin into contact with the brewers. In the case of the latter the local breweries that supplied the pubs — still mostly independently owned at this stage — with their beer also became the wholesalers of wines and spirits. This was an arrangement that was more than a mere convenience for all concerned: wine and spirit merchants could conceivably have acted as independent wholesalers and in some cases did, especially in country districts; but local brewers already had the premises, the drays and their horses, the workforce both manual and clerical, and all the facilities necessary to service the pub trade; so by shouldering the burden of distribution they relieved the wine and spirit dealers of the effort and expense of having to reinvent the wheel. But there were downsides: the brewers took their cut, which was only fair, but they also got to choose whose products they distributed, giving them an irksome degree of influence over the fortunes of individual distillers. And the brewers, both the London brewers themselves and the Burton brewers who were trying to establish a presence in the capital, were predatory, always seeking to expand their tied estates either through straightforward purchase on the open market, through product-tied loans, or through the credit trap — extending more and more credit to their trade customers and foreclosing when it became clear that the customer couldn't pay, and thus gaining control over more and more of the remaining free trade. More and more of the distillers' channel to market therefore came under the control of the brewers. Some distillers naturally tried to maintain a degree of independence: Nicholson's, for example, bought a small pub chain of its own when it moved from its native Clerkenwell to the Three Mills distillery at West Ham in 1872. But for the most part, distillers accepted both the positives and the negatives of having the brewers as their principal wholesale channel to the pub trade, albeit supping with a judiciously long spoon.

There was another downside for the gin distillers, though. With all categories of liquor now spread out on the counter before the drinking public, all for the first time equally accessible, it turned out that gin was not the popular favorite it had previously been. It was cheap, but not aspirational. Its character might have been transformed by continuous distillation, but not its image. And when Prince Albert, in 1852, bought Balmoral Castle as a Highland haven for his wife, all things Scottish came into vogue; and that included Scotch. The continuous still was in the process of transforming Scotch as it had gin, producing a nearly neutral spirit to act as a clean canvas for the blenders as they mixed and matched single malts in almost infinite variety to produce consistent brands that an unfamiliar public could take to. And if Prince Albert could take to it — he and his Queen were the Lochnagar distillery's new neighbors and were rumored to be fond of a dram of its product — then so could the unfamiliar public. Whiskey was still expensive, though, until 1860 when it was made far more affordable by the launch of blended Scotches and by a concession in the Budget putting back the point at which duty fell due until after ageing and blending. The tying up of capital in prepayment had long been a serious hindrance to gin and whiskey distillers alike, holding back investment and deterring start-ups. One commentator wrote:

> The metropolitan distilleries, of which the number is small, are establishments of considerable magnitude, necessitating a large supply of capital; indeed the capital required is one of the reasons why they are few in number. The revenue raised by the excise duty in British made spirits is very

> large; and as the money must be paid before the spirit leaves the distilleries, there is always a large amount of capital thus locked up.[142]

Gladstone, however, was a laissez-faire unilateralist free-trade economist who believed that tax should only be raised to fund government spending, not for any deterrent or punitive purpose, and that rationalizing duties and purchase taxes would eventually stimulate the economy to the point where income tax was no longer necessary; during his spell as Chancellor he slashed the number of customs and excise levies from 419 to 48 and reduced all surviving duties as far as possible. Of all these reductions, that of wine duty, and in particular the licensing reform that went with it, proved to have the most enduring effect.

The developments of the 1840s and 1850s may have been a mixed blessing for gin distillers, but the licensing and taxation reforms introduced in 1860–1861 were more than enough to bring the broadest of smiles to their corporate faces. The Refreshment House Act allowed shopkeepers and eating-house keepers[143] to sell "foreign wine" in single bottles without a justice's license on payment of an annual fee ranging from 10 shillings 6 pence to 3 guineas, depending on the rentable value of the premises, for a non-discretionary excise license. At the same time, in order to encourage people to turn from spirits to the less alcoholic and more genteel wine (and to placate the French, with whom Britain was at serious loggerheads), Gladstone cut the duty from 5 shillings 10 pence to 3 shillings a gallon. The following year in a further reform he cut the duty again and also introduced the modern system of taxation according to alcoholic strength: wine of above 26% proof or in modern terms 15% ABV (i.e., fortified wine) was charged at 2 shillings a gallon, whereas table wine of above 15% proof or 8.5% ABV was charged at 1 shilling 6 pence. This had a radical effect, if not quite the one Gladstone intended: although at first it prohibited the sale of spirits his "grocer's license" turned out to be the precursor of the off-license (and the restricted on-license or restaurant license too, for that matter). Wine consumption soared immediately following the passage of the Act and the 1860 Budget: sales increased tenfold by 1880 to 7 million gallons, mainly of French table wines rather than the heavier fortified wines of the past. However, and despite hopes that drinkers would switch from beer and spirits to wine, sales of beer and spirits also increased. The huge increase in wine sales, it seemed, was wholly incremental and was largely confined to the dinner-tables of the burgeoning and highly aspirational middle classes.[144] Perhaps as a result of this disappointment the 1872 Licensing Act, whose main claim to fame was its introduction of permitted "hors,"[145] simply disregarded the distinction between beer, wines and spirits, enabling off-license chains such as Victoria Wines (founded 1865) and Threshers (founded a little later, in 1897) to stock not only "foreign wines" but all other intoxicating liquors too.[146]

Such open competition was something of a novelty for the distillers, and they coped with it in a variety of ways. Nicholson's, as we have seen, bought a chain of pubs. W & A Gilbey — an unusually enterprising firm of wine merchants that had established itself by importing Cape wines at a reduced rate of duty and had opened its gin distillery at Camden Lock only in 1872 — attacked on a broad front. First it appointed a network of exclusive regional distributors on terms that looked a lot like a modern franchise, with offices in Dublin and Edinburgh; next it bought a vineyard in Bordeaux; and finally it started diversifying into the Scotch whiskey business. It had for some time had an own-label blend in its portfolio of brands, and in 1887 it bought the Glen Spey malt distillery, followed by Strathmill in 1895 and Knockando in 1903. Diversification and acquisition are classic gambits in a market approaching saturation; another is merger followed by rationalization. That's the path that Gordon's and Tanqueray chose to follow in 1898. Tanqueray had been founded in 1830 by the scion of a dynasty of Huguenot clerics and had become a strong export brand with a network of agents round the world and a significant following in America. Gordon's, on the other hand, had a much stronger presence in the domestic market. They were a perfect fit.

For most, though, tackling the new challenges boiled down to brand building. Boord's, as we have seen, led the pack, trademarking its Cat & Barrel brand of Old Tom-style gin as early as 1849. By that time Booth's had already been using its red lion logo for many years, despite its rather macabre provenance: the original Red Lion in Turnmill Street, just round the corner from Booth's distillery (or possibly in West Street — accounts vary), was the legendary headquarters of the early 18th-century gangster Jonathan Wild, the self-styled Thief-taker General, and was a folkloric warren of tiny rooms and narrow passageways overhanging the noxious Fleet, where Wild's men worked as forgers, Wild's friends were hidden from the law, and Wild's enemies were wont to be disappeared.[147] In 1817 Booth's bought a distillery in Brentford, which eventually became one the biggest in Britain, and in 1832 it added a neighboring brewery to its portfolio, renaming it the Red Lion brewery. The Red Lion graced the label of the bottle, and when the original distillery in Clerkenwell was rebuilt in 1959, it too was named the Red Lion distillery. Burnett's White Satin looked back, too: "white satin" was a nickname for gin familiar from the Georgian era. The overnight success of the Beefeater brand proved how important an instantly recognizable identity was: the Chelsea distillery was taken over by a young entrepreneur named James Burrough in 1862 with a portfolio including Old Chelsea, London Dry, and Old Tom. In 1876 Burrough launched Beefeater with its strong branding and eye-catching label, and it immediately became the company's bestseller. Distinctive bottles were favorites with gin distillers too: perhaps inspired by the case-bottle used by many brands of genever, a number of English distillers chose bottles that were square (and in the case of Booth's High & Dry, polygonal) in section. Plymouth bottles were often oval in section while Tanqueray's tall domed cylinder was more than a little reminiscent of a cocktail shaker. Perhaps it was the model?

It's an old saw in marketing, though, that brand-oriented promotion might build market share but rarely builds the market, and it was as true then as it is today. Yes, gin was now available in more retail outlets, both pubs and shops, than ever before. But not only did it face open competition from other spirits, which threatened its urban and working-class dominance, the whole liquor sector was being challenged as well. From the 1840s onwards the disposable income of the working class as a whole, pockets of desperate poverty and more or less regular recessions notwithstanding, was generally rising, and with it the choice of how to spend it. Other attractions such as organized sports became more and more popular until home match crowds could almost drain the surrounding pubs of customers twice a week: Manchester United's average home attendance, for instance, shot up from 3,727 in the 1889–1890 season to a prewar peak of 23,368 in 1907–1908[148] — not a huge number in itself, but then Manchester United was only one of the city's league sides, and its fans were almost exclusively working-class males, the very same demographic the pubs were aiming for. Then there was the temperance movement. It never reached the same position of strength as that occupied by its American counterpart, but by promoting cafes that provided cheap dinners with tea or coffee instead of beer, often with a free read of the day's papers, it did break the working class's reliance on pubs for daytime meals. Earlier in the century it had been common for workers on their dinner break to buy a couple of chops or some sausages and have them cooked in the pub accompanied by a quart or two of porter or a quartern of well-watered gin. By the 1880s liquor, whether beer or spirits, was no longer the only alternative. It would be a huge exaggeration to portray the working class as abandoning the pub en masse, although liquor consumption overall (except of wine, which was mostly drunk in the home) was by the end of the 19th century in general decline. Spirits were hardest hit: the increasing tax differential arising from the 1830 Beer Act, the 1860 Refreshment House Act, and Gladstone's 1880 Budget meant that for drinkers on a budget spirits were increasingly a luxury — a garnish to round off an evening's session or mark a special occasion rather than an alcoholic snack to be enjoyed at random throughout the day.

It was the bourgeoisie that came to gin's rescue. The disposable income available to the working class as a whole might have been rising, but both in numbers and prosperity it was the middle class and upper working class that saw the real growth spurt in the second half of the 19th century. For every protective shell of Victorian workers' terraces, Britain's towns and cities also possess a bulwark of neat villas, detached or semi-detached, plain brick or brick with stone facings, and with a set of attics or just a back bedroom for a live-in maid of all work or maybe a cook, a kitchen-maid, and a housemaid. Foremen, book-keepers, commercial travellers, teachers, shopkeepers, town hall clerks, dentists, doctors, solicitors — their incomes and expectations might have covered a very broad waterfront, but as English middle-class families their values were the same. A quiet, respectable life free of scandal or sensation; hard work; church or chapel on Sunday; acceptance of your place and respect for your betters — these ruling principles scarcely changed between the 1860s and the 1960s. As for pubs — well, they weren't entirely taboo for the menfolk of the British bourgeoisie, but you would find no piano in the saloon bar of a pub in a respectable suburb, and no singing, and certainly no knees-ups; and if there were any spirits they would be a parting dram of whiskey and soda, not gin with its still-lingering connotations. Really, though, the middle class preferred the theatre to the pub, for every town had its rep; they liked formal Masonic or other dinners at the town's leading hotel, preferably involving a starched shirtfront and archaic toasting rituals; but best of all they liked entertaining at home, hence the rise in wine sales that Gladstone had hoped for. And here was another change: by the middle of the century, as the working day lengthened, the dinner hour started moving further back, to 8 pm or even later; and as it was considered polite to arrive half an hour early, the window for drinking was getting narrower and narrower. It therefore became the custom among the upper classes to offer guests a pre-dinner drink or *apéritif*, a French term originally identical to "aperient" but now meant as opening the evening's proceedings rather than the guests' pores.[149] Today this would probably be a chilled *fino* or possibly a glass of Champagne; in the early 20th century, when sherry and Champagne were both offered as table wines, it was more likely to be a pink gin, a Gin & It, or a gimlet, all of them lighter and more delicate than whiskey or brandy, possessing sharp flavors ideal for awakening a tired palate. It is also worth noting that dinner parties at home were among the few entertainments, along with the theatre, where women were equal participants; and like Mrs. Mann and Sairey Gamp their tastes tended to run — or perhaps men simply presumed that their tastes tended to run — to lighter drinks: to hock over claret, to tea over coffee, and to gin over whiskey or brandy. Beginning in the last years of the 19th century, therefore, middle-class women had the same impact on the gin market as London's female migrant laborers had had more than 100 years before, vastly increasing it. Thus, alongside the military connotations mentioned above, did gin gain favor among the English middle classes.

Tomorrow the World

Given the limited possibilities for expansion in an overcrowded and increasingly promiscuous home market, exports were the only way forward; so, dressed in their fine liveries and fancy bottles, England's regiment of gin brands set out to conquer the world — or, more accurately, to conquer the British Empire.

The phylloxera that coincidentally devastated France's vineyards in 1863 and reduced output of wine and its derivatives to a trickle was a great opportunity for Scotch, the best of which made a more than passable substitute for Cognac and Armagnac; not so for gin, for obvious reasons. But while gin was just beginning to feel the force of competition from blended whiskies in the home market, among the armed forces, colonial administrators, and "box-wallahs" or commercial exploiters of Empire, awareness of Scotch was still low and gin was still king, especially when taken with quinine-infused tonic water or (in naval circles) aromatic bitters such as Angostura that were supposed to be little depth-charges of prophylactic vegetals. White colonialists were permanently — and justifiably — terrified of the tropical diseases against which they had no inbuilt defenses; and as anything that tasted bitter was probably good for you, they drank an awful lot of gin and tonics and Harry Pinkers. If anyone made gin middle-class, it was Indian Army officers and their wives petrified by the prospect of malaria. The officer class (other ranks retaining their fondness for rum) brought their taste for gin home with them to their messes and wardrooms, to their London clubs, and eventually to the 19th holes, hotel saloon bars and Masonic lodges of the spas and seaside towns to which they retired, and where admiring civilians soon came to emulate the manners and drinking habits of their esteemed martial neighbors.

It's something of a surprise to find that despite the Empire's prestige; despite the fact that Imperial possessions virtually surrounded the United States — Canada to the north, British Honduras and British Guyana on the Central and South American mainland and, in the Caribbean, the shining star of Jamaica and a constellation of smaller islands; and despite constant cultural, political and economic contact and exchange, especially in the upper reaches of society, the English signally failed to infect the Americans with a love of gin. Of course the United States was familiar with gin: indeed it may very well have been the first spirit distilled on mainland America. But it was not English gin they favored. Dutch traders had set up a fur-trading post on Manhattan Island in 1613, patented it as a colony, New Netherlands, in 1621, and started sending settlers in 1624. According to one source the early colonists brought pot stills with them and immediately started making *brandewijn*, although what from is not stated.[150] The tillage was poor and the settlers were more interested in furs than farming, so perhaps those "pot stills" were primarily brewing or even washing coppers? Be that as it may, by 1640 the governor, Willem Kieft, had established a distillery in the settlement of New Amsterdam that was still busily at work producing genever when in 1664 an English expeditionary force arrived, accepted the colony's surrender, and renamed its principal town New York. What happened to Kieft's distillery is unrecorded, but as the small but well-established Dutch community elected to remain in "New York" rather than migrate *en bloc* to the Dutch Antilles or Suriname, and as many other Dutch cultural elements including a distinctive patois survived into living memory, it seems unlikely that the settlers' descendants relinquished their ancestral fondness for genever. But for the time being its production remained unrecorded, eclipsed by the rum distilling for which the 13 Colonies became renowned.[151] In fact the neighboring British set up a rum distillery, the first in North America, on Staten Island no more than a dozen miles from Manhattan in the very same year that they obliged the Dutch to hand over the keys of New Amsterdam; and until tobacco and cotton came into their full growth rum remained the Colonies' principal export.

But just as rum had eclipsed genever, so whiskey eclipsed rum. From the early 17th century right up to 1783 when independence put a stop to it, Britain sent convicts and debtors by the shipload to the Colonies, perhaps as many as 120,000 of them over the years, many of them Scottish and Irish Jacobite rebels captured in the uprisings of 1690, 1715 and 1745, and all of them possessed of a powerful thirst for whiskey[152] if not necessarily the wherewithal to make it. And here the New York Dutch were able to help. They could supply the necessary brewing kettles and pot stills, and the Irish and Highland farmers who had constituted a fair part of the various Jacobite armies were perfectly familiar with their use. The fermentable materials were a different matter. Irish and Scottish smallholders were used to growing and processing oats and barley, but here in the maritime Northwest with its ferocious winters, oats and barley would thrive only in favored spots of deep soil and sunny but sheltered aspect. The Dutch, however, also put a premium on good arable, coming from a country not yet properly drained where the best grain was a scarce and expensive resource, but where rye made an excellent cover crop for wet ground. Their neighbors the Germans and, further east, the Poles and Russians, had also learnt the virtues of rye as a rugged and durable winter crop, an enormous advantage in New York and surrounding states. It was a lesson the Dutch seem to have applied in their new home and passed on to the Irish and Scottish: Gary Gillman[153] in his online paper "*Rye and Bourbon: Shared Bloodline With Dutch Gin*?" argues very strongly that rye is the common ancestor of both American whiskey and gin, citing contemporary manuals that describe the process of brewing a wash of rye and pot-distilling it as the base spirit for either gin or whiskey. This takes us right back to the 15th and 16th centuries; for as we know from the earliest days of making grain-based distillates, the only difference between whiskey and white spirits lies in the processing. Whiskey is stored in oak to carry value forward from fat years to lean, while white spirits are aromatized and liquored down for a quick sale. Whiskey is the farmer's product, gin the apothecary's. And just as it was with malted barley in Britain and Northern Europe in the early modern period, so it was with rye in 18th-century North America.

With the Scottish and Irish immigrants surging deep into the countryside to take up distilling where they had left off when forced to abandon their homes,[154] and the "Knickerbockers" confined largely to what had been the New Netherlands, whiskey emerged the clear winner over gin in the late colonial years and the nascent US. This whiskey may have started life as exactly the same rye-based wash, pot-distilled just as the Dutch did it; but left in oak where it took on flavor and color and lost some of its harsher edges, it soon lived up to its potential and supplanted rum and applejack as North America's favorite spirit. There was even an armed insurrection in 1791 when President Washington tried to tax it. If the Knickerbockers continued to distill their gin after the absorption of the New Netherlands by the surrounding British, it went unrecorded and can only have been on a domestic scale until 1808 when Hezekiah Pierrepont, a serial entrepreneur with interests in foreign trade and land development, bought a burnt-out brewery in New York and converted it into a gin distillery producing both a rye-based variant or descendant of Klieft's genever and a gin in the English style. Gillman's researches have revealed advertisements in an 1818 issue of the *Northern Budget* published in Troy, NY, up the Hudson from Manhattan and originally settled by the

Dutch. Evidently the original colonists' cultural traditions had persisted: one advertisement still touts "Dutch goods" 154 years after the British took over the New Netherlands. A merchant named E. Warren advertises Pierrepont's gin by name; another advertises unnamed "American gin" and "Holland gin" which can only have come from the Anchor distillery.

Sadly, the distillery was closed in 1819 to provide Pierrepont with capital for a huge land development venture he was planning, and gin seems to have retired into the background once more. That there was still a demand for it is witnessed by the fact that Gabriel van't Wout, the financier who had just bought the venerable Bols concern, started exporting genever and Dutch liqueurs to the US in 1823; but when in 1842 Charles Dickens embarked on the first of his American literary tours, gin was still very much a minor player. His American hosts, generous to a fault, thought that his frequent resort to liquor as a metaphor reflected his personal habits and plied him with alcohol of every description.[155] And although he claimed to have actually drunk very little of what was put before him, the great man was enchanted by the variety of the concoctions he was offered, particularly that "wonderful invention" the sherry cobbler. "The mounds of ices and the bowls of mint julep and sherry cobbler they make in these latitudes, are refreshments never to be thought of afterwards in summer by those who would preserve contented minds," he wrote.[156] The sherry cobbler returned a couple of years later to restore the dejected spirits of Martin Chuzzlewit, defrauded in an American land deal, as "a very large tumbler, piled to the brim with little blocks of clear transparent ice through which one or two thin slices of lemon and a golden liquid of delicious appearance appealed to the loving eye of the spectator." Not many of the assorted juleps, cocktails, toddies and cobblers that came Dickens's way were gin-based, though, apart from the gin sling (gin and fresh-squeezed lemon or bitters, well-watered and with plenty of ice) and spider (much the same but with sweet lemonade instead of the juice or bitters). On his second US trip in the late 1860s he resorted to sending his tour manager to buy two cases of gin from the Cunarder which had just deposited them ashore, so hard was it to buy in America. And legendary bartender Jerry "The Professor" Thomas's ground-breaking book of cocktail recipes, *How to Mix Drinks or The Bon-Vivant's Companion*, published in 1862, shows how far gin had to go before finding its place in the pantheon of American spirits: of its 243 recipes, a mere 17 were gin-based.

Even if an America whose spirits mostly had a Celtic flavor was proving an unpromising hunting ground, London's distillers during the latter decades of the 19th century still faced the reality that while the middle classes were drinking more gin the workers were drinking less, and that there was only one direction in which to expand: overseas. Export sales both within and beyond the confines of the Empire therefore represented an important opportunity for growth, a potential which a prescient Sir Felix Booth had both foreseen and facilitated in 1850 when he promoted a Private Member's Bill abolishing excise duty on spirit intended for export. Of course the measure came to favor whiskey just as much gin, and perhaps more so; but within the Empire itself gin (and Pimm's, bottled and exported after the sale of the whole concern to hotel and restaurant entrepreneur Sir Horatio Davies in 1880) remained the more popular choices for the white ruling class and became so among the native élites too. But these represented only a tiny fragment of the overall colonial populations, most of whom generally stuck to their traditional spirits such as the enguli or waragi of East Africa, thought to descend from arrak thanks to regular contact with Arab merchants over many centuries, and *ogogori* or *kaikai*, the distilled palm wine and maize beer of Nigeria and Cameroon possibly introduced by Portuguese or even American slave traders. Since import duties on spirits made up a large part of the colonial administrations' budgets — more than two-thirds in Nigeria in 1913 — every means was used to brand these traditional competitors as moonshine and stamp out their production, including the use of informers as well as heavy fines and long prison sentences.[157] But — and this will sound familiar — as the attempts at repression grew stronger, the native distillers retreated from towns to countryside, often to forested swamps where firewood and water were easily to hand, and where narrow and shallow waterways allowed the finished liquor to be transported by canoe where the handful of police motor launches couldn't follow. In keeping with the generous British spirit of equality of repression, the attempt by the colonial authorities to stamp out traditional drinks in favor of British-distilled spirits was not confined to black Africans: the only genever distillery licensed by the Boer government of the Transvaal, AH Nellmapius's *Die Erste Fabrieke* at Hetherly near Pretoria, ceased production at the start of the Boer War in 1899, and after the British victory the Dutchman's license was never renewed.

There was another obstacle to the expansion of export of British gin to the colonies as well: the temperance movement. At a series of international meetings initiated at the ironically named Brussels Convention in 1890, such delightfully named bodies as the Native Races Liquor Traffic United Committee and the Aborigines' Protection Society solemnly pronounced that spirits were bad for natives, who were unused to distilled spirits (they weren't — see above) and who should not be allowed to waste what little money they had on drink anyway. The various imperial powers paid grudging lip-service to these pious concerns but failed to coordinate their efforts at border control and in the main contented themselves with increasing the duty on imports, until by 1913 in British colonies it stood at 5 shillings 6 pence a gallon, raising £1.14 million for the Nigerian colonial government.[158] The principal result was that the price of a bottle of imported spirits rose to 5 shillings 6 pence, and the local distributors frequently watered it down by as much as half; and with the price of a bottle of *ogogoro* at anything from just a shilling to 4 shillings, the war against moonshining and smuggling was effectively lost, as such battles inevitably are. Having said all that, the total annual export of mostly British spirits to Nigeria alone stood, on the eve of World War I, at nearly 25 million bottles — a hardly inconsiderable figure, even if most of it was whiskey, and in a context of rising British exports not just in the Empire but round the world. In the last quarter of the 19th century competition from Germany and America cut into British exports of heavy machinery while rising costs made coal less competitive internationally. To make matters worse a recession that lasted for most of the 1870s and 1880s affected the prices that British exporters could charge for their goods, which made high-value products like spirits especially important. Despite the economic problems of the period, then, by the end of the century the UK (which then included southern Ireland) was comfortably the world's largest trading nation and spirits were an increasingly important part of the mix.

America, though, remained stubborn. It accounted for only 10% of British exports; and given that in 1860 the United States possessed more than 1,100 (legal) stills between them producing nearly 90 million proof gallons for a population of 31 million, there wasn't all that much room in the market for imports anyway. Nearly all of that was whiskey, of course, but from 1870 America did have one very successful gin distillery as well, Fleischmann Brothers of Cincinnati, Ohio. Charles and Maximilian Fleischmann were Hungarians whose father was a distillery owner, and Charles had himself managed a distillery in Vienna. As immigrants to an America with a fast-developing railway network and therefore a potential for national distribution, the brothers decided that the gap in the market was for baker's yeast of sound industrial quality and consistency; and with the financial backing of a whiskey distiller, Thomas Gaff, they opened a propagation plant in 1868. The gin distillery came two years later, and with it a vinegar culture; and in time the company also started producing whiskeys in decorative ceramic pots and colored glass flasks. The vinegar and yeast operations saw Fleischmann through Prohibition, and a gin by that name is still made today at Barton Distillers of Bardstown, Kentucky.

Fleischmann Brothers remained a *rara avis*, though: only the Western Mediterranean, effectively the Royal Navy's summer playground, saw any effort by local entrepreneurs to create a London dry of their own. Larios was founded in 1866 in Malaga by Fernando Jimenez and a French entrepreneur, Charles Lamothe, with financial backing from an aristocrat with strong Gibraltarian connections, Jose Aurelio Larios, whose family later took control of the company and renamed it after themselves. It's still one of the world's top-selling brands today. Less well known but far more intriguing is Xoriguer from Port Mahon, Menorca. Xoriguer is a throwback to a different world: wine, rather than malt wash, is distilled to 38% ABV in a single pass through a direct-fired pot still; the botanicals are vapor-infused in copper baskets; and the new make is briefly barrel-aged before bottling. You could be describing *moutwijn*, and indeed there may well be some Dutch influence in the background. Menorca was captured by an Anglo-Dutch fleet (16 British and six Dutch men o' war) as part of a long campaign for control of the eastern Mediterranean during the War of the Spanish Succession. The Allied fleet took Gibraltar, then not much more than a fishing village whose harbor was as yet undeveloped, in 1702. They then turned to Catalonia, which supported the Habsburg candidate for the throne of Spain, Charles, against the French candidate, Philip, established a base at Barcelona, and recruited a considerable army. Finally, attracted by Port Mahon's large natural harbor (which the British had frequently used in the late 17th-century campaigns against the Barbary Corsairs), they invaded and took Menorca — also Catalan and pro-Habsburg — almost bloodlessly from a small pro-French garrison in 1708. At some point someone then taught the islanders how to make gin for the English and Dutch sailors to enjoy when ashore and to ship as a substitute for their official beer ration. There is a tradition that the original gin was corn-based, and only later did the island's distillers turn to using wine as the base liquor; this seems unlikely. Grain must have been scarce on a small and, in terms of farming practice, somewhat backward island,[159] but Menorca had been a wine-producer since ancient times. There must have been stills on the island before 1708 too, because it's a safe bet that the fleet wasn't carrying them on the off chance. The most sensible conclusion is that the Menorcans were already making brandy from their wine, and that Dutch sailors taught them to distill the spirit only to potable strength and to infuse it with botanicals (the juniper was imported from Catalonia). Xoriguer (windmill) is the last example being produced today; the distillery at Port Mahon still belongs to the founding family of Pons and can be visited. The distinctive bottle with its decorative handle has been in use since the early 20th century: before then the gin was generally dispensed straight from the barrel. Menorca was returned to Spain at the Peace of Amiens in 1802 after almost a century of on and off British occupation; but with its cheddar-derived Mahon cheese and its gin, it's always been something of a haven for Britons even if lemonade is the preferred mixer over tonic.

A more significant Mediterranean contributor to what you might call gin culture is vermouth, a close cousin to gin itself and the third in the holy trinity of curatives. Juniper and quinine we have met. Wormwood, a prolific shrub fond of dry, sandy soils and high, rocky places, is the most bitter and least genuinely therapeutic of the three. It's also one of the hardest to pin down because there's such a wide range of drinks and traditions that call themselves vermouth.

Using wine as a solvent to release the therapeutic alkaloids contained in many herbs, spice, roots and barks but insoluble in water is a practice as old as wine itself: in the 17th century, as we have seen, it was usual to dissolve powdered cinchona bark in sweetened and flavored wine to combat malaria; and of course apothecaries from the Islamic Enlightenment onwards used distilled wine for the same purpose. What set vermouth apart from straightforward medicated or aromatized wines was the addition of spirit, which enhanced both the flavor and the extract but was not as harsh as a tincture of pure ethanol, making it an ideal halfway house between medicine and beverage. The wormwood that characterized this particular mixture has three principal efficacious actions: its harsh bitterness encourages the appetite in anemic or otherwise chronically ill patients, including Crohn's sufferers; its artemisinin content reduces parasite populations in the blood including ringworm, pinworm and malarial plasmodia and is also a mild antibacterial helpful against most forms of dysentery including salmonella; and finally its thujone content, although not as once thought a hallucinogenic, makes it a mood elevator that interferes with the inhibitory gamma-aminobutyric acid receptors in the brain. An all-round treatment, then, that improved a patient's appetite and general sense of wellbeing while tackling (with what efficacy we can't say) many of the causes of chronic debilitation. Judging by its etymology it seems that dissolving wormwood in a sweetened fortified wine, with the addition of anise and fennel to tone down the bitterness and counteract bloating and flatulence, was a German innovation dating probably to the mid 16th century: *Wermuth* is Old High German for *Artemisia absinthium*. A wine merchant named D'Alessio was making a sweet red version in Piedmont at roughly the same time, but probably a little later since the name passed into Italian and French as straight transliterations of the German (and then appeared in English in its French form, dating its arrival perhaps to the reign of the Francophile Charles I).

From fairly obscure beginnings, differing versions of vermouth — some sweet, some dry, some red or amber, some white, some of them not even made from fermented wine but from raw must, and all infused with their proprietors' own secret blend of herbs and spices — became popular round the Western Mediterranean on their merit as aromatic, versatile, mid-strength (about 17–18% alcohol) aperitifs. A merchant and blender named Antonio Carpano successfully promoted the sweet red version (based on white wine and taking its color from brandy and caramel) in the Piedmontese capital, Turin, from the 1780s, and 20 years later another blender, Joseph Noilly of Marseillan in the southwest of the French Mediterranean coast, popularized the dry white version that still bears his name. The little Catalan city of Rues, an important center of the wine blending and shipping trade, also became famous for making sweet red vermouth: at its height it was home to 30 blenders. Three brands are still blended there and are vastly popular in Barcelona.

In the later years of the 19th century, and in the wake of phylloxera, an extreme version of vermouth, which dispensed with the wine altogether and was either a compounded or a rectified blend of wormwood, anise, fennel and neutral spirit bottled at anything up to 75% ABV, became enormously popular with the French artistic community and rakish bohemian *demi-monde.* Absinthe, nicknamed *la fée verte* for the green food coloring it was dosed with, was essentially over-strength gin but with wormwood substituting for juniper, and there was nothing hallucinatory about it. Huge alcoholic strength combined with empty stomachs, overactive imaginations, and the power of suggestion were more responsible for its reputed psychotropic qualities than any chemical quality of thujone; but to be on the safe side and under pressure from a moral panic got up by the popular press, government after government banned absinthe anyway. Most makers were quick to follow by reducing the amount of wormwood in their recipes to homeopathic quantities or deleting it altogether, blameless though it was; and it was in this emasculated form that it made its triumphant crossing of the Atlantic arm-in-arm with its natural soul mate — gin.

COCKTAILS AND KILLERS: GIN DISCOVERS AMERICA

Sorting through charter myths and comparing their respective degrees of plausibility is one of the more entertaining areas of popular history, and in particular trying to track down the derivation of vernacular names. The study of pub signs is perhaps the richest of all veins of unsupported tosh, but gin throws up a few gems of its own. The suspiciously elaborate anecdotal etymology of Old Tom is one; the meaning of the term "bathtub gin" is another; the origin of the word cocktail is a third. To many, as Andrew Barr says in a laconic footnote in *Drink: A Social History*, the last "remains an unsolved mystery." But once one has disposed of the obvious nonsense, two equally plausible solutions present themselves.

Let's start with the meaning, which is fairly straightforward. Most people today would, if asked, define a cocktail as a mixed drink, but that's not what it meant originally. In the late 18th and early 19th centuries it was a pick-me-up or stimulant, as is unambiguously stated in contemporary documents. There's a diary entry in the *New Hampshire Farmer's Cabinet*, 28th April 1803, when the columnist cured his hangover the morning after a dance with "a glass of cocktail — excellent for the head." Shortly afterwards comes a reply in a spoof Q & A column in *The Balance & Columbian Repository* of Hudson, New York, on 13th May 1806, in which the editor defines a cocktail as "a stimulating liquor composed of spirits of any kind, sugar, water, and bitters." It is vulgarly called bittered sling, and is supposed to be an excellent electioneering potion, inasmuch as it renders the heart stout and bold, at the same time that it fuddles the head. It is said also to be of great use to a Democratic candidate: because a person "having swallowed a glass of it is ready to swallow anything else." Written references to cocktails then became more and more common; and as late as 1862 when Jerry Thomas published his ground-breaking *Bartender's Guide* the word still carried its original meaning, for he characterizes the cocktail as a pick-me-up "generally used on fishing and other sporting parties, although some patients insist that it is good in the morning as a tonic."

David Wondrich, the historian of the cocktail, has pointed out that the casual tone of these early references implies that the cocktail was already well known, and indeed the word itself was first recorded almost two centuries earlier, in 1640, although evidently by the later 19th century its derivation had been forgotten. Of all the etymologies that have been dreamt up since then the three most widely peddled are, in ascending order of plausibility:

- The Haitian-born inventor of Peychaud's Bitters, Armand Amédé Peychaud, served his concoction with brandy in an egg-cup or *coquetier*, which in the vernacular pronunciation became cocktail. But remember the date above. Peychaud was born in the 1790s or possibly as late as 1803, far too late to have invented the cocktail. Besides, vernacular pronunciations of unfamiliar words tend to leave letters off rather than add new ones.

- Thrifty bartenders used to mix the dregs (tailings) from their spirit kegs (cock here meaning a tap) and sell them cheap. But why would they? Unlike beer, spirits carry no dregs and even when opened a keg will last weeks or even months before spoiling, so a bartender who couldn't sell a keg in that time should have found a business he was good at. No source is ever cited for this fanciful explanation; and while the word tailings meaning waste is standard in the extractive industries, it is unrecorded in the bar trade.

- While thoroughbreds tended not to have their tails docked, mixed-breed horses almost always did. A mixed-breed horse entered in a race was therefore easily identifiable (and not to be backed) simply by observing its "cocked" tail. The relevance of this to stimulant drinks is unexplained; cocked does not mean docked; would a "mixed-breed" horse be entering a race anyway; and remembering, again, the early date of the word's first appearance in print, a few hours spent with Google images will reveal that in the 17th and 18th century almost all horses, including thoroughbred racehorses, had their tails either docked or tied.

There is, however, a possible equine link. The word "cock" in this instance derives from the Old English *coc* which means heap or hill and appears in the Domesday Book in place-names such as Cookham and Coughton. Over many centuries its use was gradually extended to signify, as a noun, any sort of protuberance and, as a verb, any sort of lifting or raising action, especially a sharp or rapid one. By the 17th century it had come to mean a spout or tap or, of course, penis; other uses as a verb include or have included to cock the ears, to cock the hammer of a firearm, and to raise the brim of a hat either fore and aft or port and starboard; or as a noun the gnomon of a sundial, a weathervane and a horse's tail either docked or clubbed so that only the first few caudal vertebrae remain, protruding laterally from the horse's hindquarters. Literally, then, the word "cocktail" means a raised tail, either the high-carried tail of an excited or generally high-spirited horse or the puffed-out tail feathers of a gamecock psyching itself up and attempting to intimidate its opponent before a fight; and in time the expression attached itself to a drink intended to stimulate, to arouse, to lift both mind and body. To put paid, once and for all, the dizzy fantasticals of egg-cups, thrifty bartenders and 19th-century horse-racing, here is the short poem in which the word first appears. Published posthumously in 1640 in *Witt's Recreations: Selected from the Finest Fancies of Modern Muses, with 1,000 Outlandish Proverbs*, "On A Gallant" is number 386 in a book of sundry aphorisms and epigrams collected and put into verse by the metaphysical poet George Herbert.

> What gallant's that, whose oaths fly through mine ears?
> How like a lord of Pluto's court he swears!
> How Dutchman-like he swallows down his drink![160]
> How sweet he takes tobacco, til he stink!
> How lofty-sprighted, he disdains a boor!
> How faithful hearted he is to a whore!
> How cock-tail proud he doth himself advance!
> How rare his spurs do ring the Morrice dance![161]

In its earliest use, then, the word is a metaphor for male braggadocio, and it has to be acknowledged that a horse's tail carried high and either docked or clubbed at the fifth or sixth caudal vertebra looks uncannily like a rather impressive erect penis.[162] The similarity is even more explicit in the word's next surviving appearance in print in the 20th March 1798 issue of the *London Morning Post*, when it was used as a *double enten-*

dre to taunt the Prime Minister Pitt the Younger. For all his brilliance, Pitt was hopelessly shy of women, probably died a virgin, and was suspected of homosexuality.[163] The occasion for the *Morning Post*'s taunt was that a London publican who had won the lottery celebrated by excusing all his customers their bar-bills; in the spoof, Pitt's bar-bill amounts to "two petit vers of L'huile de Vénus 1s, one of parfait amour 7d, a cock-tail [vulgarly called ginger] three-quarter pence." Oil of Venus is a herbal lubricant and possibly a spermicide; *parfait amour* is a floral liqueur flavored with rose petals or violets, redolent of the boudoir; and the cock-tail signifies both the erection it so resembles and the means by which Pitt might achieve one. (Jockeys supposedly enlivened their horses before a race by rubbing cut ginger around their anuses, giving us the expression "ginger up.")

The only clue we have as to the properties that made the early cocktail such an effective energizer lies in the basic recipe given in the same edition of Thomas's *Guide*: four dashes of gum syrup (an obsolete ingredient that thickened the drink as well as sweetening it), two dashes of Bogart's (or Boker's) bitters,[164] a wineglass of spirit (gin, whiskey or brandy), two dashes of Curaçao, and a small piece of lemon peel, all shaken with fine ice and strained into a glass whose rim has been rubbed with lemon. The only way to find out whether it lives up to its billing is, of course, to try one, although the volume of alcohol suggests that it might be more soporific than stimulating — certainly the second one would be. But the characteristic common to all cocktails that would make a livener out of even so strong a potion was its serving temperature.

Drinking culture in Britain, well into recent times, was much concerned with keeping out the cold. Many of Dickens's favorite drinks — mulls, punches, neguses, bishops, jorams, beer or cider lambswools, gin or rum warm-with or warm-without,[165] early purls — were customarily served hot, from a convivially smoking bowl. In an age when most people worked outdoors the pub with its ingle nook (often equipped with copper mulling-boot) and high-backed settle, was a haven of warmth. As the novelist and travel-writer Thomas Burke had it:

> In winter the inn allures us. It is not merely shelter and refreshment: it is a beatific image of contrast. Outside are snow, ice, fog, or rain, wind, and mire. Inside, your imagination says, are glowing hearths, piquant odours, lights, drawn curtains, and soothing chairs... Indeed, most of our inns appear to have been designed with an eye only to hard weather, their narrow passages, low ceilings, small rooms, huge fireplaces and shuttered windows all making for snugness.[166]

In America, though, ice was king. True, winters in New England and the Midwest — not to mention Canada — are of a ferocity and duration that few Britons, more accustomed to a general dankness with only brief bursts of drama, can even imagine, let alone endure. Thomas's *Bartenders' Guide* duly includes a full catalogue of cockle-warmers that would have cheered Dickens to the bottom of his heart; but North America also enjoys meltingly hot summers such as maritime Britain only experiences once in a generation; and the United States therefore evolved, long before artificial refrigeration, an ice cutting and distribution trade on a heroic scale, principally to supply its burgeoning meat-packing and brewing industries, but with enough left over to produce an unceasing tide of cold drinks for every sweltering saloon and sun-struck porch in the land. The ice trade was based in the Northeastern US, a region blessed with lakes large and small which obligingly — and, more to the point, reliably — freeze thick and hard every winter, and in the days before mechanical refrigeration supplied plentiful ice, but for use only in the locality. Using bowsaws to cut the blocks by hand and sawdust from the region's equally plentiful timber yards to insulate them was a well-established business by the early 19th century, but a tricky one: for a start, ice-sawyers couldn't use full-size whipsaws because a whipsaw requires one of the sawyers to stand in a pit — not really possible on a lake! This limited the size of blocks that could be cut, and therefore their shelf-life. Insulated storage was also lacking, curtailing the length of sea-voyages possible as well as curbing the ice's longevity at its final destination.

These drawbacks were addressed in 1825 when an established but barely profitable Boston-based ice distributor, Frederic Tudor, joined forces with 23-year-old Nathaniel Wyeth, whose father owned a hotel on the banks of Fresh Pond in Cambridge, MA, which was itself harvested for ice. Between them they developed a horse-drawn ice plough and saw that could cut much bigger blocks than before; a rasp that dug grooves in the surfaces to stop them sticking together during storage and transportation; lifting gear to handle the heavier blocks; and double-skinned storage units that prolonged their life. Thus equipped, Tudor and Wyeth staged a voyage to India in 1833 on which less than half of the cargo melted, demonstrating that it was not only possible but profitable to ship ice all over the world by sea — their ice had great cachet in London clubs — and, once America's railway network started spreading, all over the continent by train. Horse-powered ice-harvesting gradually gave way to mechanical refrigeration, but by that time the whole of North America had an expectation of limitless supplies of ice, available on demand. Domestic iceboxes were introduced in the 1840s; by 1865 two-thirds of Boston homes had daily ice deliveries; and by 1880 the Northeast had 22 icehouses capable of storing 30,000 tons each.[167]

The expanding railway network that distributed ice so freely to food-processing businesses and bar owners in towns and cities across the continent brought investment and industry with it; and with investment and industry came a middle class of professionals, managers, engineers, clerical grades, public servants and other white collar workers with middle-class tastes and aspirations. Recreation appropriate to their social standing and sophistication was as important to them as the spacious, well-furnished housing, equipped with modern plumbing and kitchen appliances and laid out in the broad tree-lined streets of the most affluent late 19th century American suburbs; and it was people like Jerry "the Professor" Thomas who ensured they got it. We have already met Thomas as the author of *The Bartender's Guide: How to Mix Drinks, or The Bon-Vivant's Companion*; but he was also celebrated in his day as a practicing bartender himself. Born in New York in 1830, he first worked behind a bar in New Haven, Connecticut, then in gold-rush-era California. By the age of 21 he was back in New York with enough money to open a saloon of his own; but soon he was on the road again, working in upmarket saloons and hotel bars (which implies the presence of women among his enthralled patrons) in Chicago, St. Louis, San Francisco, Charleston and New Orleans. His theatrical flair meant that he could earn up to $100 a week, for he was supposedly the first of his profession to go in for bottle-twirling, pouring from a height, flourishing the cocktail shaker and all the other razzmatazz without mastery of which no one dares claim the title of mixologist today. As much a stage magician as a barman, his *pièce de resistance* was the creation before your very eyes of a Blue Blazer, a mixture of whiskey and boiling water set alight and tossed rapidly from one tankard to another several times in a continuous stream of blue fire. "The novice in mixing this beverage should be careful not to scald himself," warned the Professor. "To become proficient in throwing the liquid from one mug to the other, it will be necessary to practice for some time with cold water." As we have seen, though, only 17 of the 200+ recipes in the first edition of *The Bartender's Guide* called for gin. By the time of the 1887 posthumous edition (he died in poverty in 1885, ruined by speculation) the number had more than doubled to 39; but gin was still clearly the loser in the competition with darker spirits, and most of what gin was consumed was the sweeter, milder genever rather than London Dry. Figures from Bols indicate that genever outsold dry gin in the US by a ratio of six to one in 1880, while David Wondrich's research has revealed that for every 120-gallon pipe of English gin imported through New York docks in the 1850s there were 450 pipes of genever. Thomas gives recipes for many classic gin-based cocktails including the margarita, the Tom Collins, and the gin sling; but they can only have tasted very different when made with genever or even Old Tom, which was also popular. The martini, included under the name Martinez[168] in the 1887 posthumous edition and other roughly contemporary manuals, was also originally made with sweet vermouth and Old Tom in roughly equal measures, along with dashes of bitters and either Curaçao or maraschino — a very different proposition from the dry martini of today, which rose to its peak of popularity much later in the story.

London dry gin started overtaking genever (and Old Tom) in popularity in the United States after the 1880s when fast and reliable transatlantic liners made frequent travel between Britain and New York a viable proposition. Average crossing times fell from 15 days in 1860 to only three or four in the 1890s, with larger and more luxurious ships making the voyage both a pampered interlude and an opportunity for networking. The ruling élites of London and New York almost merged, as much for pleasure as for business: many a faltering noble bloodline had its fortunes rescued by a judicious American marriage; the Churchills were one such, and the House of Windsor itself was very nearly another. The first Midatlantic celebrity, P.G. Wodehouse, spent most of the years 1915–1930 as a hugely successful Broadway librettist and a slightly less successful Hollywood scriptwriter, and his Jeeves & Wooster series is peppered with American characters and episodes. The British upper classes took as enthusiastically to American cocktails as they did to American millionaires' daughters; in return, their gift to America was their preference for the cleaner, more sophisticated London dry gin (Old Tom and British-made Hollands having almost died out in England by the '90s) with its zesty, palate-stimulating botanicals, especially lemon and cardamom.

The newfound fondness for English gin among the American élites who hobnobbed so freely with dukes and earls did not, however, trickle far down the social scale. British working class men were by the 1890s drinking far more beer (and tea) than they did gin, while working-class women were coming to prefer the less heavily taxed and sweeter fortified wines; the American working class never really took to gin at all, even if their saloons were often nicknamed "gin mills"[169]; and although the English middle class was drinking more and more gin, the American middle class scarcely had the chance to try it out before, at midnight on 16th January 1920, the Volstead Act came into force and with it the 18th Amendment to the US Constitution: Prohibition.

Prohibition was one of the most ambitious attempts at social engineering in the history of the West and has perhaps understandably given rise to many misconceptions and myths. For a start, it wasn't strictly an anti-alcohol measure: it banned the production, transportation, sale and public consumption of all alcohols except medicinal spirits, sacrificial wine and industrial alcohol, but not their possession or private use. The principal target of the many organizations, largely composed of and organized by working and middle-class women, was not so much alcohol itself but the saloons that kidnapped the family breadwinners and stripped them of much of their earnings.[170] One of the most prominent of these organizations even called itself the Anti-Saloon League. And Prohibition did not arrive overnight: it was fought for state by state over more than 70 years, giving America's womenfolk the chance to operate in the political vanguard, a chance that they gleefully accepted. By the time the 18th Amendment extending it nationwide came into force, 23 of the 48 states of the Union were already dry. Maine had had prohibition since 1846, with a two-year gap from 1856–1858. Thirteen more states followed Maine's example in the 1850s, and although some of these periods of prohibition were short-lived, in other cases they lasted for decades. Vermont went dry in 1852, followed by New Hampshire in 1855;

they stayed that way until 1903. Connecticut was a prohibition state for nearly 20 years; Michigan and Minnesota for 22. In some states there was a ding-dong battle between wet and dry votes: Iowa had four periods of prohibition before Volstead, 1885–1887, 1882–1883, 1884–1894, and 1916–1917; Massachusetts was dry from 1852–1868 and again from 1869–1875; and Rhode Island was dry in 1853–1863, 1874–1875, and 1886–1889, although in 1919 it was one of only two states, the other being Connecticut, that decided not to ratify the 18th Amendment. And when in 1933 President Roosevelt had the amendment repealed, four states held out for another year and two — Alabama and Kansas — until 1937.

When Prohibition finally arrived it had substantial majority support: 65 votes in favor to 20 in the Senate; 137 to 62 in the House. Much of the public enthusiasm evaporated overnight, though, when supporters who thought it would extend only to spirits, as it had done in most of the states, found that it banned beer and wine as well. For many generations American workers had been swinging away from the country's traditionally heavy consumption of spirits and towards beer as the spreading railway network made possible the transportation and distribution of a highly perishable product. Brewers and beer-drinkers had numbered themselves among the righteous who would of course be exempt; but as the principal target was not so much the drink itself as saloon culture, they soon found they were wrong. The reduction in alcohol-related disorder and disease might have been appreciated to a limited extent, although such gains are often imperceptible in real time; but the job losses inflicted on blameless brewery and catering workers in such harsh economic times certainly were not. And then there was the mob.

One of the great misconceptions surrounding Prohibition is that it gave rise to the emergence of organized crime; but organized crime long predated Prohibition. Migrant populations crammed into urban slums had brought their own criminals with them, principally extortionists and protection racketeers such as the Sicilian Black Handers. Ethnically based street gangs founded on the protection of territory and funded by petty crime were also commonplace, and their youthful members were often recruited, usually by bosses but also on occasion by unions, as "labor sluggers" who used intimidation and violence both to sway strike ballots and to break or to enforce picket lines. Ownership of saloons, casinos, and brothels was the obvious next step as these racketeers matured: Big Jim Colosimo, for example, had been active as a pimp and union organizer in Chicago since 1895, and had a legitimate job as a street cleaner; as his clandestine enterprises flourished he abandoned the pretense of honest work and bought a luxurious nightclub on South Wabash Avenue. When Prohibition arrived the first concern of criminal entrepreneurs like Colosimo was to maintain and protect the supply of liquor to their own outlets. Once they had developed the organization, logistics, and connections[171] to achieve that, the mantle of clandestine purveyors of booze to an entire nation — a role that some of the earlier bosses including Colosimo himself had thought too ambitious to be worth attempting — fell on their shoulders almost by default.

The first commodities the gangsters wanted were whiskey and, to a lesser extent, rum. The American working class, as stated, were tending more and more to favor beer over spirits (and were indeed drinking less and less overall); but the gangster-run saloons or "speakeasies"[172] attracted a rather more rakish, free-spending clientele who drank more cocktails than beer. In the first years of Prohibition smuggling enough to supply the speakeasies was not an insuperable problem. The various American bourbon and rye distillers themselves had stockpiles amounting to 64 million gallons between them, of which 60 million rapidly went astray. Scottish and Irish distillers happily looked the other way as cases of their product were unloaded from freighters moored just outside territorial waters on to powerful motor launches easily capable of outrunning US Coastguard cutters, to be transferred to waiting trucks at some deserted cove or well-bribed fishing port. The Gulf coastline was porous to rumrunners, as was the 4,000-mile Canadian border.[173] In Windsor, Ontario, just across the Detroit River from the eponymous city, Seagram's distillery sold its whiskey in casks to the Detroit Purple Gang and the Little Jewish Navy, which specialized in coming up with devious ways of getting the casks across the river. Commercial spirits from the Gooderham & Worts and Hiram Walker distilleries in Toronto found their way across Lake Ontario in much the same manner. In country districts where prohibition had long been a day-to-day reality, moonshiners had already perfected the arts of bribery and corruption to get their goods to market without official interference. And given that state and city police were already in many cases either overstretched or open to corruption or both, the appointment in 1920 of a mere 1,500 Prohibition agents to control the clandestine distribution of spirits across the entire country was hardly even a fig leaf. True, there were arrests: it's often said, in fact, that the sheer number of prosecutions in the first two years soon filled the jails and persuaded district attorneys and magistrates to ease the pressure by introducing the plea bargain. At first, though, the flow of bootlegged whiskey and rum was enough to satisfy the immediate demand; only when that happy circumstance changed did gin begin to supplant dark spirits as the gangsters' (and hence their customers') preferred option. For supplying their own speakeasies was one thing; supplying the whole demand of 123 million thirsty Americans who had previously drunk 140 million gallons of spirits a year, was quite another. To smuggling, then, the racketeers had to add another source of spirits: they had to make their own.

Fortunately, a perfectly legal means of doing so was at hand. America's industrial economy used around 600 million gallons of industrial ethanol a year for a range of manufactures from cosmetics and solvents to military incendiaries the Islamic alchemists would have recognized a millennium earlier. Gangsters found that industrial distillers and their wholesale distributors were perfectly happy to sell them all they needed and in some cases, as with the Genna Brothers on Chicago's South Side, they actually bought the whole distillery.[174] An unnamed bootlegger, interviewed at length by the *New Yorker* in 1926,[175] described his induction into the big time:

> After I paid the president of the big liquor distributing syndicate my thousand dollars... he gave me a long talk about selling liquor. He said that rum peddling was a piker's business and that his organization had developed a scientific system just like any other organization with goods to sell, such as the Standard Oil Company or the Uneeda Baking Company, for example. The firm had a small quantity of fine liquor, he said, that came in steadily through Canada and through boats from the West Indies. But this was only for sample purposes and was not used for actual deliveries. He said: "Of course, we are not delivering genuine Scotch liquor or genuine anything else. We cannot get that stuff any longer. We have fifteen or twenty big plants which are converting alcohol into whisky and wine and cordials and I had just as soon drink it as the real stuff. I will guarantee that it would not harm a child. But, of course, the customer does not like that idea. He likes to think that he is getting the real goods. And as long as the stuff we sell does not hurt him, it helps business to make him think so. So the main job is to make him think he is getting the real goods. He just enjoys it that much more."

What the mobsters then had on their hands was pure grain or agricultural spirit produced on column stills which could be turned into a form of whiskey by adulteration and possibly even by steeping over oak chips for a few weeks, or into gin by either steeping or redistilling with easily available flavorings for a few hours. For what Americans really wanted was whiskey: before Prohibition they had drank 135 million gallons of bourbon and rye a year along with 1.5 million gallons of Scotch and Irish whiskies but only 5 million gallons of gin.[176] Under the circumstances it would have been impossible to gratify such a huge demand for real (i.e., aged) whiskey: no amount of bribery could have suborned the police into turning a blind eye to warehouses containing millions of gallons of maturing stock! The only options for determined whiskey drinkers were vastly expensive "imports" (provenance not guaranteed — see above); real whiskey legally prescribed by a doctor (8 million gallons in 1921 alone, but restricted and expensive); or industrial alcohol colored with caramel and flavored mainly with extracts and essential oils described by the *New Yorker*'s anonymous bootlegger. Prohibition-era recipes obtained by collector Matthew Rowley[177] indicate that these fake whiskies were at least innocuous: imitation rye called for 40 gallons of US proof spirit (i.e., 50% ABV), two gallons of peach flavoring, a pint of white vinegar, 12 drops of oil of cognac (an essential oil extracted from grapes) dissolved in neutral spirit, and caramel. Darker, richer, sweeter imitation bourbon was compounded of the same volume of spirit, a dram of copper sulfate solution, a gallon each of peach and brandy flavorings, a pound of glycerin, 12 drops of oil of cognac in neutral spirit, and caramel. Admittedly these recipes originated with a respectable New York doctor, Victor Lyon, whose hand-written notebook was given to Rowley by a friendly restaurateur and fellow collector; but the processes and ingredients used for the same purpose by the mob, in the early years of Prohibition at least, were probably no more noxious than the inexpensive and easily available additives favored by Dr. Lyon. However, while American drinkers were already familiar with genuine rye and genuine bourbon and could distinguish (or at least, thought they could) the counterfeits from the real McCoy, there was no such problem with gin. Most Americans knew little about it and had probably never even tasted it. And there was no need to make counterfeit gin — indeed you might even argue that there's no such thing: neutral spirit, either compounded or rectified with the appropriate flavorings and let down to potable strength quite simply *is* gin, whether the processes take place in gleaming copper vessels in the sterile environment of a modern distillery, or in a tin bath in the galley kitchen of a railroad apartment in Little Italy (see below).

The 18th Amendment took a year from passage to implementation, and the mobsters had plenty of chance to prepare. Legitimately held stocks of liquor were quickly mopped up, as we have seen (what little was left was acquired in 1924 by the National Distillers' Products Corporation). Smuggling routes were established. What few judges, court clerks, City Hall satraps and secretaries, police officers and others who hadn't already been thoroughly corrupted were probably of no account anyway. The final piece in the puzzle for more far-sighted gangsters was to acquire interests in the distilleries that would be allowed to continue making industrial ethanol — pure ethanol compulsorily contaminated with at least 5% toxins, including methanol to make it unusable as a beverage. Among these, as we have seen, were the Genna clan, six Sicilian brothers prominent in Chicago's South Side and styled the Terrible Gennas (surely self-styled, since when rival mobsters came after them in 1925 following their assassination of North Side gang boss Dion O'Banion, three were picked off almost immediately and the others ran away). The Gennas not only controlled a licensed distillery but also recruited some 1,500 "alkie-cookers" — Sicilian immigrants, supposedly already experienced in distilling back in the old country, equipped at the Gennas' expense with small pot stills and paid up to $15 dollars a day. It's sometimes said that the Gennas supplied their compatriots with a crude corn mash which they were expected to ferment, distill, and rectify in their homes, but this seems absurd if the brothers already had access to a steady source of reliable industrial ethanol. Besides, it would have been impossible in the standard railroad apartment to brew the quantity of wash it takes to boil down to a worthwhile quantity of "bathtub gin." Which rather begs the question: what was the role of the bathtub in all this?

One can easily imagine a backwoods moonshiner using a 50 or 60-gallon bathtub to ferment enough wash at 8% ABV to yield sufficient spirit for personal use and local sale, but he'd be lucky to get five or six gallons of 80% spirit from an average bathful — perhaps more, if he followed the traditional practice of fermenting on the grist; but even then, not enough to make a viable business in Little Italy. And if the Gennas' 1,500 alkie-cookers were actually mashing and fermenting in their kitchens, how did they dispose of the spent grain without attracting unwanted attention? What's much more likely is that the Gennas' alkie-cookers took delivery of carboys of denatured ethanol and rectified it to remove the contaminants while infusing it with flavorings in the form of essential oils. The galvanized tin baths, the most commonly available and easily disguised vessel in the neighborhood, filled with cold water to cool the condensing coil, made the perfect wormtub. After the heads and tails had been discarded, the original carboys could be used as spirit receivers; the finished gin would be out of the cooker's apartment only a few hours after it had arrived; and the bathtub could be rinsed out and hung back up on its nail in the galley kitchen. Frankie Yale in New York had a similar set-up until he was gunned down in 1928, but it seems that most bootleggers satisfied themselves with having their base spirits quickly and simply compounded with essential oils and other extracts in the very same galvanized tin bathtubs. Dilution and the added flavorings would have gone some way, at least in the early days of Prohibition, to concealing the taste and reducing the harm of the compulsory contaminants.

As for the cod explanations and apocryphal charter myths — well, whatever you hear about bottles half-full of gin being diluted from the bath-tap because they were too tall to stand under the taps in the kitchen sink, ignore it: the bathtubs you'd find in Little Italy didn't come with luxuries like taps. This explanation has been repeated so often that almost everyone believes it, but a single look at the kind of bathtub common in working-class homes in the 1920s is enough to dismiss it as fantasy. Besides, the bottling operation in Chicago at least was carried out at the soft drinks plant run by Al's brother, the aptly nicknamed Ralphie "Bottles" Capone; and the *New Yorker* bootlegger's description of painstakingly bottling his best and most expensive counterfeit liquor by hand implies that the run-of-the-mill hooch was diluted and bottled mechanically on one of the dozens of commercial bottling lines in the city. The humble bathtub's meagre capacity must have created an irksome bottleneck between industrial production and industrial packaging, but rectifying the denatured spirit in the community under a concealing cloud of bribery and intimidation was far less risky than trying to introduce a whole layer of extraneous processes — rectification, dilution and bottling — to a distillery that must have been under at least some legal supervision.

What can it have been like, though, this bathtub gin? Well, as one might expect, it has been excoriated with almost exactly the same calumnies as the gin of 18th-century London. In his huge biography of Al Capone, Laurence Bergreen declares authoritatively: "It was dreadful stuff, the Gennas' home-made brew. It stank, it was raw, and it was dangerous. Brewed quickly on the cheap… colored with caramel or coal tar and flavored with fusel oil, a noxious by-product of fermentation."[178] Not only is this assessment unsupported by contemporary evidence (Bergreen himself was born 25 years after the Genna brothers went out of business and never reveals how he knew how their "home-brew" tasted), it's also full of howlers. It wasn't "home-brew"; it was produced in a commercial distillery. It wasn't brewed; it was distilled. And it probably didn't contain any fusel oils: these heavier alcohols are indeed produced during fermentation and concentrated by distillation, but the rectifying columns of the continuous stills used to produce industrial alcohol condense the fusel oil separately from the ethanol. Less howler-ridden is the website of a museum (which shall remain unnamed) dedicated to all matters mob-related, which sums up the process of compounding fairly accurately[179] but then asserts, on the basis of what evidence it does not reveal: "Few could tolerate the bad taste… Bartenders in speakeasies blended ounces of it with various mixers… to hide the flavour." Well, you could say that of bartenders everywhere and all times; but the purpose of the blending is not and was not to "hide" the flavor but to complement and enhance it. That's what mixology is all about.

Those who have actually sampled Prohibition-era bathtub gins — or recreations of it — are not so dismissive. In 2013 Cameron Collins of Distilled History recreated as faithfully as possible two authentic recipes from the 1920s for a tasting held at the Campbell House Museum in St. Louis. The verdict was generally favorable, with one taster recording: "To our surprise, we didn't spit it all out… We'll take a hip-flask of bathtub gin any day." Indeed it's doubtful if the mob could have sold as much of its hooch as it did — possibly as much as 120 million gallons a year by the time Roosevelt rode to America's rescue — if the stuff had been no good. And the acid test was that people liked it — especially those young middle-class women who "cut their hair short, shortened their skirts and flattened their breasts… sipped cocktails and served at tennis."[180] In an extraordinary echo of 18th-century London, where migrant women workers were able to frequent dram shops and more or less doubled the size of the gin market at a stroke, young American women who would never have been allowed into an old-school saloon were regular customers in gangster-owned speakeasies with their dangerous charm, relaxed protocols, and red-carpet welcome for anyone with money. This was, after all, the Roaring Twenties, the era of the flapper, the Charleston and the Black Bottom. Fortune's unsigned contemporary account of November 1933 makes no specific mention of the quality of the product, but implies that it was at least adequate, specifically mentions the new female custom, and predicts (accurately, as it turned out) a rosy future:

> The bootleg industry discovered that the one thing Prohibition prohibited was the manufacture of the native US drink, rye and bourbon whiskey, and so it gave the thirsty citizens something else and changed the taste of a generation... Before prohibition, gin went into Martinis and Negronis. The alcohol industry of the 1920s made it a drink. The younger drinking generation was weaned on it and an entirely new body of drinkers, women, preferred it to whiskey, possibly because it is reputed to contain some of the medicinal properties of essence of peppermint and Lydia E Pinkham's vegetable remedy.[181] Furthermore, gin can be sold more cheaply than even the worst whiskey. Two classes of businessmen are confident that during the first year of repeal as much gin will be sold as whiskey: they are the officials of the alcohol companies and the bathtub chemists.

As for the quality of the better counterfeit gin, the *New Yorker's* bootlegger — whose customer base was founded on the clientele of the Fifth Avenue restaurant Sherry's, where he had previously been a waiter — was inordinately proud of his.

> Nearly everybody needs gin, and everybody knows that the so-called Gordon's Gin is fake stuff. You can't get any real Gordon's in this country. But I struck upon the idea of a different package. I put out two packages, calling one of them a London Gin and the other a South American — that is, English manufacture in a South American package, export stuff. I sent a trial case of the London package to the president of a leading New York bank, but in about three days he sent it back. It wasn't real stuff, he said, and he couldn't drink it. I went down to pay him a personal call, and

> explained that… the London stuff was all I had at the moment. If he was willing to wait a week, I told him, a South American ship would be in with a quantity of real London gin, packed for Brazilian export. The price I gave him on this was much higher than the original sale, but I explained that the South American stuff was really a rare article and cost me a lot. The bank president was very eager, and said he would wait. Well, in a week I sent him down a case of the South American stuff and took his check. He called me up that night to tell me how fine it was, and that he wanted some more, at any price. Of course, it was exactly the same gin that I had sent him in the London bottles. But he was having a great time fooling himself, the liquor would not hurt him, and he could afford to pay for it… I assure you, you couldn't have told my product from the genuine article to save your life. Unless you were a real expert, just come from England, or from a stock of pre-war stuff, you could not have found any difference ... On the whole, I was selling pretty pure and smooth liquor, even if it was fake.

If bathtub gin owed its lethal reputation to anyone it wasn't the mob: it was the Federal Government. In 1906, when the tax imposed on industrial alcohol during the Civil War was finally lifted, the Government, ordained that it should be "denatured" — that is, as we have seen, a charge of contaminants including up to 4% methanol should be added to make it undrinkable. Even though methanol tends to "stick" to ethanol during redistilling, careful rectification could remove most of the noxious additives, while dilution could reduce what remained to more or less harmless levels, and by the mid-20s so much legally distilled industrial alcohol was being diverted either through illegal purchase or outright theft that the Government felt it had to act. Enforcement had clearly failed, even though the number of Prohibition agents had doubled and their budget, originally set at $4.4 million, was to rise to $13.4 million, with a further $13 million a year being spent by the coastguard. The administration of Calvin Coolidge therefore decided simply to make industrial alcohol much harder to refine by increasing its methanol content to 10% and authorizing the addition of other poisons harder to remove including kerosene, brucine (a plant alkaloid closely related to strychnine), gasoline, benzene, cadmium, iodine, zinc, mercury salts, nicotine, ether, formaldehyde, chloroform, camphor, carbolic acid, quinine and acetone.[182] Deaths from methanol poisoning had already risen sharply from 1,000 in 1920 to just over 4,000 in 1925; now the rate took off, with 400 in New York City alone in 1926, 700 in 1927, and possibly as many as 50,000 across the country by the time of repeal. Some estimates are even higher. Deborah Blum writes:

> Public health officials responded with shock. "The government knows it is not stopping drinking by putting poison in alcohol," New York City medical examiner Charles Norris said. "Yet it continues its poisoning processes, heedless of the fact that people determined to drink are daily absorbing that poison. Knowing this to be true, the United States government must be charged with the moral responsibility for the deaths that poisoned liquor causes, although it cannot be held legally responsible." His department issued warnings to citizens, detailing the dangers in whiskey circulating in the city: "Practically all the liquor that is sold in New York today is toxic," read one 1928 alert. Norris also condemned the federal program for its disproportionate effect on the country's poorest residents. Wealthy people, he pointed out, could afford the best whiskey available. Most of those sickened and

> dying were those "who cannot afford expensive protection and deal in low-grade stuff."[183]

It's impossible to determine how much of America's industrial alcohol output was diverted to make illegal beverage during Prohibition since throughout the booming 1920s legitimate demand for it was rising and "gasohol" — a motor fuel of gasoline blended with up to 12% ethanol — was being actively promoted. Alcohol consumption in America had been falling steadily when Prohibition was introduced; in fact 1921 saw it hit a record low. In 1922 it started to creep up again as entrepreneurs in the underground economy improved their techniques and expanded output while consumers began to realize the folly of the ban. Consumption of pure alcohol per head rose from a mere quarter of a pint in 1920 to 1.2 gallons in 1929, while spirits began to displace beer in popular favor: before Prohibition the spend had been roughly 60:40 in beer's favor, but during Prohibition itself beer was so hard to get that its price shot up by 700% while the price of spirits rose only 270%. As a result the spend ratio about-faced to 70:30 in favor of spirits. The ratio soon settled down again as beer became cheaper and more widely available; but gin, as the author of the Fortune magazine article had predicted, was now firmly established in the popular taste. Prohibition, then, wasn't a complete failure. It was a win for the mob, a win for female emancipation, and most definitely a win for gin.

Drinkie~poos: The Gentrification of Gin

War, slump, stock market crash, slow recovery, north-south divide, more war... for the British drinks industry, the first half of the 20th century included some proverbially interesting times, the thrust of which was to damage the habits, customs and traditions of the working classes while elevating the improving impulses of their bourgeois superiors. It was also to lead to the more or less complete gentrification of gin.

The licensed trade in particular had for decades been a social and political cotillion in which none of the dancers appeared to share any notion as to the steps; but while laissez-faire conservatives, grasping brewers, high-minded liberals, aggressive socialists, hidebound magistrates, churchmen high and low, and temperance campaigners of all spots and stripes warred over whether the existing small and unappealing pubs, which many considered so unedifying as to constitute a positive deterrent to drinking, should be allowed to soldier on; whether they should lose their licenses and be replaced by large, well-designed, civilized (for which read bourgeois) pubs that would attract a much wider and more respectable demographic, and which many believed would merely lure even more poor souls to perdition; whether licenses should be strictly rationed according to local "need" (a nebulous concept only overturned in the 1980s by the J.D. Wetherspoon Organisation pub chain); or whether there should be no pubs at all.

Into this maelstrom liberal chancellors — first Gladstone in 1880, then Lloyd Georgein 1909 — lobbed duty increases tailored to create the price differential between beer, wine, and spirits that still persists today. At the outbreak of World War I the duty per proof gallon was 6 shillings 9 pence on wine, 7 shillings 8 pence on beer, and 14shillings 9 pence on spirits, a state of affairs that made wine, especially Empire wines from South Africa and Australia, affordable even for working-class drinkers[184] while redefining spirit-drinking (for the working class) as an occasional treat or (for the middle class) a sign of status. The trend, in fact, was very similar to that prevailing in the United States, where the working classes were drinking less and less whiskey and gin and more and more beer. During the period 1870–1914 beer accounted for 60% of Britain's alcohol consumption, with 30% accounted for by spirits and 10% by wine, a large proportion of it fortified. Annual spirits consumption per head fell from 11 liters of pure alcohol (LPA)[185] or 27.5 standard bottles in 1900 to 8.5 LPA or 17 bottles in 1910; and as well as the price premium arising from the widening duty differential the decline was also driven by well-organized temperance campaigning which attracted huge popular support.

The prewar years saw turmoil in the Scotch industry following the catastrophic collapse in 1898 of Pattison Brothers of Leith, a blender and merchant founded on credit which went bust when the banks called the loans in, taking with it 60 of its unpaid suppliers, mostly small malt distillers. Many of them were bought out of receivership by the Distillers Company Ltd., cementing the conglomerate's dominance over the industry. Meanwhile the gin distillers continued to thrive on their diet of middle-class women and export sales. The outbreak of World War I, however, very nearly led to the demise of the entire distilling industry.

The direction of the war by the Liberal Prime Minister Herbert Asquith and Chancellor David Lloyd George (Prime Minister himself from 1916) was much bedeviled by a social issue whose place in the political front line carried over naturally from a peacetime issue to a (supposed) matter of life and death in the nation's great struggle. Excise and licensing were already live issues, and as soon as hostilities commenced Britain's army of temperance campaigners were on the streets, handing out pamphlets to all who failed to slip past quickly enough and persuading thousands to take the pledge for as long the war lasted. The King and Queen themselves took the pledge on behalf of their entire household, although a rather ambiguous report in the Daily Express in April 1915 suggests that while servants and guests were treated only to soft drinks (and woe betide any guest who tried to smuggle a hip-flask into the palace!), Their Majesties allowed themselves a modest ration of French wine at dinner (the hock and Moselle remaining, of course, under lock and key for the duration). But the pledge was not as popular among the elite as among the bourgeoisie: Asquith himself was a notorious alcoholic nicknamed "Squiffy" for his frequent unsteadiness at public occasions; and although Lloyd George had made his political bones as a fiery temperance campaigner in the fine old Welsh Nonconformist tradition he was probably not, as is so widely reported, teetotal and never took the pledge.[186] In the early months of the war his attitude to liquor was the conventional one: it was a cash-cow to be milked to pay for armaments, and in November 1914 he duly upped the duty on a standard barrel of beer from 7 shillings 9 pence to 23 shillings, assuring the Commons: "This is not a temperance proposal: it is a fiscal proposal to raise money for the war." However he decided against an increase in the tax on spirits, narrowing the price differential and leading to a spike in spirit-drinking: duty was charged on 2.3 million proof gallons of home-produced spirits in October but 2.7 million gallons in November and 2.9 million in December. In April 2015 the error of judgment was corrected when spirit duty was doubled from its prewar 14 shillings 9 pence a gallon.

It was not long before the two aims of financing the war and furthering the cause of temperance insensibly merged. As always seems the case, Britain's first encounter with modern warfare war was a catalogue of rude awakenings. The 60,000 casualties suffered by the original 160,000-strong British Expeditionary Force — the "old contemptibles" — in the Ypres salient in October-November 1914, Germany's declaration of unrestricted U-boat warfare in February 1915, and the "shell crisis" that emerged in March 1915 caused a political panic in Whitehall, and Lloyd George rallied his political power base to his side by blaming the calamities on his old enemy. Two speeches in spring 1915 produced perhaps his most memorable, if not very deeply researched, quotations. On February 28th at Bangor, a temperance stronghold, he reiterated a theme as common in the temperance movement then as it had been in 1720–1751, and one in which a sympathetic audience will have found most gratifying vindication: that drinking undermined the fitness of the worker. He said:

> I hear of workmen in armaments who refuse to work a full week for the nation's need. The vast majority belong to a class we can depend upon. The others are a minority. But, you must remember, a small minority of workmen can throw a whole works out of gear. What is the reason? Sometimes it is one thing, sometimes it is another, but let us be perfectly candid. It is mostly the lure of the drink. They refuse to work full time, and when they return their strength and efficiency are impaired by the way in which they have spent their leisure. Drink is doing more damage in the war than all the German submarines put together.

Two weeks later he told the Shipbuilding Employers Federation that Britain was "fighting Germany, Austria and drink, and as far as I can see the greatest of these three deadly foes is drink." A new front had been opened in the fight; and despite the lack of evidence for any drink-related loss of industrial efficiency at all, Lloyd George as Chancellor, then as Munitions Minister, and from 1916 as Prime Minister overrode objections that he was baselessly maligning the entire working class and put the control of drink from raw materials to retail very publicly at the center of his policies. The restrictions (enabled by the catch-all 1914 Defence of the Realm Act) on brewing and retailing beer that followed — the creation of a Central Control Board with almost plenary powers to regulate; the nationalization of breweries and pubs in districts with key defense industries; the reduction in beer's alcoholic strength through the rationing of malting barley (a device copied in World War II); the cuts in permitted opening hours for pubs; the fourfold duty increase — were draconian, and are fully described and analyzed in *Pubs & Patriots*. Equally severe restrictions were imposed on the distilling industry.

Having remarked publicly that the Tsar's ban on vodka was "a great act of nationalism and sacrifice," Lloyd George was talked out of outright prohibition by advisers seconded from industry to the Ministry of Munitions, including James Stevenson of Johnnie Walker. In the event alcohol was never rationed, or not formally, at least: even after many staples such as butter, jam, sugar and bacon were rationed following the stepping up of the U-boat campaign in spring 1917, liquor was limited only by price and availability. However a sharp brake had already been put on whiskey production by the Immature Spirits Act of May 1915, which outlawed (on all sorts of spurious grounds including the fiction that new make was bad for the health) the sale for retail of spirits at less than three years old. This suited the Scotch distillers — in fact it was Stevenson's idea in the first place — as it allowed the whiskies of the 1912–1914 harvests to be eked out for future fillings, while the shortage of product meant that what they lost in volume they could hope to make up in value.[187] However a specific exemption for "spirits delivered to licensed rectifiers" meant that there was not quite such a dearth of gin, a fact noted with disapproval by John Henderson, MP for Aberdeenshire West.[188] He said in a Commons debate during the passage of the Act:

> We all know that gin is just as great a cause of drunkenness as whisky. As a matter of fact, I have been shown the number of bottles of whisky and the number of bottles of gin sold in a great many places in London, and I know that gin very nearly comes up to whisky... We know that when beer does not get a man far enough on, he adds gin to the beer; that is a very common drink.[189]

Henderson's censure was not enough to persuade the Government to withdraw the exemption, though; as the Attorney General Sir John Simon said in the same debate: "Whatever may help to defeat the Germans the shutting of gin up in warehouses most certainly will not." Besides, even if the malt distillers' pot stills were effectively mothballed, especially when 1916's poor harvests and the U-boat offensive really began to bite into grain supplies in 1917, the great column stills were busily at work producing the ethanol[190] for which the munitions factories had as great a thirst as (according to Lloyd George, at any rate!) the munitions workers themselves. There was always bound to be some left over for the rectifiers.

But there were other ways to restrict supply. The obvious one was to stretch it by adding water, a device to which the brewing industry was already freely resorting and which in 1916 became compulsory for distillers. The effect of the dilution ordered by the Central Control Board has, however, often been overstated as halving the strength of spirits. Before the war spirits had usually been bottled at 15–22% under UK proof or 44.6–48.6% ABV. In 1915 the CCB recommended a cut to 35% under proof or 37.2% ABV, but then sought a further reduction to 50% under proof or 28.5% ABV. In the end the CCB and the Whisky Association settled on 25% under or 43% ABV. That lasted until 1917 when the CCB got a further reduction to today's 30% under or 40% ABV, which has been the minimum bottle-strength for Scotch ever since. Only in the designated munitions areas such as those around Enfield and Woolwich in London, Carlisle in Cumbria and Gretna in Southwest Scotland and the Invergordon naval base in Western Scotland was it lowered to the oft-repeated 50% under proof.

The simplest way to limit the supply of spirits, though, as with beer, was to limit the supply of fermentable materials. In 1916 the Ministry of Food Control was hived off from the Ministry of Agriculture, charged with the task of allocating resources appropriately and knitting together supply and demand as effectively as possible. To meet the challenges of 1917 it transferred more than a million acres of grassland to tillage, but little was allocated for barley and the additional yield was a mere 24,000 tons as compared to a million tons of wheat and 1.5 million tons of oats. You can, of course, ferment almost anything to charge a column still with, which is one of its beauties; but other cereals and sugar were as closely controlled as malted barley, and under all these pressures UK spirits consumption per head dwindled from 4 LPA or 10 bottles per head per annum in 1915 to 3 LPA or 7 1/2 bottles in 1918. (For comparison, the same figure for 1980 was 6 LPA or 15 bottles.)

If the privations of war saw spirits consumption including gin-drinking severely curtailed, especially among the less affluent, worse was to follow when the armies began to come home. Before the war rum had been very popular among a fairly narrow distribution base in the catchment areas of the principal ports of entry including Plymouth, Bristol and Glasgow and among sailors of almost all varieties.[191] During the war, however, soldiers like their maritime opposite numbers received a rum ration. For men in the front line it was half a gill, the liquid equivalent of a treble; but at 54% ABV it packed rather more punch than the same quantity in a pub, especially as it was customary to down it in one. In some units a double ration was served immediately before an attack, so many of those who died as cattle must have been mercifully anaesthetized, at least to an extent, before the monstrous anger of the guns became their passing bells. The rum ration was always controversial: the commander-in-chief General Sir Douglas Haig, living the life of a well-off country gentleman at his HQ 40 miles behind the lines and drinking and dining with commensurate extravagance, heartily wished it could be withdrawn.[192] General Reginald Pinney, son of the vicarage and commander of 33 Division, actually did withdraw it and made his men drink tea instead. Nevertheless, the men mostly had their rum and came home with a great fondness for it — a constituency of well over two million working-class men pretty much lost to the gin distillers for good, as it turned out.

Gin held on through the hard years thanks to the loyalty of its core constituents: army officers and box-wallahs in the tropics to whom the quinine-rich tonic was supposedly as important as the gin; naval officers, for whom gin had the virtue of not being the proletarian rum (army officers on the Western front favored whiskey for much the same reason); and women of gentility or of some pretense to it. In short, during World War I gin finally shook off its working-class image and started the journey to bourgeois respectability in earnest.

The war changed the economic, political and social status of women for good. It was not a smooth journey: for instance, returning soldiers got back many of the industrial jobs that women had been performing in their absence; and although women over 30 got the vote in 1918 it was another decade before women over 21 got it too. But if the progress of emancipation in the economic and political spheres was slow — and indeed is still a work in progress — it was much more rapid in the social sphere. With more than two million men away at war pubs needed customers and women needed friendship and, in all too many cases, emotional support. And with well-paid jobs in the munitions factories, they had the money to afford it. As one soldier on leave from the front and trying to order a drink recalled: "One girl forestalled me saying, 'you keep your money, Corporal. This is on us,' and with no more ado she pulled up her frock, turned back her stocking from under the flashy garter, and produced a roll of notes big enough to choke a cow. Many of the girls earned ten times my pay as a full Corporal, and they were generously big-hearted where we were concerned."[193] There was, as might be expected, a great deal of scandalized comment on the sudden prevalence of female custom in the nation's pubs, and outrage on a scale that almost matched the moral panic of 1720–1751 — "Alarmed social workers wrote to The Times that women who insisted their children were starving were 'all the time puffing into our faces fumes of whisky, gin and the like.'"[194] But this time round there were wiser heads, mainly in the form of senior police officers, who had no axes to grind and a more sophisticated approach to gathering statistics and who found that reports of drunkenness and debauchery among female workers were, if not completely untrue, at least wildly exaggerated. In particular, they found very little evidence of spirit-drinking among working women — not, at least, in pubs. A report into drinking in Woolwich found that on occasion "a great many smartly dressed girls throng the Beresford Square House [the Arsenal's main gate] after 8 o'clock, drifting from house to house[195] and consuming ports and spirits… they seem little the worse for this kind of amusement;" but in general it found that "very few [munitions girls] call at any of the public houses, and then only get a glass of stout."[196]

Middle-class women could and did use the better-class snugs and (a new phenomenon) lounge bars of more upmarket pubs; but in general they preferred to entertain more discreetly at home, with gin and Angostura bitters (the Navy's "harry pinkers"), vermouth (either "It" or French) or lime (the gimlet) being particular favorites, and sherry replacing the heavier fortified wines popular before the war. The choice of the lighter-bodied gin and sherry over the more muscular whiskey, brandy, Port, Madeira and Marsala probably reflects the hour at which people entertained. The informal "at home" was normally an afternoon affair[197] when lighter drinks were preferred; meanwhile dinner grew later and later, so the aperitif was more important than the digestif. "Perhaps it was the nerve-strain of the war which led to a great increase in the consumption of spirits and the general desire to put away not one but several drinks before dinner; or it may have been that the fashionable hour for dining had been growing later and later," wrote the novelist Dennis Wheatley.[198]

Perhaps the epitome of the genteel female gin drinker was Lady Elizabeth Bowes-Lyon, daughter of the Earl of Strathmore. She spent the war itself mostly at the family home, Glamis Castle in Scotland, which had been commandeered as convalescent unit for wounded servicemen and where Lady Bowes-Lyon herself as a teenager worked as a humble ward assistant. After the war, though, the 19-year-old headed south to the family's other stately home, St. Paul's Walden near Hertford, and its London house in Grosvenor Gardens, and hit town where she captured the hearts of her male peers. Although very far from the contemporary ideal of androgynous flapper she was, according to the historian Lucy Moore:

> ...enormously attractive, with what Evelyn Waugh described as "creamy English charm" — milky skin, sparkling blue eyes, gentle curves — and what one of her biographers calls an "innocent sensuality"... When she announced her engagement to the Duke of York in January 1923, the diarist Henry "Chips" Channon said: "The clubs are in gloom."[199]

Perhaps it was the Duke of York — George V's second son Prince Albert, later George VI — who introduced her to gin. As a naval sub-lieutenant aboard the battleship HMS Collingwood he was mentioned in dispatches for his conduct during the Battle of Jutland. He had joined the navy at the age of 14 and had grown up on harry pinkers; his wife — they married in 1923 — became a devotee of both gin and Dubonnet and martinis for the rest of her life. Adrian Tinniswood's *Behind the Throne: A Domestic History of the Royal Household* (Jonathan Cape, 2018) cites Margaret Rhodes, the Queen's niece and former lady of the bedchamber, as saying her habit of taking gin and Dubonnet before lunch, wine with the meal, a martini before dinner and then a glass of Champagne never varied. Her equerry in later life, Colin Burgess, said her routine could be rather more flexible than that, sometimes extending to a glass of port after lunch and two martinis before dinner, although he was careful to add: "Contrary to popular myth, her alcohol consumption was steady rather than excessive." (The Queen is also said to be partial to a gin and Dubonnet as an aperitif.) As a young married couple the Yorks were frequently called upon to entertain official visitors as well as family friends at 145 Piccadilly, their cavernous 25-bedroom, five-story London mansion overlooking Green Park. And although it seems impossible to discover exactly when it was first coined, the expression "drinkie-poos" — a babified euphemism both for pre-prandial sharpeners and informal drinks parties, preferred by the royals to the Americanism "cocktail"[200] — sums up a common pattern of socializing among the middle and upper classes in the interwar years.

In the 1920s and 1930s the middle classes, especially the urban middle classes, pretty much eschewed pubs. There were important exceptions: historic coaching inns (especially those with the acumen to have equipped themselves with petrol pumps) and quaint country pubs became popular resorts in the dawning automobile age, while newly built Tudorbethan roadhouses (again, especially those with petrol pumps) were necessary conveniences. But whole swathes of suburbs were built almost entirely without pubs. Metroland in North-west London has a handful, mainly roadhouses, but at nothing like the concentration found in the London suburbs built only a couple of generations earlier. Alwoodley, a suburb of north Leeds, was built in the late 1920s and early 1930s with four golf courses and a rugby club but only got a pub when a retail development including a giant Sainsbury was added in the early 1980s. The same pattern is to be found in the interwar suburbs of cities all over Britain: even the "improved" pubs built to attract a much wider clientele never really got off the ground. So where did the middle classes choose to congregate?

Among the provincial and suburban bourgeoisie sports club bars, especially tennis and golf clubs where the hoi-polloi was not welcome, were the watering-holes most favored by the likes of Miss Joan Hunter-Dunn and her ardent Subaltern suitor, with lime-juice and gin their preferred livener before setting off for the golf club dance.[201] Most towns also had a principal hotel (in many cases a coaching inn built or rebuilt in grand style just as the coaching age was drawing to a close, or a hydro left behind by scientific medicine) which had been eking out a living on the strength of a trickle of room lets, a reasonable dining-room favored by Rotarians, Lions and Freemasons, and possession of the only ballroom for miles around. Here the old coffee-room might find a new lease of life as a *soi-disant* cocktail bar, manned by a superannuated ostler with a shaky grip on a handful of recipes, striving to bring the sophistication of the Savoy[202] to Sudbury or Sunderland or Stafford.

These provincial efforts mimicked, or tried to, a West End that was becoming increasingly cosmopolitan and that was staying up later and later. From the mid-19th century onwards London's huge wealth and political stability attracted ambitious Europeans, many of them — then as now — chefs and restaurateurs. The Café Royal in Regent Street opened in 1863; Stucchi's in Rupert Street two years after that; Kettner's in Romilly Street two years after Stucchi's. The kitchens of the grandest hotels hired the finest French chefs — Adolphe Dugléré, the inventor of the tornedos rossini; Brillat-Savarin himself; Napoleon III's personal chef Pierre LeComte. Alexis Soyer cooked at the Reform Club for 13 years. The food and wine at the great hotels was of the highest quality and the highest price too, because traditionally the bedrooms were no more than self-financing while the profit came from the kitchen and the cellar.[203] There was intense pressure to make the bars and restaurants ever more attractive in order to pay for the huge capital investment poured into building and equipping the hotels on a scale lavish enough to compete; there was, fortunately, a complementary demand from guests for after-theatre dinners and early hours dancing and cabaret; hence, in the last years of the 19th century, the night-club was born.

Demand soon outstripped supply, however; and the great hotels had priced their lobster, Champagne, and cocktails well beyond the wallets of ordinary mortals. In the decade before the First World War, therefore, according to the novelist and social commentator Thomas Burke,[204] a new kind of night-club started appearing in London, smaller, more intimate, and less expensive than the grander institutions.

> The first of these was started by Mme. Strindberg and Austin Harrison, who was then editing the *English Review*. It was in Heddon Street, and was named the Cave of the Golden Calf. It was intended as a conversation club, with a little occasional entertainment, a chanteur or a diseuse, on the lines of Le Chat Noir. It opened after the theatre, and was a place to which one could go after closing time at the Café Royal. For a time it was the fashion. Some of the young found a new excitement in having breakfast at four in the morning… in an atmosphere of moderns and intellectuals and futurism.
>
> Then came more elaborate and more expensive places. Murray's was, I believe, the first of them. Later came the Embassy and a number of others;

> and the night-club, which earlier had been a rather furtive, limited, masculine affair, became generally the vogue. In the form of a smart supper and dancing club, it was a pleasure which the most respectable could enjoy. Much later, a swarm of little two-room places in West End cellars made the term night-club again synonymous with the furtive and disreputable. Through the last war, and through the years between that war and this, those small obscure places grew in number and variety. They were not, of course, real clubs like the smart places. They had no committee, no formal election, no scrutiny of candidates' social qualifications. Their prices were high, and they offered little comfort or amenity. Most of them were just places for drinking after hours. A few of them gave some sort of entertainment in the way of singers, and a dance floor, and a crashing and howling band, but they were too small to be comfortable.
>
> Almost every street in Soho had one or two, mostly in a basement, and almost every provincial town had one or two. They came and went like a bat. Closed in one place, they took a new name and opened in another.[205]

Burke's frankly censorious attitude is echoed by a vignette in his contemporary H.V. Morton's *The Nights of London* (Methuen 1926) in which an innocent young subaltern, home on leave, demands to be taken to his first night-club and meets an attractive "dance instructress" — one of the "new professions," as Morton euphemistically explains. After some dancing and a few drinks the young man suddenly realizes that his companion's father is an old friend of the family and storms out in dismay that she should have "gone bad" in "these filthy night-clubs." Morton infers that the girl's problem is more likely to be narcotics than cocktails[206]; but gin had not yet quite lost its old bad name. It's the snare from which Charlie Allnut (*The African Queen*, C.S. Forester, 1941) and Captain Anson (*Ice Cold In Alex*, Christopher Landon, 1957) have to be redeemed before they can rise to the challenge of their odysseys; it's the sweet temptation that undermines traditional values in the officers' mess in Joan Wyndham's World War II memoir *Love Is Blue* (1986), along with Benzedrine, crème de menthe, rum and Algerian wine.

Burke, the tireless observer of London's social life, also witnessed the genesis of the cocktail party, the bourgeois equivalent of the royal "drinkie-poos." Their invention is variously attributed to the artist CRW Newison in 1924, the author Alec Waugh in 1925, an American socialite called Mme. Alfredo de Peña, and a group of American Oxford undergraduates,[207] all seeking a cheap and easy way to entertain informally at home. Burke, who could be very scathing about the Londoners he appraised, saw the "six o' clock cocktails and snacks" as the natural consequence of a dinner hour that had been getting later and later since the 1850s — itself the natural consequence of businesses and professions becoming more and more concentrated in city-center offices while the homes of the business and professional people employed in them receded ever further into the suburbs. But it seems that these at-homes were pretty sedate affairs — after all, everybody had work in the morning! How abstemious these affairs could be was explained by the author's father (1908–1985), a gin and French drinker who favored Booth's and Noilly, 50:50, with no ice. The classic gin and French was thus a good deal stronger than gin and tonic; but the remains of the set of mid-1930s engraved glasses he left on his death were tell a different story. The wine glasses were only 100 ml, the sherry glasses 50 ml, and the delicate little stemmed port or liqueur glasses 30 ml. The tall, narrow spirit glasses, true, were 150 ml to the brim, but this allowed space for both spirit and mixer. These Lilliputian measures were partly due to the parsimony of the times: table wine was expensive and you expected to get 10 glasses out of a 750 ml bottle; partly due to a strong bourgeois inhibition against public drunkenness; and partly due to the fact that ice cubes hadn't been invented. Slabs of ice from Norway had at one time been imported at a rate of 30–50,000 tons a year,[208] mainly destined for the catering trade and various food and drink processing industries; middle-class households had it delivered in blocks for their ice-boxes. From 1900 on a domestic ice-making industry supplanted the import trade, but the ice still came in unwieldy blocks not exactly tailored for dunking in a glass of gin. Domestic fridges with trays for ice-cubes came on the US market in the 1920s; but as late as 1950 only two per cent of British households had one. Unless, therefore, someone was prepared to detach a chunk from the slab with an icepick, then take dish-cloth and rolling pin to the chunk to produce a batch of crushed ice, cocktails in most households were taken at room temperature. Even in later years the author's father preferred his gin and French or Scotch and a splash without ice. If he found himself at a party or reception he would drink in the 1930s way: one short but very strong drink swallowed straight down to get himself up, and a second nursed and sipped at intervals to keep him there. In the former instance a block of ice would merely get in the way; in the latter it would melt and turn the drink into a feeble mush.

While respectable middle-class Brits were happy to take their gin at room temperature at golf club dances and cocktail parties, the working class had more or less given it up completely. *The Pub and the People* is a massive study of pubs and their customers in "Worktown" (actually the big Lancashire mill-town of Bolton) conducted by the anthropological survey group Mass Observation in 1938–1939 and published by Victor Gollancz in 1943. Its 150,000-odd words cover almost every conceivable aspect of the pub trade in a major northern industrial center; but the book scarcely mentions spirits and when it does, whiskey[209] clearly predominates over gin. Price was certainly one reason for the poor take-up of spirits generally: in a city where the average weekly wage was 32 shillings 5 pence and where the unemployment rate was more than 10% a measure of spirits — 1/5 gill, or 1 fl. oz. — cost 6 pence, a penny more than the ubiquitous pint of mild but carrying less alcohol. But there was more to it than that. Beer was still regarded as wholesome and nourishing, good for energy and for regulating the digestive system, whereas spirits might have been seen as efficacious specifics for digestive and respiratory ailments, but taken regularly they "do you no good," as one respondent put it. Women were occasionally treated to a gin and lime, but they usually preferred port (sweeter and 2 pence cheaper) or bottled stout, which was the same price but lasted longer. Dennis Wheatley's view of spirit-drinking during the first war notwithstanding, by the outbreak of the second it had pretty much crashed. A Commons committee on national debt and taxation reported in 1926 that in 1913 the poorest had drunk, on average, four bottles of spirits a year each and the most affluent 30; by 1923 the same figures were none at all and 12.[210] In 1935 a survey of alcohol production revealed that average consumption of spirits had fallen to slightly more than a bottle a head at a fifth of a gallon — not strictly comparable, but a solid indication of the slide. In 1938 Bolton more than half of the 300 pubs sold no spirits at all; licensees of many of the pubs that did sell spirits estimated that beer made up 90% of their sales or more; one reasonably upmarket city-center pub had in its cellar 9 1/2 barrels (i.e., 2,736 pints) of draught beer, nearly all of it mild; 200 bottles of stout; 10 bottles of whiskey; four each of gin and rum; eight of port; and nine of sherry.

While spirits sales were in sharp decline among working class drinkers, the pub trade was signally failing to recruit new consumers. Only 10% of frequent pub goers in Bolton were under 25. The pub was still a bastion of male adults, which held little attraction for the young. We have already seen how popular football was becoming before the war; in the interwar years it was joined by other more technically advanced sports such as mechanized greyhound racing, first seen in 1926 in Manchester, and speedway, first staged in 1927, also in Manchester. Rugby League, which broke away from Union in 1895, was becoming more and more popular, partly because it could seduce the best players away from amateur Union simply by paying them. But these sports were not too grave a challenge to pubs because until floodlighting was improved in the 1950s they could really only be played in daylight, and the compulsory afternoon closing introduced under the Defence of the Realm Act had never been revoked. A much more serious threat came from the cinema. In 1938, the year that Bolton was surveyed by Mass Observation, a young couple could spend an evening at the flicks for 10 pence each, share three pen'orth of chips on their way home, and still have a penny's change of two bob. More to the point they could be alone, unsupervised by their elders, in the cozy darkness of the fleapit for maybe three hours while enjoying, or more likely ignoring, the newsreel, the cartoon, the second feature, and finally the main event. They might have spent a little less at the pub — 6 pence for two port and lemons and 10 pence for two pints of mild — but the extra 5 pence bought them privacy, which in the crowded back-to-backs of Worktown was beyond price. Small wonder that there were 987 million cinema admissions in the UK that year![211] From our point of view, though, what matters is that when that young man turned 25 and decided to spend less time at home with that young woman and more down the pub with male relatives and workmates, he had never learned to drink spirits. Whiskey was a treat — to wet the baby's head with, perhaps, when he and his girl settled down? But gin was as alien to him as absinthe.

The Name's Smirnoff... Pyotr Smirnoff

The end of Prohibition found America with a much greater demand for gin than before and, for the time being at least, insufficient means of satisfying it. British distillers, though, having weathered the storms of war and depression, were ready, willing and able to step in.

There was, of course, some production capacity in the US, despite Prohibition. Six companies had obtained distilling licenses to allow them to maintain the necessary stocks of medicinal spirits: they were Brown-Forman, Glenmore, Frankfort Distilleries, Schenley, American Medicinal Spirits (which became National Distillers) and Stitzel-Weller. They, of course, could expect to profit most from repeal. But in the most entrepreneurial nation on the planet there were plenty of businesspeople positioning themselves to join the race as soon as Roosevelt fired the starting gun. From as early as 1926 companies were being formed and trademarks registered by would-be distillers who planned, in the main, to supply the USA's huge thirst for whiskey. As they couldn't actually start distilling, they contented themselves with reserving bonded stocks of Canadian and even Scottish and Irish malts (not enough, alas, to save the 118[212] Scottish malt distillers that were either mothballed or closed for good as a result of Prohibition, including every last one in Campbeltown) which they planned to blend with newly legal ethanol and as much genuine rye or bourbon as they could lay hands on to produce something not entirely unlike the mob-made whiskey substitutes.

The same ethanol could, of course, be used to manufacture the newly popular gin quickly, cheaply, and in unlimited quantities; and before long the country's liberated saloons and hotel bars were dispensing new and unfamiliar brands like Old Colony, Coronet, Gold Seal and, this being the jazz age, Rhythm to the world's most affluent clientele. But beyond America's borders British competitors were just as eager for the opportunity; and they had every advantage. During the 13 years when America's distillers slept the currency of their brands had expired, their plant had moldered, and their master blenders and sorcerer's apprentices had drifted away, taking their expertize with them. The upstarts had none of these assets, and precious little capital either. The British had it all — brands with prestige, oceans of spare capacity, regiments of technicians and salesmen, and all the capital in the world.

First off the mark was W&A Gilbey, which had for many years employed a sales agent named Charles Preston Douglas. Douglas had worked for the company in West Africa and the West Indies before marrying a Canadian and settling there, separated from the great forbidden sales territory of the United States by no more than an imaginary line. In 1931, with opposition to US Prohibition mounting, Douglas registered W&A Gilbey (Canada) and started planning a modest new distillery in Entobicoke, a suburb of Toronto conveniently placed for the US border at Buffalo and no more than a mile from the shore of Lake Ontario. Work on the three-acre site took not much more than a year and cost $64,000; the plant was ready by late summer 1933, a few months before Prohibition came to an end; the first spirit ran on 11th September.[213] In 1936 the plant was extended to import and distribute a portfolio including Harvey's sherries, French wines, and Italian vermouth, and to make Smirnoff vodka, Black Velvet, Very Best, Golden Velvet, Old Gold and Special Old Canadian whiskeys, Governor General rums, and several liqueurs; but for the first decade it turned out nothing but Gilbey's London Dry Gin.

Tanqueray Gordon was not far behind, opening its first US distillery at Linden, New Jersey, in 1934. Tanqueray of Bloomsbury and Gordon's had merged in 1898 to meet the challenge of declining spirits consumption in Britain by rationalization and by attacking export markets. Its brands were performing strongly, especially in America, until Prohibition spoiled the party. A surprising amount of both main brands — or at least, something that looked very like them — continued to be enjoyed in the states; nevertheless, in 1922 Tanqueray Gordon became the Distillers Company's first gin acquisition, although not its last.

The US was not the only target for the British distilling industry's global expansionists. Australia had a burgeoning distilling industry.[214] Brandy had been made since the mid 19th century not as a by-product of winemaking but to mop up a glut of table grapes, which make bad wine but good brandy. Rum had been made in Queensland for almost as long: Bundaberg, possibly Australia's most famous brand, was founded by a consortium of sugar-mill owners in 1888. But the Australians seem to have been happy with imported whiskey and gin until after the Great War, when large import tariffs were imposed across the board to protect domestic industries. These included an increase of 8 pence per proof gallon on imported spirits, which prompted the Distillers Company both to buy a controlling interest in Australia's only operating whiskey distiller, Federated Distillers of Port Melbourne, Victoria, and also to take a 51% stake in a new venture at Geelong a few miles along the coast. This latter, the Corio Distillery, opened in 1929 and was to become the biggest distillery in the Southern hemisphere, and while the first stocks of its Corio Special whiskey were maturing it was earning a crust by producing Burnett's White Satin under licence. In its first 25 years Corio produced 12 million proof gallons of whiskey and five million proof gallons of gin — half of Australia's entire gin consumption.[215] However its whiskies never gained a reputation for quality, and in 1989 the distillery was closed.

Gilbey's, which was also active in the Australian market, at first responded to the duty increase by exploiting a loophole and importing a high-strength version of its gin in bulk to be diluted and bottled in West Melbourne. Only in the 1930s did the company decide to build a new £50,000 distillery of its own at Moorabbin, a suburb of Melbourne. It opened in November 1937 and was substantially extended in 1960 to allow the centralization of all bottling and distribution on the one site. Gilbey's products by then included Australian whiskies, Jim Beam, Hennessy and Smirnoff as well as gin, but Moorabbin closed in 1985 when Grand Metropolitan, which had bought Gilbey's in 1972, moved its regional operations to New Zealand.

Seager Evans chose a different route to the world's markets, opening a gin distillery in Chile in 1929 and another in Brazil in 1934. At the time South American economies were developing strongly, and countries such as Brazil and Argentina were important trading partners for the UK with significant expat populations.[216] However Seager's main activities were in the Scotch industry, where it acquired a host of famous distilleries and built a good number of new ones too. This brought it to the attention of Schenley Industries, which duly snapped it up in 1956.

World War II, of course, brought an abrupt halt to the nascent corporate imperialism within the spirits industry, even if it was not quite as painful an interruption to business as usual as the previous conflict had been. There was, as before, no formal rationing except by price and availability. Successive duty increases meant that a bottle of spirits that had cost 12 shillings 6 pence in 1939 was well over £1 by 1945. Malting barley was not in short supply: the acreage of Britain's arable land under barley doubled in the first years of war to just under

2 1/2 million acres, but the allocation of malt to the distilling industry under the wartime Limitation of Supply Orders in 1940 was 30% of prewar levels; in 1942 it was cut by 10%; and in 1943 there was no allocation at all and distillers had to make do with the previous harvest's leftovers. The restriction on supply was compounded by bomb damage: the Plymouth gin distillery narrowly escaped during the blitz on the city of March 1941, but a number of London's historic distilleries, clustered in the industrial target areas of Clerkenwell and the East End, were hit and damaged. What little gin was produced mainly went either for export to the USA or to the armed forces; by the end of the war it was virtually unobtainable at home. At least the industry didn't have to fight its own politicians as it had done in WWI: they were all heavy drinkers themselves. Stalin was frequently incapacitated by vodka; Churchill probably didn't drink as much as he made out but was still alcohol-dependent by modern standards; and Roosevelt, although sober when on duty, went on some astonishing binges when the opportunity arose. Both Churchill and Roosevelt are said to have enjoyed mixing their own martinis, although Roosevelt's generally seem to have included far too much vermouth and Churchill's far too little.[217]

Once the dust of World War II had settled the corporate merry-go-round resumed and even intensified, but from being an expression of British imperialism it became a multinational game in which American, Japanese, French and other contenders joined enthusiastically. It would be tedious to recount even in outline the various episodes in this corporate Game of Thrones, especially as gin only forms a small part of it: as witness the demise of Seager Evans, above, dominance in the international whiskey market has generally been seen as the real prize in the saga of takeover, merger and discard of the last half-century. But it's instructive to look at a few snapshots just to get an idea of the scale and impact of the continual change in ownership and provenance of brands. Of the six "medicinal" distillers of the Prohibition era, for instance, only one — Brown

Forman of Louisville, Kentucky, proprietor of Jack Daniels and Southern Comfort — remains independent, although heavily reliant on Bacardi for distribution in many international markets. Glenmore, Stitzel-Weller and Schenley itself have all fallen into the hands of Diageo, itself the amalgam of a tectonic series of mergers and takeovers going all the way back to the Distillers Company buyout of Tanqueray-Gordon sometime in the Pleistocene. Frankfort was bought by Seagram soon after Repeal; and finally National Distillers which had bought up all the remaining pre-Prohibition stocks of maturing whiskey and was perhaps best-known for Old Grand Dad, survived as an independent concern until 1987 when it was bought out by Jim Beam, now a subsidiary of Suntory. Gilbey's itself disappeared in a grand corporate avalanche: in 1962 it sought to increase its power and presence in both domestic and foreign markets by merging with United Wine Traders, proprietor of J&B Rare, and thus establishing a cross-category portfolio of strong brands in a company with deep pockets and a broad presence. Not quite strong or deep or broad enough, though: 10 years later it fell victim to an even bigger player, the London brewer Watney Mann. Then only six months after that, following a ferocious battle that made headlines well beyond the business pages, hotel and catering giant Grand Metropolitan took over Watney Mann to create a lumbering behemoth that for many years fought for dominance with the likes of Allied Breweries, also owner of many leading wines and spirits brands; Guinness with its combined Bell's/Distillers Company spirits portfolio; and Whitbread, whose Long John International spirits arms was actually based on the former Seagar Evans portfolio that was bought by Schenley in 1956, acquired by Whitbread in 1975, sold on to Allied in 1994, and finally (so far) picked up by Pernod Ricard in 2005. By the late 1980s the misbehavior of Britain's biggest breweries had invited the attention of the competition authorities, and while that's a story for another day the upshot was that all of them disintegrated, including

Grand Metropolitan. IDV was sold to Guinness in 1997, forming Diageo.

That story alone should be enough to excuse the author's decision not to go into greater detail: the wholesale corporate meltdowns of the 1980s and 1990s were bewildering enough then and have become no less so with the passage of time. A clear narrative is not nearly as important as the impact the whole impenetrable muddle had on the object of our study.

Gin, as has been pointed out, has almost always played second fiddle to whiskey anyway; and in post-war Britain and North America it was facing new competition, which devalued it further in the eyes of the finance departments of its increasingly distant parent companies. The most striking difference between the companies that plunged into the takeover maelstrom early in the 20th century and those that emerged at its end was that the latter were more likely to operate in a single category and often only ran one or two brands, perhaps with closely linked extensions, whereas the millennial giants and their immediate precursors generally had numerous brands in numerous categories. The former, with only one revenue stream to depend on, would fight with real passion to defend and extend it. For the latter, the challenge was to rationalize their sprawling portfolios and select drivers to focus their marketing and promotional efforts on. It's all part of the natural business cycle: small businesses grow by expanding sales, taking on more staff, opening new sites; big businesses grow by acquiring weaker rivals, cannibalizing their sales, laying off staff and closing sites. In the case of gin, the weaker brands in the big conglomerates' portfolios found themselves facing competition not just from their stronger stable mates but also from entirely new categories, namely vodka and white rum, often under the same ownership or distributorship — for example Gilbey's, as we have seen, acquiring the right to produce and distribute Smirnoff in most of the world's biggest markets. From the moment in *Dr. No* (1962) when James Bond asked for a dry vodka martini (it was Dr. No himself who added the "shaken not stirred" rider), gin sales were in trouble.

Truth to tell, gin was already being painted further and further into its unfashionably bourgeois corner when Bond — the Bond of the cinema, that is — turned up to compound its misery by presenting an exotic and exciting alternative. Ironically, in the very first of the 12 Fleming-authored novels, *Casino Royale* (1953), Bond orders not just a gin but a particular brand:

> "A dry martini," he said. "One. In a deep Champagne goblet."
>
> "Oui, monsieur."
>
> "Just a moment. Three measures of Gordon's, one of vodka, half a measure of Kina Lillet. Shake it very well until it's ice-cold, then add a large thin slice of lemon peel. Got it?"
>
> "Certainly monsieur." The barman seemed pleased with the idea.
>
> "Gosh, that's certainly a drink," said Leiter.

And in truth, the Bond of the books is the very type who was to give gin a bad name: educated at a minor public school and conscious of not being quite top-drawer, smoked custom-made cigarettes but was otherwise a brand snob and shameless status-signaler — in short, the bourgeois par excellence only made interesting by being a sex-addicted narcissistic psychopath. In the books he drinks (in order of frequency) Champagne; Scotch or bourbon with or without soda; and only then martinis, sometimes unspecified but with vodka and gin variants named in almost equal number. Other cocktails are mentioned occasionally, as are other wines, but beer comes up only once, in the form of black velvet ordered at Scott's to accompany oysters. He could almost be one of the 100,000-odd[218] gin-swilling post-independence returnees from India, doubtless good news for the bar stewards at the 19th holes they (like Bond himself in 1959's *Goldfinger*) preferred to frequent, but antediluvian relics as far as their host communities were concerned. It was they, though, who chiefly popularized tonic water, and by the 1990s 57% of the gin consumed in Britain was drunk with it.[219] The Bond of the films, however, was a very different kettle of cultural fish: the Bond of the films drives an Aston Martin with ejector seat, machine guns and rocket launchers; the Bond of the novels drives a Bentley. *Moonraker* the movie is set in California, Rio, Venice, the Amazon rainforest and outer space. *Moonraker* the novel is set in Kent. To make matters worse, just as the movie Bond was promoting vodka at gin's expense, Jaguar launched its Mark II. And with it came the gin and Jag belt.

> The expression "gin and Jag" probably stems from the 1960s when the Jaguar marque, having struggled through the previous decade, had a great success with its Mark II model. This Jag, with its wire wheels, walnut dashboard and deep leather seats, was executive plush. Earlier Jaguar sports cars had been rare beasts, owned by the likes of Clark Gable. Now, with the Mark II, senior managers could aspire easily to a gleaming roadster in which to roar out to the country pubs around Egham and Epsom, Marlow and Maidenhead, there to sink gin and ignore the loose drink-driving laws of the day.[220]

With teenage rebellion breaking out all around, this denunciation of bourgeois culture was as final a condemnation among the young as the verdict of any witch-trial. Mods and rockers, flower-children, Angry Young Men and all the multifarious manifestations of youth culture, were united despite all their apparent conflicts by one thing: their mums and dads may have been gin-drinkers, but they most definitely weren't. That James Bond had ordered vodka did not in itself, of course, make converts of all these disparate tribes and cults; but it did make a market for an entirely new, cosmopolitan, and female-friendly alternative that was big enough to be worth exploiting. A single gin, sweetened with a shot of orange squash and dashingly garnished with a plastic épée piercing a single cocktail cherry was not an uncommon offering from boyfriend to girlfriend on a Friday or a Saturday night; somehow substituting vodka for gin made it a little less sad and, of course, a little less spirity, a little blander, a little easier to swallow without coughing. A vodka and orange or, even better, a Bacardi and Coke (no slice of lime yet — this is, after all, the 1960s) with a sad little berg bobbing forlornly as it melted became the *dernier cri* of sophistication in public bars and workingmens' clubs up and down the UK; and to gladden the hearts of the drinks industry's accountants the usual ABV of both vodka and white rum was 37.5% which, given the quantities involved, added up to a vast saving in duty.

To add to the pressure, there were other competitors for gin's female market. The 1950s and 1960s were the golden age of "babies" — Moussec, Pony, Cherry B, premixed snowballs and, of course, Babycham — all sweet and sparkly in their four-ounce single-serve bottles. They came mostly from the cider and British[221] wine industries and were hugely popular, particularly in the on-trade. Like bottled sweet stout or port and lemon in the 1930s, they were usually treat drinks bought by men for their wives and girlfriends and, it might be argued, created a particular pattern of social drinking that led to wine coolers, alcopops, RTDs, and fruit-flavored cider. Perhaps more seriously for gin distillers was the abolition in 1966 of price controls on alcohol, which came during a 25-year period when duties on table wines were progressively reduced and at a time when supermarkets, starting with Sainsbury in 1962, started applying for liquor licenses as a regular feature of their stores.[222] Home consumption of wine shot up as prices fell and choice and availability mushroomed: in 1960 average annual wine consumption was 3.6 gallons; in 1990 it was 27 1/2 gallons; and it's been growing ever since. At first the demographic behind the growth of wine sales was women shopping for the family dining-table, a new departure for most British households, and as home entertainment and dining out began to outpace the pub trade, for informal drinking in front of a video or with dinner in a restaurant.

The inevitable upshot of the double whammy of concentration of ownership in a contracting market was fewer and fewer owners putting less and less effort behind fewer and fewer brands; and as a result of that, once-familiar brands dwindled and disappeared. To compound matters, the establishment of the supermarket's dominance over the take-home liquor trade meant that less and less variety was presented to the public. Supermarkets could not carry as many facings as specialist wine-merchants and off-license chains, and their cut-throat pricing was too much for many drinks companies to endure; and labels that had once seemed ubiquitous became harder to find: Lemon Hart rum; Haig, White Horse, Black & White, 100 Pipers, Dewar's, VAT 69 and even Teacher's whiskies; and Burnett's, Booth's, Nicholson's, Seagar's and Gilbey's gins. Some were simply priced off the shelves of the major retailers; others were designated as export brands; others were restricted to regional distribution; others were withdrawn altogether. Concentration of pub ownership through brewery takeovers had a similar effect. The number of tied estates contracted while the size of each estate expanded, and as each estate tended to stock its own range of spirits; so the on-trade market polarized into a handful of national brands and an even smaller handful of top-shelf brands.

The effect of all this on the consumer was underestimated in the boardroom. The various takeovers and mergers were undertaken in the name of returning value to investors; the fate of each particular brand was determined in the same spirit. But the bond between consumer and brand is one of love, or something very like it. The corporation behind the brand is invisible and unknown unless, as in the case of some breweries, it has a strong and benign local personality. But when, for instance, a merger such as the creation of IDV in 1962 results in one of the protagonists abandoning its century-old distillery in Camden Town and moving to Harlow new town in Essex[223]; or when after various changes of ownership production of Gordon's, the leading brand, originally a true Londoner from Clerkenwell, is settled in Scotland after a 14-year interlude at a purpose-built ultramodern distillery in Laindon, Essex, the consumer loses that vital sense of connection. The recipe will have been unaltered; the matching process may have been scrupulous; the product itself may be indistinguishable from its old self. But — and this is perhaps more true of beer than of gin — any notion that the relationship between fan and brand is a two-way street, a partnership, will have been sacrificed. The love is succeeded by a grudging acceptance. It's a phenomenon the author has observed time after time in 13 years of working for the Campaign for Real Ale, where production transfers are generally — and usually rightly — seen as a sign that the brewer has lost faith either in the brand, or its home brewery, or both. And if the brewer has no faith, why should the consumer? The own-label is indistinguishable and a good deal cheaper, and if the brand has thrown away its cachet, why not opt for the own-label?

Grudging acceptance turned to cynicism in 1992 when Gordon's, having valiantly maintained its ABV at 40% after 30 years of being undercut, reluctantly stepped down to 37.5% in line with its competitors. A temporary wobble at the revered Plymouth gin shortly after, when the strength was cut from 41.2% to 37.5% and (or so it was said) molasses was used instead of malt to make the base spirit (both expedients very soon reversed) prompted more cynicism, and it was even rumored (although never substantiated) that the traditional botanical grist had had its proportion of orris root reduced to lighten the flavor.

This sort of negativity contrasted with activity in the vodka market, where in the 1980s importers had read the runes of big hair and shoulder pads correctly. British distillers had been somewhat dubious about responding to Smirnoff in the 1960s and 1970s. Gordon's itself briefly introduced a vodka in the late 1960s but seems to have withdrawn it again as soon as decency permitted; it's still made and widely distributed in the US, though, where it's regarded as one of the more acceptable bottom-shelf brands. The challenger from the Warrington distiller and brewer Greenall Whitley, marketed with its characteristic tongue-in-cheek cheeriness, was more successful. Greenalls already had its own house lager, wittily entitled "Grünhalle," one of whose slogans was "have you been grabbed by the Grünhalles?"; and although it has been suggested that Grünhalle wasn't just keg pale ale served very cold but was actually bottom-fermented and even contained some genuine lager malt, nobody who has tried it will believe it. Greenall's Vladivar vodka, launched in 1971, was promoted in like vein as "the vodka from Varrington," which was an interesting inversion: first you give your brand a cod-Russian name like Borzoi, Cossack or Romanoff; then in your advertising you tell everybody you're faking it and isn't really Russian at all. As a shared joke, though, it worked. Vladivar is with us still whereas Borzoi, Cossack and Romanoff are all long-forgotten. (They really existed, by the way.)

In the 1980s, though, vodka got serious. In the age of Thatcherism, the Big Bang, red braces, barrow-boys, yuppies, Sloane rangers and all the other social atrocities of the time expensive imports — the more expensive and imported the better — were an integral component of vulgar display. Weird cloudy Hoegaarden at twice the price of everyday beers; Stella Artois, the wifebeater, at its full 5.2% ABV and "reassuringly expensive" (although — shh! — actually brewed in South Wales); and of course cataracts of Champagne all flowed across the counters of City wine bars, and with them came the first wave of genuine imported vodkas. Stolichnaya from the Soviet Union itself; Absolut from Sweden; Zubrowka and Wyborowa from Poland; Finlandia from... well, Finland — these were brands with provenance, authenticity, character, freshness, life!

And it wasn't just vodka that challenged gin's place as the most popular white spirit in the west: white rum — well, Bacardi, which like Guinness is effectively the sole representative of its category — was being heavily promoted too. These brands had not been shaken and stirred by amalgamation, takeover, relocation, production under license, regional designation, local listing, delisting and other devices and stratagems into a thick, opaque, corporate soup from which nothing stood out. They were not to be taken for granted.

Gin had never been further from the forefront of the action

Return of the Alchemists

If, through takeover, rationalization, and the inexorable devaluing of brands, Britain's gin distillers had got themselves into the soup, it was up to them to get themselves out. And they tried — or at least, some of them did; and not surprisingly it was the smaller of them, those with most to lose, who were first to try their hands at turning things round.

It started in 1987, when IDV found itself with a problem brand that needed more than merely cosmetic surgery. Bombay Dry was actually Greenall's Dry repackaged by an American entrepreneur for the US market back in 1960, when for millions of white-collar workers the day's labors still ended with a dry martini and the dry martini was still based on gin. By the early 1980s gin was being squeezed not only by vodka and white rum, as we have seen, but also by a new enemy — physical fitness. Jogging as a form of recreation rather than serious athletic training began in the early 1960s but only went mainstream in the late 1970s thanks to celebrity endorsement, sportswear branding and promotion and, not least, rising heart disease figures. As VHS won its battle with Betamax in the mid-80s, exercise videos such as Jane Fonda's Aerobics (1982) invaded homes all over the western world and for many, a brisk workout replaced a stiff martini as the preferred means of relaxation. As so often happens in a squeeze, the leading brands, Tanqueray and Beefeater, could take the hit; further down the ladder the overall market decline posed an existential threat.

Faced with gentle decline as the only possible future for a brand that was just another London dry gin in town, IDV decided on a radical overhaul. A new name, a new bottle (blue, like the name), a new botanical grist with cubeb and grains of paradise included, and a new rectification regime using Carterhead stills all created a radically different gin: softer, richer, rounder, and fatter than London dry, and the first of a new generation of superbrands.[224] Bombay Sapphire didn't set the world alight from the word go; but then superbrands don't need to sell huge volumes to make solid profits — that is, after all, the whole point of superbrands. It changed hands very quickly in the continuing corporate shuffle, first when IDV was sold to United Distillers to become Diageo in 1997 and then to Bacardi in 1998 when Diageo had to divest to satisfy the competition authorities. Bacardi recognized the brand's potential and gave it more prominence,[225] especially in America, just in time for the emergence of two more superbrands: Tanqueray 10 from Diageo and Hendrick's from Glenfiddich distiller William Grant, both launched in 2000. Both echoed Bombay Sapphire in selecting botanicals that were less juniper-led and, it has to be said, more feminine than the leading brands: gin had traditionally been slewed towards women, as we have seen, with darker spirits being regarded as more assertively masculine. Perhaps the designers of the new brands were trying to push the category further in the traditional direction with flavors that had a much broader appeal, especially to novice drinkers. It's interesting but perhaps coincidental that Hendrick's was actually formulated by a woman, Lesley Gracey, a highly respected chemist whose previous job had been as a flavor analyst working on William Grant's Glenfiddich and Balvenie single malts. The new gin was a blend of spirits rectified on two old stills that the doyen of the company, Charles Gordon, had picked up at auction in 1960, a 1948 Carterhead and a small pot still from the 1860s. The two produced very different results which, once blended, were dosed with essences of cucumber and roses and packaged in distinctive brown-glass flasks. (It's not too cynical to note that upmarket packaging is a vital ingredient in the consumer's perception of value: the Bombay Sapphire bottle, as we have observed, is a brilliant blue, while Tanqueray 10 comes in a stylized version of the brand's green cocktail-shaker pattern).

It could hardly be said that these three brands led a charge into the US superpremium market: in the first few years sales hovered steadily around $10 million and 50 million cases.[226] But for the British distillers who made them, they were good high-margin performers with potential for growth — potential that was also spotted, completely independently, by two imaginative entrepreneurs who decided to launch superpremium export brands of their own. In 2005 Johnny Neill, a direct descendant of the Greenall distilling dynasty, launched Whitley Neill, which included in its botanicals baobab fruit and physallis from his wife's native South Africa and which was made under contract. The following year Anshuman Vohra, a City financier, launched Bulldog, made by G&J in Warrington and initially sold only in New York before being rolled out to the world. In 2007 G&J itself, perhaps inspired by Lesley Gracie and Hendrick's, came out with Bloom, created by Britain's only female master distiller, Joanna Moore, and infused with camomile, honeysuckle and pomelo.

If these initiatives from mainstream distillers and established businesspeople seem to have left the artisan distillers behind somewhat, they weren't slow to catch up. Perhaps surprisingly, gin had not been a large part of the artisan distilling mix on either side of the Atlantic, where the initial excitement had been about speciality spirits. In California, Jörg Rupf, a lawyer from the Black Forest in Germany, bought himself a small still and in 1982 set up St. George's Spirits to produce the fruit *eaux-de-vie* he was used to back home. It was a similar story in Britain, where the King Offa Distillery was established at the Hereford Cider Museum to make cider brandy, in 1984.

It proved short-lived, but the second craft distillery to be founded in the UK — Somerset Royal in 1989 — also made and indeed makes cider brandy and has proved enduring and iconic. But most of the earliest craft distillers on both sides of the Atlantic and in Australia too concentrated very much on whiskey. Fritz Maytag, owner of the Anchor Brewery in San Francisco, start distilling rye whiskey in 1993, adding Junipero Gin in 1997; but Britain had to wait until 2008 — well after the appearance of whiskey distillers Speyside (1990), Isle of Arran (1995), Penderyn (2000), Kilchoman (2004) and St. George's (2006) — for its first artisan gin. This was produced by Worcestershire potato-grower William Chase, who had already built a successful brand of crisps and sold it for a fortune. Mashing and distilling his potatoes would be more entertaining and more rewarding than frying them, he decided; soon afterwards he made more headlines by turning cider into gin too.

But the bigger headlines went to two microdistilleries that opened in London in 2009. Perhaps the fuss was because Sipsmith and Sacred Spirits were making new-wave gin in London, its spiritual home (and entirely coincidentally the media's back yard). Sipsmith was started by two drinks industry executives, Fairfax Hall and Sam Galsworthy, who had been friends since childhood, and an experienced American distiller, Jared Brown. Hall and Galsworthy had been working in America and were impressed by what they saw: "While we were there we saw lots of microdistilleries popping up," Galsworthy said in an interview with *Daily Telegraph* in November 2015. "We thought, why isn't this happening anywhere in London?" An appeal to tradition was an important part of Sipsmith's appeal: its recipes were based on 18th-century originals, and the German 300-liter (or 66-gallon) rectifying still the partners installed[227] was copper — the first such in London since 1820, they claimed, and they're probably right: by 1820 small independent rectifiers had almost died out, and the last surviving small pots such as this were not being installed but carted away for smelting.[228] From this small start, in the hands of experienced professionals who knew what they were doing, Sipsmith grew and grew until December 2016, when it was bought by Beam Suntory for £50 million.

The second of the two new London gin distillers, Sacred Spirits, could hardly be more different. It was set up in an outhouse in Cambridge natural science graduate Ian Hart and his partner Hilary Whitney's back garden in Highgate, and there is not a scrap of copper to be seen because it's a vacuum still, custom-made of laboratory glass to Hart's own design. The great advantage of the method is that once the air is pumped out of the still and the pressure falls to zero, the ethanol will vaporize at 22° C — pretty much ambient. The botanicals, which at Sacred are steeped in spirit for up to six weeks beforehand, therefore don't cook as they do at the usual 78.3° C, and their raw flavors in the finished product are therefore much more intense and distinct. Sacred also steeps each ingredient separately, blending them only at the end of the process. Vacuum distillation has been taken up by newer gin distillers including Cambridge in England and Durham in the US.

The arrival of Sipsmith and Sacred marks the end, as far as this book is concerned, of the historical narrative. From now on it becomes reportage, and reporting the living story of events as they unfold is journalism, not history. It's always going to be a matter of subjective perception where to mark the spot or draw the line that has "history" on one side and "news" on the other — why end the medieval and define the start of the modern at Bosworth and not the fall of Byzantium or the Dissolution of the Monasteries? — but in this case the return of small-scale rectification to its historic city of origin is as good a point as any.

And the use of the word "rectification" is important here. A full 13 years before Jared Brown first fired up Constance the copper pot-still Charles Maxwell, eighth generation of the family that had once owned the recently defunct Finsbury Distillery, set up Thames Distillers in Clapham with, among his main investors, Christopher Hayman. Hayman is also a London distilling blueblood, the fifth generation of the Burroughs family that founded and owned Beefeater until it was bought by Whitbread in 1987. He was able to buy out the firm's bottling plant at Witham, Essex, and to establish a contract distillery there. Maxwell set up Thames with a similar idea in mind, and also had plans to launch a brand of his own to be called Old Chelsea. Thames's opening, though, coincided with the sudden rise of alcopops, the launch of Two Dogs carbonated lemon wine (really!) being swiftly followed by the much more successful Hooper's Hooch — not a wine, but a mixture of lemon concentrate, neutral spirit, carbonated water, and sugar. Its success prompted a sudden rush of imitators — 90 within a single year! — and a consequent shortage of spirit: one of Thames's first contracts was to supply the alcohol for the co-op's own-label alcopop.[229] At the same time the Langley Green contract distillery in Birmingham installed a 10,000-liter still, Jenny, to cope with the rush. The relevance of these developments to the nascent craft gin scene was that when it came along, there was plenty of expertly produced base spirit for the new alchemists to rectify — one of the many factors, as we shall see, that made the "ginaissance" possible at all.

One element that no one can really command and without which success is almost impossible is timing, and either by luck or by judgment Chase, Sipsmith and Spirit got their timing right. For a start, public taste right across the socio-economic board was veering in a direction that favored them: demand for lighter, fresher, and often fruitier flavors, more authentic, more innovative, or more just plain eccentric was growing fast. J20, often ordered by color rather than flavor, was launched in 1998 and the range evolved in garishness and weirdness over the following decade. Fever-Tree, the ultimate in premium soft drinks, formulated by ex-Plymouth boss Charles Rolls to do justice to gin, was launched in 2005. In 2001 the first Michelin stars were conferred on Indian restaurants, and while many traditionally minded proprietors remained stuck in the mud and suffered as a consequence others started presenting regional cuisines and lighter menus. Chinese restaurants gained a new reputation for healthy eating thanks to their vegetable dishes, their steamers and their woks (in 2001 65% of British households owned a wok). Thai restaurants, with their emphasis on fresh herbs, spices and vegetables, spread out of the big cities and into provincial high streets, often taking over underused pub kitchens. The fresh faces of British food were cheeky geezer Jamie Oliver, Hugh Fearnley-Whittingstall with his placenta pâté, and Heston Blumenthal, the snail porridge man. And in the very same year that Sipsmith and Sacred gins appeared, so did Kopparberg's first fruit-flavored cider. Craft beer with its fervent pursuit of flavor and near-obsessive focus on hops, especially the more aromatic varieties, had not quite arrived in 2009, but it was well on its way. Were its earliest exponents inspired in their olfactory excesses by the botanical debauchery of the first artisan gins? For one of the most powerful appeals of gin-making to the new artisans has been the opportunity to experiment with all sorts of botanicals until the juniper which, by law in both Europe and the US, should predominate has rather faded into the background.

Apart from juniper, that bush so commonly known, the distiller's botanical palette has traditionally been fairly limited, with the final flavor of the gin determined both by the balance of ingredients and the method of extraction. Compounders will usually simply steep their grists in spirit, often warmed, for as long as they see fit and then add the resulting liquor to their base, or even use a blend of oils. Rectifiers sometimes, like compounders, steep their grists in warm spirit and add them to the base ethanol which they then redistill; alternatively they put their grists in baskets which are then hung in a chamber in the neck of the rectifying still — the Carter head — for their aromatics to be gently released into the rising vapor. Subtle alterations in the process can have quite marked effects on the intensity of the outcome. Apart from juniper itself the range of botanicals has generally included coriander seed, angelica root, orange and lemon peel, dried orris (or iris) root, cardamom, cinnamon or cassia bark, and licorice root. Over the centuries many other herbs, fruits and flowers have also been called into service from time to time — aniseed-type flavorings such as star anise, wormwood and caraway prominent among them but also the various mints, thyme, rosemary, basil, sage and other table herbs, and saps and resins including birch and the wrongly maligned pine. In the last decade, though, the range has been limited only by imagination and experiment. Baobab fruit we have already met, in Whitley Neill, and cucumber and rose petals in G&J's Bloom; but these are tame by comparison with some of the exotics that have found their way into the world's little copper pots. Anything and everything is fair game to the gin distiller. The peel of distinctive citrus varieties is a favorite, naturally; not just common-or-garden orange, lemon and lime but also bitter orange, mandarin orange, grapefruit, pomelo, bergamot, kuzu, calamansi and kaffir lime (normally its leaves rather than its peel). Then there's almond, apricot kernel, black pepper, blue butterfly pea, bog myrtle, buchu, chocolate, clove, clover, coconut, dandelion leaves, dragon eye, elderflower, galangal, ginseng, hibiscus, honeysuckle, hops, kampot pepper, lavender, lotus leaf, nettles, nutmeg, oak chips, olives, pomegranate, poppy leaf, quince, raspberry, rhubarb, rose root, rowanberry, saffron, savory, seaweed, shamrock, spruce tips, tarragon, tea, thyme, truffles, vanilla… oh, and ants. And fresh forest elephant dung. And — well, the list was out of date before it was even typed. Artisan distillers are like craft brewers in at least this respect: they are pragmatic and at the same time playful. They have no regard for tradition but will gleefully batten on any old aromatic that chances across their paths and if it works, they'll use it.

In the pursuit of flavor, the artisan gin distiller has one great advantage over the craft brewer. The matrix, the stock, the medium in which the botanicals and aromatics are melted and mingled comes ready-made in a 25-liter tub or, if business is good, a 1,000-liter cubitainer. Most artisan distillers have to learn the disciplines of mashing and fermentation just as every brewer does. Indeed for many of them a fermented mash is the existential starting point. Whether you're Julian Temperley with his apples or Jason Barber with his whey, the process of creating cider brandy or unusually creamy vodka depends as much on the creation of a wash as on the distilling itself. Artisan gin distillers can and often do go through these preliminary processes themselves, and if you aim to make gin out of cider like Chase, or out of wine like Chilgrove, then you have to. But most choose not to. Not only do they prefer to buy in expertly made ethanol from an experienced and well-equipped contractor, but depending on their resources they might even choose to have their gin formulated, tested and produced by a contractor like (in Britain) Thames, Wharf, Hayman, Langley Green or G&J or (in the US) Midwest Grain Products of Kansas, Southern Distilling of North Carolina, or Citrus Distillers of Florida. They might, like Spencerfield Spirits in Scotland, start out with a contractor but take their brand in-house once it has proved itself to investors. The same journey has also been taken in the opposite direction — starting out on a small scale and then as the brand grows contracting it out rather than invest in extra capacity. This is a relationship that is often characterized as somehow dishonest, especially by farm-to-fork whiskey distillers who see the completeness of the process as integral to the brand's authenticity; and in the case of whiskey they might be right. But in the case of gin they are not. The best base spirit is the purest base spirit; any residual congeners or proteins or other materials that might provide a hint of its origin are debit points. A steady supply of top-quality base spirit that rectifiers can take for granted allows them to get on with the real work of… well, of rectifying. And it's perhaps worth remembering that while the Old Masters generally made their own paints, they didn't weave their own canvas as well.

The innovations of the last decade or so have certainly stirred the gin industry out of its somnolence. Once pigeonholed, gin is now flying free — and not just in Britain and North America: Spain, Germany and Belgium have all seen their gin booms, and the global brands have benefited vastly from innovation, promotion, imaginative extensions, and the general globalization of consumer taste. The artisan brands have surfed to success on a wave of flavor but also, in the UK at least, on the back of a generation of duty freezes that have boosted profit margins and allowed big returns on small sales. The fact that gin sells straight from the still has been responsible for the creation of a good few brands, too: while your cherished malt whiskey is still slumbering in its oaken incubator, making not a penny, your gin is out there hustling.

After its storm-tossed voyage from new phenomenon to scapegoat to drinkie-poo to speakeasy to Blimp's tipple, gin has arrived at an odd position: surging ahead hand-in-hand with hipsters and sophisticates, regularly turning in double-digit annual sales growths, with new breeders and brands proliferating wherever you look. And yet it's still a tiny minority drink with a share of only 11% of Britain's spirits market and 5% of America's,[230] and already it's being written off by the prophets and predictors in favor of a rum renaissance. So that's the end of the history of gin: the rest is futurology. But whether gin is really running out of steam or not, any category that could give us Shnoodlepip, created by Bristol's Wild Beer Co. by deconstructing the elements of the eponymous beer — a sour saison brewed with pink peppercorns, hibiscus, and passion fruit and aged in red wine barrels — then reconstituting them as gin will surely never be anything less than magic.

Alchemy, in fact.

APPENDIX

Further reading

Barr, Andrew, *Drink: A Social History*, Pimlico, 1995

Blue, Anthony Dias, *The Complete Book of Spirits*, Harper Collins, 2004

Brander, Michael, *The Georgian Gentleman*, Saxon House, 1973.

Burnett, John, *Liquid Pleasures: A Social History of Drink in Britain*, Routledge 1999

Clark, Peter, *The English Alehouse* 1200–1830, Longman 1983; *The Mother Gin Controversy in the early Eighteenth Century*, Transactions of the Royal Historical Society, 1988

Cornell, Martyn, *Beer: The Story Of The Pint*, Headline, 2003

Dillon, Patrick, *The Much-Lamented Death of Madame Geneva*, Review, 2002

George, Dorothy, *London Life in the 18th Century*, Kegan Paul, 1925

Hornsey, Ian, *A History of Beer & Brewing*, Royal Society of Chemistry, 2003

Moore, Lucy, *The Thieves' Opera*, Viking, 1997

Pullar, Philippa, *Consuming Passions*, Hamish Hamilton, 1970

Rodger, N.A.M., *The Wooden World*, Collins, 1986

Tannahill, Reay, *Food in History*, Penguin, 1988

Unwin, Tim, *Wine & the Vine*, Routledge, 1991.

Van Schoonenberghe, Eric, "Genever: a Spirit Full of Story, Science, and Technology," *Journal of the Sarton Chair of the History of Science*, vol. 12, University of Ghent, 1999.

Warner, Jessica, *Craze: Gin and Debauchery in an Age of Reason*, Profile, 2002

Online resources

Only a generation ago it would have been impossible for anyone less elevated than a full-time academic with a salary, long vacations, and access to a well-stocked university library to tackle such a large subject as this. Today, while the salary and the leisure-time wouldn't come amiss, at least the library is available. For that's what the internet is, among many other things: you can play games on it, make friends on it, wage political war on it, furnish your house and fill your wardrobe from it, fill the gaps in your love-life on it, and you can also browse its theoretically infinite shelves of books, theses, papers, historic texts and even whole archives on it. In short, any researcher into any subject now has access to source material that would have been the stuff of dreams to an earlier generation. The one thing it doesn't have that a print library does is a catalogue. To search it efficiently you have to know at least what questions to ask it and how to frame them, so that it can understand what you don't know and produce the information you might not even have realized you needed. Either that or you need an index which, for any researcher into the whole field of alcoholic drink, is Difford's Guide. Founded in 2001 before most people even knew they needed it, www.diffordsguide.com is a truly, staggeringly vast compendium of drink-related information which includes, among so much else, an outline of the history of gin. It won't tell you everything you want to know, but it will alert you to what you don't know and thereby enable you to find out. Which is all you need and far more than you could, in the past, have expected.

Notes

1 Sailors, it was said, would at need boil seawater and catch the vapor in a sponge. Sheepskins could serve the same purpose.
2 On top of a spirit-lamp is set a large bowl, on top of that a smaller bowl, and on top of that an upside-down metal cone. Fermented wash is placed in the larger bowl and set to boil; the vapor rises around and above the second bowl, or spirit receiver; the ethanol fraction of the steam condenses on the cone, runs down it, and drips from its tip into the receiver.
3 The Greek poet and physician Nicander of Colophon (183–135 BCE) mentions rose oil, which can only be extracted by distillation, as an ingredient in snake-repellent. Glass alembics were known and even drawn from his time onwards, but never apparently with a condenser that could separate alcohol.
4 Andre Simon, "The Art of Distillation." Lecture delivered at Vintners' Hall by the Wine Trade Club, 1912.
5 Barnard, Alfred, *The Whisky Distilleries of the United Kingdom*, 1887.
6 Smith, George, *The Compleat Body of Distilling.*
7 Morewood, Samuel, *Inebriating Liquors,* Dublin 1838.
8 In France and Spain de Villeneuve (1240–1311) is popularly credited with the introduction of distilling. By de Villeneuve's day, though, Andalucia had been almost entirely reconquered, and its science was freely available to Christian Spaniards.
9 al-Hassan, Ahmad, *The History of Science & Technology in Islam*, UNESCO 2017.
10 The salt acts as a separating agent by increasing the volatility of the mixture and breaking any azeotropes that might form.
11 *The Book of Turning Potential into Action*
12 *The Book of the Chemistry of Perfume & Distillations*
13 al-Hassan *op. cit.*
14 al-Hassan, *op. cit.*
15 Paul Strathern: *Mendeleyev's Dream*, Crux Publishing 2018.
16 *De Aquae Ardentae*, by Magister Salernus.
17 Peter Mulryan, *Bushmills: 400 Years in the Making*, Appletree Press 2008.
18 Not, presumably, meaning a water-clock in this case but only its outflow pipe, the "thief of water."
19 *On the Early Use of Aqua Vitae in Ireland*, Ulster Journal of Archaeology vol. vi, 1858.
20 Anthony Dias Blue, *The Complete Book of Spirits*, Harper Collins 2004.
21 Christian, David & Deborah, *Living Water: Vodka & Russian Society on the Eve of Emancipation,* Clarendon Press 1990.
22 Simon *op. cit.*
23 Anthony Dias Blue *op. cit.*
Gilbertus Anglicus was one of the great medical writers of the time, and still well-enough known

more than a century later to be included by Chaucer in the company of the all-time greats:
"Wel knew he the olde Esculapius
And Deyscorides and eek Rufus,
Olde Ypocras, Haly and Galyen,
Serapion, Razis and Avycen,
Averrois, Damascien and Constantyn,Bernard and Gatesden and Gilbertyn." (*Canterbury Tales, The Prologue.*)

24 Linda Ehrlam Voigts, *The Master of the King's Stillatories*, Harlaxton Medieval Studies, vol. 13, 2001, cited by Guthrie Stewart in Alchemy, distillatio.wordpress.com

25 Voigts, *op. cit.*

26 Simon, *op.cit*

27 A colorful fruit-bearing shrub.

28 Barnard *op. cit.*

29 Eric Van Schoonenberghe, *Genever: A Spirit Full of Story, Science, and Technology*, Sartoriana, The Journal of the Sarton Chair of the History Of Science, University of Ghent, 1999 vol. 12.

30 Tim Unwin, *Wine & the Vine*, Routledge 1991.

31 Nicholas Culpeper, *Compleat Herbal*, 1653.

32 The study of the chemical causes of and remedies for medical conditions.

33 A juniper tisane is still used by modern herbalists as both a diuretic and an antiseptic and in the treatment of cystitis, indigestion and flatulence.

34 Van Schoonenberghe, *op. cit.*

35 Daniel Defoe, *A Brief Case of the Distillers and of the Distilling Trade In ENGLAND, shewing how far it is the Interest of England to encourage the said Trade*, 1726.

36 Peter Clark, *The English Alehouse 1200–1830 A Social History*, Longman 1983.

37 Defoe, *op.cit.*

38 Martyn Cornell, *Beer: The Story of the Pint*, Headline 2003.

39 Or earlier, if the scholars who believe Francis Beaumont (d. 1616) to have been one of its authors are correct.

40 Clark, *op. cit.*

41 Clark, *op. cit.*

42 Many of the British tobacco-planters went into exile in Virginia and Carolina, where they resumed their calling with rather more success.

43 Defoe, *op. cit.*

44 Clark *op. cit.*

45 By which he might well have meant gin.

46 Quoted by Stephen Inwood, *A History of London*, Macmillan 1998.

47 Defoe, *op. cit.*

48 Coffee and chocolate both made their debuts in 1657, whereas tea-drinking can be less certainly dated to 1660.

49 Defoe, *op. cit.*

50 John Bickerdyke, *Curiosities of Ale & Beer*, 1889.

51 It should be explained that the process of distilling gin before the column still was invented comprised a minimum of three stages. First, the fermented malt liquor went into the wash or stripping still for a quick cleansing distillation to 25 or 30% ABV — the "low wines." Then it went into the spirit still for a finer, slower distillation up to the desired alcohol content — around 50% in the case of Dutch moutwijn; 60–80% for neutral malt spirits. The spirits then left the distillery and went to the compounder/rectifier to be either infused or redistilled with juniper and other herbs and spices.

52 Defoe, *op. cit.*

53 P. Mathias, *The First Industrial Nation: An Economic History Of Britain 1700–1914*, Methuen, 1983.

54 Confusingly, these low wines would be measured and charged as proof gallons, a gallon of low wines being about half a proof gallon.

55 Clark, *op. cit.*

56 Patrick Dillon, *The Much-Lamented Death of Madame Geneva*, Review, 2002.

57 Defoe, *op. cit.*

58 Hence porter's nicknames, "entire butt" and the metathetical "three threads."

59 Ambrose Cooper, *The Complete Distiller,* 1757; still common practice in America.
60 Peter Mathias, *The Brewing Industry in England 1700-1830,* Cambridge University Press 1959.
61 Boyle also isolated and identified methanol in 1661.
62 British "proof" is the strength at which gunpowder soaked in spirit will still catch fire. If the spirit is any more dilute than that it will still ignite, but the powder won't because it will be waterlogged. It might seem an odd test of alcoholic strength, but spirits and gunpowder were constant companions among gunners, especially in the navy: a paste of the two was used to waterproof linstocks and fuses, and spirit was often used instead of water to swab out the guns between broadsides because water in the barrel could dampen the next powder charge and stop it going off. The Dutch had a more practical method of determining proof, which was universally used by British distillers for day-to-day use: they half-filled a bottle with the spirit to be tested, sealed it, and gave it a vigorous shake. The denser the liquid — i.e., the more water it contained — the more slowly the bubbles or "blebs" would disperse. At proof, a distinct foamy head would form. 100° proof in the UK is 57.15% ABV; in the US, and by the Dutch method of testing, it's a more convenient 50%. To make matters more complicated, British proof was historically commonly expressed as a percentage of 57.15: "26% proof" may sound like a nonsense but was adopted in 1861 as the dividing line between table and fortified wines and equated roughly to 15% ABV. To add to the confusion, "degrees below proof" was another common means of expressing alcoholic strength.
63 Ian Hornsey, *A History of Beer & Brewing,* Royal Society of Chemistry 2003.
64 Hornsey, *op. cit.*
65 Mathias, *op. cit.*
66 Clark, *op. cit.*
67 Clark, *op. cit.*
68 Joseph Haines, *A Satyr Against Brandy,* 1700.
69 Mandeville, *op.cit.*
70 Although, as Lucy Moore points out (*The Thieves' Opera,* Viking 1997), the cohort that supplied most of the victims of the gallows in the early 18th century was not indigent ex-servicemen at all, but disgruntled ex-apprentices like Jack Sheppard (and like Tom Idle, Hogarth's Idle 'Prentice), who were too wild to submit to seven years' indentures during most of which they were used as cheap labor but who found, having broken their indentures early, that they were not allowed to practice a trade and had only crime to fall back on.
71 Moore, *op. cit.*
72 Dillon, *op. cit.*
73 Always excepting the wonderfully titled *Dissertation Upon Drunkenness: Shewing to what an Intolerable Pitch that Vice is Arriv'd at in this Kingdom. Together with the Astonishing Number of Taverns, Coffee-houses, Alehouses, Brandy-shops, &c. Now Extant in London, the Like Not to be Parallel'd by Any Other City in the Christian World. Also an Account of the Pride, Insolence, and Exorbitance of Brewers, Vintners, Victuallers, Coffee-house-keepers, and Distillers; with the Various Arts and Methods by which They Allure and Excite People to Drink and Debauch Themselves. The Whole Proving, that If this Drinking Does Not soon abate, All Our Arts, Sciences, Trade, and Manufactures Will be Entirely Lost, and the Land Become Nothing But a Brewery Or Distillery, and the Inhabitants All Drunkards.*
74 Many of who were obliged by the terms of their leases to grow two crops of barley in each four-year rotation.
75 Recent writers prefer the spelling "Defour," but I have stuck with Dorothy George's version.
76 The Irish adventurer Dudley Bradstreet in his memoirs published in 1755 claimed to have opened the first "puss-mew" house in Blue Anchor Alley, fixing a plaque of a cat with a lead pipe through its paw and a coin-slot for a mouth into a window frame and pouring a measure of gin down the pipe whenever a coin fell through the slot. Bradstreet was a notorious fantasist — it was he, he claimed, who had persuaded Bonnie Prince Charlie to turn back at Derby — and the story is obvious nonsense: Bradstreet's cat would have made a target no informer could resist. The same could be said of the whole puss-mew construct: fixed slots would have been veritable beacons to informers; and "puss-mew" itself can only be a metaphor for password-controlled dram shops as a genre: they can't all have had the same password! The Beefeater Visitor Centre in Kennington does possess a very primitive cat-plaque, complete with lead pipe and coin-slot mouth as described by Bradstreet, but has no provenance for it at all. It looks rather earlier than 1736 and may originally

have been some sort of retailer's novelty, and clearly Bradstreet had seen it or something very like it. It is also suspiciously similar to the Maneki-Neko or Fortune Cat often found in Chinese restaurants, which actually originated in 17th or 18th-century Japan. Rather mysteriously the barrel on which the cat sits has the words "Old Tom" inscribed on it in raised lettering which looks rather less worn than the rest of the piece and is in a completely un-18th century typeface.

77 Dillon, *op. cit.*

78 Sidney & Beatrice Webb, *The History of Liquor Licensing in England,* 1903.

79 Dillon, *op. cit.*

80 The claim that he was paid for the paintings by the brewers has never been substantiated.

81 In the 1730s as many as 20% of infants died before reaching the age of two, according to Clive Emsley, Tim Hitchcock, and Robert Shoemaker in *A Population History of London*, Old Bailey Proceedings Online (www.oldbaileyonline.org).

82 Quoted in Dillon, *op. cit.*

83 Clark, *The English Alehouse.*

84 Jessica Warner, *Craze: Gin and Debauchery in an Age of Reason,* Profile 2002.

85 *The Servant's Calling, With Some Advice to the Apprentice*, 1725.

86 *Population History of London*, Old Bailey Proceedings.

87 This last may be why Corbyn Morris and others thought the birth-rate was declining: they got their numbers from parish records, and neither matrimony nor baptism figured in the lives of a great number of the footloose and fancy-free young immigrants.

88 Typically, 3 pence for a quart of porter compared to 1 1/2 pence for a quartern of gin. The quartern probably contained slightly less alcohol than the quart but still represented better value.

89 Clark (Mother Gin) records that in 1725–1726, 24% of a sample of Middlesex spirit-sellers were female, compared with 10% of victuallers; in 1735–1736 women comprised 23% of spirit-sellers and 15% of victuallers. The female proportion of unlicensed spirit-sellers in the City in 1751 was nearly a third.

90 Barr, *op. cit.* The opposite charge, that unscrupulous rectifiers and publicans watered the gin until it was virtually innocuous and used pepper and ginger to make it taste stronger, is made equally commonly; the two are not mutually exclusive, but neither is supported by evidence.

91 A unit being 10 ml, 8 g or 0.35 fl. oz. of pure alcohol

92 According to the Webbs, citing a report of the Commissioners of Inland Revenue, "The records begin in 1684, when the total was only 527,492 gallons, and it did not reach a million until 1696. It then rose rapidly to 2,200,721 in 1710, 3,879,695 in 1722, 4,612,275 in 1727 and 6,074,562 in 1734, the known production being thus at the latter date about one gallon per head of the estimated population of England. The first Gin Act of 1729–1733 effected no reduction at all. The second, of 1736–1743, caused the amount to fall off for the first three years only, the increase for the last four years of its operation being at a greater rate than before. This was again checked by the Acts of 1751 and 1753, when the total amount fell from 7,049,822 gallons in 1751 to only 4,483,341 in 1752 and to 1,849,370 in 1758."

93 At the same time, people were drinking less beer. The population of England Wales rose from 5.5 to 9.5 million over the course of the 18th century, but beer production rose by only 6%.

94 Henry Fielding, *An Enquiry into the Causes of the Late Increase in Robbers*, 1751.

95 Wilson, *Distilled Spirituous Liquors the Bane of the Nation*, 1736.

96 What is true of gin, however, is not necessarily true of whiskey!

97 Patrick Boyle, *The Publican and Spirit-Dealer's Daily Companion*, first published 1795, long after the gin scare had become but a distant memory. Also the source for the author's calculation of the usual alcoholic strength of 18th-century gin.

98 This is not to say that sulfuric acid wasn't used in other contexts as a cheap substitute for other substances, especially vinegar. Pickles, popular for their long shelf-life, were commonly preserved in sulfuric acid well-diluted with water colored and flavored with oak-chips, especially by naval chandlers for ships' stores. No sailors, however, are recorded as having taken harm from eating them.

99 Clark, *Mother Gin.*

100 Michael Brander, *The Georgian Gentleman*, Saxon House, 1973.

101 N.A.M. Rodger, *The Wooden World*, Collins, 1986.

102 And much of it being rather stronger than we are used to today. Martyn Cornell (*Beer: The Story Of The Pint*, Headline, 2003) calculates the original gravities of the different styles of porter on the market in the mid-18th century as ranging from 1040–1090. Their actual ABV would

depend on how well–attenuated they were but would range from 4 to 10%.

103 Indeed they sometimes combined the two in one pot: "early purl" was a pint of porter with sugar, ginger, and a slug of gin added, served hot, and a breakfast beverage far preferable to tea or coffee for many a laborer on a frosty winter's morning. It wassold not only in pubs but also from the bumboats that plied the Pool of London up until the 1870s selling small luxuries to ships' crews. A cold variant including nutmeg is mentioned inDickens's *Pickwick Papers* (1836–1837), and was known as a "dog's nose."

104 De Saussure also observed: "Though water is to be had in abundance in London, and of fairly good quality, absolutely none is drunk. In this country beer is what everyone drinks when thirsty." Not gin!

105 Eric Williams, *Capitalism & Slavery*, 1944.

106 The directory appears to be incomplete. It lists Booth's, Cowcross Street; Bush & Co, Wandsworth; Cooke & Co, Stratford; Gordon & Foott, Clerkenwell; Gosse, Benwell & Co, Battersea: Hatch, Smith & Currie, Bromley-by-Bow; Hodgson, Weller & Alloway, Battersea: William Johnson & Co, Vauxhall: John Liptrap & Co, Whitechapel Road; and P Metcalfe & Co, Three Mills, West Ham; but not the earliest of the major companies, Boord & Sons of Tooley Street (founded 1726), or Finsbury Distillery (founded 1740 but at the time of the Directory operating under the name Walsingham's).

107 One of the losses in that year was due neither to falling demand nor to increasing duty: Langdales of Holborn Hill, which had supposedly supplied the gin for Dudley Bradstreet's "puss-mew" speakeasy in 1738, was burnt to the ground during the Gordon Riots amid scenes so memorably recorded by Dickens in *Barnaby Rudge*.

108 John J. McCusker, "The Business of Distilling," in *The Early Modern Atlantic Economy*, ed. John J. McCusker & Kenneth Morgan, Cambridge University Press, 2000. The forerunners of today's G&J and Plymouth Gin were founded in 1761 and 1793 respectively.

109 Three Mills's place in the history of London's distilling industry has been brilliantly described in *The Three Mills Distillery in the Georgian Era* by Keith Fairclough, published by the River Lea Tidal Mill Trust.

110 McCusker & Morgan, *op. cit.*

111 For all the Scotch industry's hauteur, gin enthusiasts might take pride in the fact that there is nothing in Scotland to compare with Three Mills for age and scale — although there are quite a few Highland malt distilleries that outrank it in terms of locale!

112 Julian Woodford, www.historylondon.org

113 Woodford, *The Boss of Bethnal Green*, Spitalfields Life Books, 2016.

114 A near neighbor was Josiah Spode, originator of bone china. The ground-up bones of pigs from the distilleries comprised 30% of the mixture.

115 McCusker & Morgan, *op. cit.*

116 E.W. Brayley, *A Topographical History of Surrey*, 1841.

117 Interestingly, the copper kettles used for boiling hops in porter breweries were of similar dimensions, but designed with the intention of caramelizing the lowest stratum of liquid for added color and flavor.

118 Peter Mulryan, *The Whiskeys of Ireland*, O'Brien Press, 2002.

119 The percentage at which no more water can be separated.

120 Not actually the case: Cruikshank's illustration of this very passage shows all the huge butts as being of exactly the same size. Besides, they were only dummies. The real spirit casks of a manageable 32 gallons were either kept on the bar-back or in a secure spirit room from which the gin was piped to taps mounted on the bar. It's also unclear whether all the different names represent different types or brands: customers are rarely represented as asking for a particular gin by name, only by quantity.

121 The spread of the bar-counter from dram-shop to pub turned out to be a transformative development, but in the history of the pub rather than the history of gin. Suffice it to say that in the early years of the 19th century many pubs were installing bar-counters in imitation of the dram-shop, while many dram-shops were installing "accommodations" in imitation of the pub; so that by mid-century if you looked from dram-shop to pub, and from pub to dram-shop, and from dram-shop to pub again it would be impossible to say which was which.

122 *On Tour with Inspector Field, Household Words*, June 1851.

123 *Ins and Outs of London,* Philadelphia 1859.

124 Literally upright: like most shops, Thompson & Fearon had no seating.

125 Built in an unusual style best described as "Italianate," it was demolished in the 1860s along with the rest of Holborn Hill to make way for Holborn Viaduct and Holborn Circus; but unusually, a full set of drawings survives.

126 Peter Jonas, *The Distiller's Guide,* 1816.

127 David Wondrich, *Solving the Riddle of Old Tom Gin*, the Daily Beast, March 2017.

128 Anonymous, *History of the Remarkable Lives and Actions of Jonathan Wild, Thief-taker, Joseph Blake alias Blueskin, Footpad, and John Sheppard, Housebreaker,* 1725. One of Blueskin's frauds was to charge women considerable sums to "reset their tow-vows," which he accomplished by means the reader can surmise.

129 Although it might well have been: duty on tea rose to a ridiculous 119% by the late 18th century, and smuggling and the Government's attempts to prevent it almost amounted to guerrilla warfare along the south coast of England. In 1784 duty was slashed to 12.5%, and the consequent increase in consumption was checked only by two decades of war with France before tea began to overhaul beer and gin as the favorite beverage of the working class.

130 It might also have been a gin-based infusion of fruit, heavily sweetened, such as today's sloe and damson variants. Dickens himself mentions in various works such "cordials" made with cherries, cowslip, Seville oranges, lemons, almonds, caraway seed, rue, tansy, cloves, peppermint and much else besides.

131 John Burnett, *Liquid Pleasures*, Routledge, 1999.

132 Including a British version of genever known as "Hollands," which may simply have been a particularly well-rounded and possibly more alcoholic variant of Old Tom, barrel-aged for color and body and often taken as a digestif in place of brandy or whiskey.

133 Teemu Strengell, whiskyscience.blogspot.com, January 8, 2013.

134 Rum and shrub and brandy and lovage were popular until as recently as the 1960s; in the current climate they are perhaps due a comeback.

135 Sidney W. Mintz, *Sweetness and Power: The Place of Sugar in Modern History*. Penguin, 1987.

136 Mike Paterson, londonhistorians.wordpress.com 2010/2011

137 The Royal Navy's rum ration was a regulatory oddity in that it never officially existed. As N.A.M. Rodger points out (op. cit.): "There was no official issue of spirits in the Navy. Men drank beer, except on long voyages when it ran out and on foreign stations where it could not be had. Then they drank watered wine, or as a last resort watered spirits, usually rum in the West Indies, arrack in the East Indies, and brandy elsewhere." The rum that was doled out to matelots until "Black Tot Day" — July 31st ,1970 — was in legal fiction a substitute for beer.

138 Gin and lime constitutes a gimlet, but the charter-myth that it was named after Admiral Dr. Sir Thomas Desmond Gimlette is unattributed and surely apocryphal given that he joined the navy in 1879, by which time it had been using lime juice as an antiscorbutic for at least 150 years.

139 Or, after 1867, Rose's lime juice cordial.

140 George Dodd, *op. cit.*

141 While the wine and spirit bottle had long been accepted as a sixth of a gallon or 26 2/3 fl. oz., wine for consumption on the premises was sold in half-pints, pints, and (for sharing, one hopes) quarts, so when Tennyson bade the plump head waiter at the Cock to "go fetch a pint of Port," that's exactly what he meant.

142 James Nicholls; *Wine, Supermarkets & Alcohol Policy,* www.historyandpolicy.org, 2011.

143 Or, in plainer English, compulsory closing times. For most pubs the Act forbade breakfast-time opening, which was the final nail in the coffin of Dickens's "early purl" and also put a stop to the widespread habit of stopping off on the way to work for a fortifying dose of gin or rum.

144 It was so unpopular with temperance MPs who made up part of Gladstone's increasingly shambolic coalition, though, that it played a significant role in the utter collapse of the Liberals in the 1874 election.

145 When the Red Lion and the neighboring buildings were demolished in 1844, human remains and a knife with "J. Wild" engraved on the hilt were conveniently "found" among the rubble. Actually, though, Wild had chambers very close to the Old Bailey. Still, *se non e vero...*

146 www.red11.org

147 Andrew Barr, *op. cit.*

148 It seems the *brandewijn* may have been the latchlifter for the Dutch settlers' purchase of Manhattan from the Canarsee tribe for a valuable consignment of lead ingots and manufactured

goods including cauldrons, knives and axes (not beads, and worth rather more than the $24 of legend!), as there are early accounts of the Dutch plying native peoples who had never encountered so much as beer before with gin — an abuse that white settlers were only too happy to repeat as they steamrolled indigenous populations on their remorseless progress westward.

149 Applejack, or freeze-concentrated cider, was also a popular spirit. Barley being so hard to grow in many parts of the North-Eastern colonies, cidermaking was widespread. The apples were pressed and left to ferment late in the summer in large wooden butts kept outdoors or in unheated barns: during the winter the exothermic fermentation and the concentration of CO2 prevented freezing; but by its second winter the mature cider in the butt would be stable enough for much of the water to freeze, and enough ice could be scooped out to leave a residue of 40% ABV or more. Further south, peach brandy was distilled from the local variant of jerkum, the stone-fruit wine indigenous to Worcestershire.

150 Or indeed whiskey. The distinction is purely one of jumbled orthography and has nothing to do with different ingredients or processes, whatever anyone tells you.

151 Gary Gillman, www.beeretseq.com, September 2017.

152 Hugely reinforced by streams of desperate emigrants driven off their land during the Highland Clearances of 1790–1830 and the Irish Potato Famine of 1845–1855.

153 Edward Hewett & W.F. Axton, *Convivial Dickens,* Ohio University Press, 1983.

154 *American Notes*, 1842.

155 Ovie Felix Forie, *The Prohibition of Illicit Alcohol in Colonial Nigeria 1910–1950.* Journal of Innovative Research and Development, March 2013.

156 Simon Heap, *The Quality of Liquor in Nigeria in the Colonial Era*. International Journal on the History of European Expansion, July 1999.

157 The governor from 1712–1736, Richard Kane, devoted himself to developing the island's economy through road building, water conservation works, and agricultural improvements including the introduction the Friesian cow. He also improved the island's viticulture.

158 An early gin-drinker, perhaps?

159 The exclamation marks are all Herbert's.

160 The timing is interesting here, although possibly of no consequence: The first Arabian stallion in Britain, the Markham Arab, was imported by James I in 1616; a high-carried tail is a breed conformation trait of the Arabian. And the early 17th century was also the time when cockfighting reached the peak of its popularity, with the first book on the subject being published in 1607.

161 William Hague, *William Pitt the Younger: A Biography*, Harper, 2004.

162 This has been reverse-engineered from surviving bottles and launched commercially; and although the ingredients have naturally not been published, the bitters is said to be more rich and chocolaty than sharp and astringent.

163 Sugar.

164 Thomas, Burke, *The English Inn,* Longman, 1930.

165 *Ice Industry & Ice Wagons*, Carriage Museum of America, www.carriagemuseumlibrary.org

166 Possibly after the eponymous San Francisco suburb, where one of many charter-myths claims it was first formulated during the 1849 gold rush; although as early cocktail recipe books cite it as a gin-based variant on the Manhattan, its origins perhaps lie in New York. Another possible and perhaps more likely place of origin is Reus, 50 km from Barcelona. Gin has been distilled in Barcelona since1866, while vermouth was made in Reus from 1892. It is inconceivable that the two never met.

167 The description of Rick's Café Americain in *Casablanca* as a "gin-joint" seems more a matter of euphony than fact, since of the 33 alcoholic drinks ordered throughout the movie not one is gin. Other than three whiskies, every single drink in the movie is French. Hardly surprising, since it's set in the Vichy Empire during wartime!

168 This is not a history of Prohibition, but it is necessary to mention that racism also seems to have been a powerful force behind its introduction: The 70 years leading up to Volstead were the decades when the tired, the poor, and the huddled masses yearning to breathe free arrived quite literally by the boatload bringing with them, according to those who felt challenged by them, saloons, casinos, brothels and booze.

169 "Connections" here implying members of the police, judiciary and political establishment susceptible to bribery, blackmail or intimidation. Organized crime is impossible unless these institutions are thoroughly subverted and as Al Capone found out, it only takes a single uncorrupted

branch of government — in his case the IRS — to bring down even the most powerful individual. In 1920s America the gangsters were helped enormously by the ethnic divisions in society that left the loyalties of many public officials irreconcilably divided between state and community.

170 A term first recorded by the *New York Voice* in 1889 denoting an unlicensed bar. The "easy" in this usage means "quietly" — i.e., don't blab!

171 Canada introduced a mild form of Prohibition as a wartime measure in 1918. Most territories repealed it in 1920 but in Ontario it lingered until 1927. However it exempted weak beer, Canadian-made wine, and spirits intended for export.

172 Six pre-Prohibition distilleries were licensed to maintain supplies of medicinal whiskey; producers of industrial ethanol were not regulated because their product was not classified as a beverage.

173 The piece, *A Bootlegger's Story*, purports to be autobiographical but the confidence of the writing and some shakiness on detail strongly suggest that it is based on interviews by a professional journalist.

174 *Fortune Magazine*, "Whiskey and America: A post-prohibition reunion," November 1933.

175 Matthew Rowley, *Lost Recipes of Prohibition: Notes from a Bootlegger's Journal*, Countryman Press, 2015.

176 Laurence Bergreen, *Al Capone, the Man and the Era*, Simon & Schuster, 1994.

177 Although it does aver that "they (the alkie-cookers) used a small still to ferment a mash from corn sugar or fruit," which betrays such a fundamental ignorance of the processes involved as to call into question the validity of the entire piece.

178 Philippa Pullar, *Consuming Passions*, Hamish Hamilton, 1970.

179 Pinkham was immortalized in song as Lily the Pink, whose 20% ABV medicinal compound was "most efficacious in every case."

180 Deborah Blum, *The Chemists' War*, www.slate.com, February 2010.

181 Blum, *op. cit.*

182 Yates's Wine Lodges, one of the first non-brewing pub chains in Britain, was founded in Oldham in 1884 and quickly expanded across the industrial cities of the north of England. Its specialty was "Blob," a toddy of Australian (both phylloxera-free and subject to a preferential rate of duty) sweet white wine and brandy, with sugar, lemon juice, and hot water. A bottled version, technically "shrub," was later released.

183 The standard bulk measurement that has replaced proof gallons.

184 Robert Duncan, PhD thesis subsequently published as *Pubs & Patriots: The Drink Crisis in Britain During World War I*, Liverpool University Press, 2013.

185 The 3-year minimum age requirement has been retained to this day as a guarantee of quality exceeding even that of VS Cognac, which has to be aged for only two years.

186 Western Aberdeenshire was even more of a whiskey constituency then than it is now, and is still the home of noble drams such as Glendronach and Ardmore.

187 A drink known to Dickens as a "dog's nose."

188 Derivatives such as glycerol and acetone were vital ingredients in explosives and propellants. Column stills also produced alcohol for medicines and as solvents to waterproof clothing for sailors at sea and soldiers in the trenches. Surplus yeast from fermentation went to the country's bakers.

189 The author's father recalled holidays in Lyme Regis in the mid-1930s, and treating local fishermen in the pub to a tot added to their pints until the liquid content was more rum than cider.

190 "The fact that his men slept in muddy holes was no reason for Haig to decline a soft bed in a luxurious château. Grouse, salmon, fine wines and the best brandy were sent to him by rich friends at home. Nor did he perceive anything wrong with sending whole lambs and butter from the army stores to his wife so that she would not have to endure food shortages… Few objections were raized about the luxuries Haig enjoyed during the war, or the rewards he received after it." Gerard DeGroot, *Blighty* (Longman 1996).

191 Duncan, *op. cit.*

192 Duncan, *op. cit.*

193 i.e., public house.

194 Duncan, *op. cit.*

195 As in George Bernard Shaw's famous rebuff: "Lady Randolph Churchill will be at home on Thursday afternoon next at four o' clock. RSVP." "So will George Bernard Shaw."

196 Quoted by Andrew Barr in *Drink: A Social History.*
197 *The Observer*, March 31st, 2002.
198 Martin Pugh, *We Danced All Night*, Vintage Books, 2009. The slang name "mother's ruin" seems to date from the same period and attests to gin's popularity with women. Although many people think it's older, it was first used in print by the surely pseudonymous W. Juniper in *A True Drunkard's Delight* as recently as 1933.
199 *A Subaltern's Love Song*, John Betjeman, 1941.
200 Its legendary American Bar opened in 1892 and is still going strong. Jacket and tie required!
201 Derek Taylor and David Bush, *The Golden Age of British Hotels*, Northwood, 1974.
202 Thomas Burke, *English Night Life*, Batsford, 1941
203 Burke, *op. cit.*
204 Burke also implies that drug use underpinned the nightclubs' popularity among "a small section that stayed up all night (and) expressed its high spirits… by an ugly and newly imported American word, Whoopee."
205 Barr, *op. cit.*
206 Martin Pugh, *op.cit.*
207 Rather oddly spelled "whiskey" throughout, although without any indication that the book was referring to Irish whiskey.
208 John Burnett, *Liquid Pleasures: A Social History of Drink in Britain,* Routledge, 1999
209 Cinema statistics, www.terramedia.co.uk
210 Out of 133.
211 New Toronto Historical Society: Celebrating Our Golden Jubilee, 1963. www.newtoronto-historical.co/gilbey
212 Except Tasmania, where a whiskey distillery had been founded in 1822 to be followed by three more before 1839, when the Distillation Prohibition Act banned it. The Act was in force until 1992!
213 *Melbourne Argus*, October 6th, 1938.
214 Brazil joined the Allies in WWII, declaring war in 1942 as a result of U-boat attacks on its merchantmen. A Brazilian division fought with distinction in Italy alongside US ground forces, and the Brazilian navy and air force played an active part in suppressing U-boat activity in the Western Atlantic.
215 Brian Abrams, "FDR: Portrait of a Drinking President," *Modern Drunkard Magazine*, June/July 2006.
216 The 1941 Indian census lists 155,000 people recording themselves as British; by the 1951 census it had shrunk to 28,000. An unknown number of those who left migrated to the tea-growing regions of Kenya and South Africa.
217 Barr, *op.cit.*
218 Quentin Letts, *Daily Telegraph*, January 5th, 2003.
219 "British" here signifying wine, often fortified, fermented in Britain from imported grape concentrate.
220 Burnett, *op. cit.*
221 This, to be fair, was not entirely Gilbey's own decision. In the early 1960s the Government was trying its hardest to reinvent congested, overcrowded, smoky and bomb-scarred London as a modern-ish city where it was possible to live, work, breathe, and move about. Gilbey's was one of many inner-city factories induced to make way for redevelopment by moving out to one of many new towns planned for the purpose. The policy was not a complete success in that many large companies fled as expected but the hoped-for redevelopment did not always follow. The enormous ABC bakery in Camden Road remained standing and empty until the 1980s; the vast Carreras cigarette factory in Mornington Crescent is there to this day, but is an office-block.
222 In 1993, the author was privileged to be shown how to make the perfect martini by Salim Khoury, legendary manager of the Savoy Hotel's American Bar. The gin he chose was Tanqueray for its 43.1% alcohol content and its simple but classic botanicals. His recipe was very, very dry: nine parts gin to one of dry Martini with a thumbnail-size piece of lemon zest squeezed to release its oils and dropped into the glass after pouring. All the ingredients came from the fridge, but there was also plenty of ice in the shaker.
223 Including the $150,000 endorsement of Las Vegas mayor and former mob lawyer Oscar Goodman.

224 www.discus.org/heritage/spirits

225 In the house in Hammersmith, which until his death in 2007 had been the home of the world's most celebrated beer writer, Michael Jackson.

226 Sipsmith is not entirely correct to say that it overturned the rule that stills must have a minimum capacity of 1,800 L (396 imperial gallons). The legal minimum capacity for spirit stills had been set at 40 gallons in the 1823 Excise Act; but Customs wouldn't actually license such small stills because they would be impossible to supervise. In 2004 Loch Ewe managed to get its 120-liter spirit still licensed; but it still took Sipsmith two years of legal argument before it could exploit Loch Ewe's precedent. The requirement has now been quietly dropped.

227 Second-generation white ciders, made not of filtered cider but of spent pomace, the cheapest possible neutral spirit, sugar and carbonated water, boosted the demand for ethanol yet further.

228 www.statista.com. America's leading gin brand, Seagram's, is only at number 6 in the spirits sales chart; Smirnoff and Bacardi are at 3 and 2 respectively, and Jack Daniels whiskey is at number 1.

INDEX

CPSIA information can be obtained
at www.ICGtesting.com
Printed in the USA
BVHW081428151021
618873BV00004B/252